Shaping the Preschool Agenda

SUNY SERIES, LITERACY, CULTURE, AND LEARNING:
THEORY AND PRACTICE
ALAN C. PURVES, EDITOR

SHAPING THE PRESCHOOL AGENDA

Early Literacy, Public Policy, and Professional Beliefs

Anne McGill-Franzen

STATE UNIVERSITY OF NEW YORK PRESS

Published by
State University of New York Press, Albany

Printed in the United States of America

For information, address State University of New York
Press, State University Plaza, Albany, N.Y., 12246

Production by E. Moore
Marketing by Fran Keneston

Library of Congress Cataloging-in-Publication Data

McGill-Franzen, Anne
Shaping the preschool agenda : early literacy, public policy, and professional beliefs / Anne McGill-Franzen.
p. cm. — (SUNY series, literacy, culture, and learning)
Includes bibliographical references (p.) and index.
ISBN 0-7914-1195-8 ISBN 0-7914-1196-6 (pbk.)
1. Readiness for school. 2. Education, Preschool—United States—Curricula. 3. Socially handicapped children—Education—Reading. 4. Educational equalization—United States. I. Title. II. Series.
LB1132.M33 1993
372-21'0973—dc20 91-34722
CIP

10 9 8 7 6 5 4 3 2 1

CONTENTS

1. MAKING CHILDREN READY FOR SCHOOL: AN ISSUE FOR THE 1990s

By the year 2000, all children in America will start school ready to learn.

—President Bush, State of the Union Message, 1990 and National Governors' Association, 1990.

IN THE WINTER of 1990 and for the first time in history, a sitting president and all the governors convened a national education summit and jointly set an education agenda to improve the public schools (Walker, 1990). The very first national goal set at this education summit was "readiness" for school among the nation's children. President Bush announced in his 1990 State of the Union address that, by the turn of the century, every child in America would start school "ready to learn."[1]

Children who start school behind rarely catch up. Mostly, they do not learn to read on schedule[2] with their peers. Schools respond by flunking children in the early grades or by labelling them as "impaired" in some way so that they can qualify for special help (Smith & Shepard, 1987). Children respond by not believing in themselves as learners (Martin, 1988).

As Marilyn Jager Adams writes in *Beginning to Read: Thinking and Learning about Print* (1990), it is unlikely that first-grade teachers can make up for the vast differences among children's preschool experiences. Among families who routinely read stories to their children, Adams estimates that the children spend from 1,000 to 1,700 hours in one-to-one literacy activities[3] before entering school. Adams suggests that these children experience another 2,000 hours of print "guidance" by watching "Sesame Street" and perhaps another 1,000 or 2,000 hours by playing with magnetic alphabet letters, participating in reading and writing activities in playgroup or preschool, exploring with paper and pencils and playing alphabet games on a computer (p. 85).

But for children in many other families,[4] there are no storybook routines, no magnetic letters on the refrigerator, no easy access to paper and pencils for creating messages, and no literacy games to play on a computer. Perhaps there is not even "Sesame Street." Such children will begin first grade without the "thousands of hours of school-like reading experience" (Adams, 1990, p. 90) that other families have the resources to provide.

Adams notes that first-grade teachers typically allocate about 360 hours of classroom instruction to language arts, and any one child must share his first-grade teacher with at least twenty other children. This is not much time at all when compared with the approximately 4,000 to 6,000 hours of literacy activities—including one-to-one tutorials—that more advantaged children receive prior to first grade.

I began this project in the late 1980s. By that time, policy people—education commissioners, mayors, governors—had begun to talk seriously about providing public school to all four-year-olds. At about the same time, a consensus seemed to be developing among researchers that children's experiences with print before first grade were at least as important as their experiences with print after they started school. I wondered what policymakers hoped public schooling for four-year-olds might accomplish. Did they believe—as I did—that entitling all four-year-olds to educational programs could be the first step in entitling all children to literacy?

This book is about beliefs and understandings. It is an account of the historical ties between early childhood education and literacy learning. It is also my account of what contemporary policymakers in one state believe about early childhood education. I describe how these policy participants define readiness for school, who they identify as the child development experts, what they say about preschool and literacy learning, and what even counts as "school" for young children.

This book is also a study of agenda setting. Public school for four-year-olds is an idea that is clearly getting on the agenda. The term *agenda setting* was originally used by anthropologists to describe the way tribal societies brought problems to the attention of their leaders. More recently, its use has been appropriated by political scientists to explain how certain demands by groups in the population actually become "translated into items vying for the serious attention of public officials" (Cobb, Ross & Ross, 1976, p. 126). Borrowing the agenda-setting paradigm from anthropology and political science, I describe how contemporary policymakers perceive the issue of "education" for children who are not yet of school age.

A NATIONAL GOAL

The ideal of making all children ready to learn—every child starting off on common ground—has universal appeal, but there is no consensus on what school readiness means or on the best way to achieve it. Do we improve the *parents* of poor children, as some suggest, so that every parent takes an "active role in his or her child's early learning, particularly by reading to them on a daily basis" (NGA, 1990, p. 16), or do we develop school readiness by sending children to *school*? If we send children to school, what should the school teach? Should teachers make it their number-one priority to read every day to the children as parents are urged to do? And should we send only *poor* children? Some would argue that children are born "ready to learn," but that the learning of the preschool years is qualitatively different from that of the school years. Do we actually know the connection between early childhood education and the literate society we envision for the future?

The governors, in fact, initially scrapped an amendment to their proposal that would have called for a national assessment of school readiness, because there was so little agreement about what such an instrument would measure. However, once they are made "ready," American children are expected to read, write, and think at a level that will challenge the best of our global competitors.

Despite the murkiness of the 'school readiness' concept, the education summit was itself a groundbreaking event. Education is and always has been a function reserved to the states, with individual states and localities exercising considerable autonomy in setting educational standards. Further, the education summit tackled issues not typically under the purview of the educational system. Developing readiness for school is one of these issues. Until now, the development of children prior to school-age has been considered the family's responsibility. In the introduction to its January, 1992 report on readiness, "Ready to Learn: A Mandate for the Nation," the Carnegie Foundation for the Advancement of Teaching acknowledges that the question of who is responsible for children's preschool development has not yet been adequately addressed by government:

> Surely, America has within its power the means to make the earliest years enriching and productive for all our children. But whose responsibility is it to ensure the school readiness of children? Who should take the lead in seeing to it that every child receives not just food, protection and love, but also the guidance to succeed in school and to proceed confidently in life? (Boyer, 1991, p. M5)

Not since the enactment of Head Start in 1965 as part of Lyndon Johnson's War on Poverty has the education of preschoolers been the focus of such sustained public attention. Recently Congress reauthorized Chapter 1 of the Elementary and Secondary Education Act and, in doing so, earmarked $50 million for Even Start, a new federal program to support parental literacy and early childhood education. In addition to this modest appropriation for Even Start, three major early childhood bills, each with profound fiscal and programmatic implications for the future of preschool programs, were also before Congress. Smart Start (S. 123) proposed that more than $4 billion be allocated over several years to the states for educational programs for low-income four-year-olds; Early Childhood Education and Development Act (H.R. 3) authorized close to $2 billion each year for an array of educational and child-care services, including an expanded Head Start; and the Act for Better Child Care Services (S. 5) authorized about $2.7 billion each year to improve the quality, access to, and affordability of child care, particularly for low-income parents. Each of these bills defines the federal interest in early schooling somewhat differently.

In addition, across the country, many more states are allocating funds to help support preschool programs. At least thiry-one states now contribute either to state-directed preschool programs or to the federal Head Start programs, an increase that quadruples the participation rate of a decade ago (Mitchell, 1989). Public school for four-year-olds is now available in New York City and Los Angeles, with other big city school boards and, increasingly, state boards of education considering at least optional programs for parents who desire them (Morado, 1985; Schweinhart & Mazur, 1987).

Education commissioners in California, New York, and Connecticut have endorsed the concept of universal public school for four-year-olds, and gubernatorial panels in Kentucky, Massachusetts, North Carolina, South Carolina, Connecticut, and Michigan have recommended policy initiatives for the care and schooling of three- and four-year-olds (National Governors' Association, 1986). The California School Readiness Task Force, established by the state superintendent for instruction to examine how California might make its children ready for school, has recommended increased state support for the education of four-year-olds (California State Department of Education, 1988). Likewise, Mario Cuomo, governor of the state of New York, has recommended in his State of the State messages (1987, 1988) that New York provide free education for all of the state's four-year-old children.

The highly publicized benefits of the early intervention programs for poor children and the dramatic rise in numbers of mothers of young children in the work force have compelled federal and state policymakers to take a hard look at what is happening to the children. At this juncture, the issue appears to be not whether early schooling is appropriate but rather what form early schooling should take. What do we think four-year-olds should be learning, and what do we want early schooling to accomplish (Fiske, 1986)?

THE ARGUMENT FOR EARLY SCHOOLING

Almost no one is arguing against the need for more programs for preschool-aged children. By the turn of the century, the Bureau of the Census estimates that 80 percent of all mothers of children under the age of six will be in the work force, and half of them will need formal child care (Kamerman, 1984). Between 1970 and 1983 the percentage of four-year-old children in child day care or nursery school programs tripled, so that now more than 48 percent are in such programs. The majority—two-thirds—are in private programs. While half of all four-year-olds are in school now, about 25 percent are actually in kindergarten, not child day care or even preschool (Ambach, 1985). The age for entry into public school is being lowered and raised as state policymakers grapple with issues of readiness. The question for the 1990s is what kind of programs should we be providing?

Parents who can afford to enroll their children in formal preschool educational programs generally do so, according to the sponsors of the Act for Better Child Care Services (Kennedy, 1989). Gordon Ambach, the director of the Council of Chief State School Officers and former New York state education commissioner, also notes that access to educational or school-based programs is a class issue (Ambach, 1985). One distinction he noted between child care and educational programs for four-year-olds was that 70 percent of all four-year-olds from families with incomes above $25,000 were in school, not day care, whereas only thirty-three percent from families with incomes below $15,000 were in school programs (Ambach, 1985). In fact, census data suggest that it is the preschool enrollment of White four-year-olds whose mothers *do not work* that has dramatically increased the participation rates of this age group in programs across the country. From 1970 through the mid-1980s, a relatively stable percentage of White children with working mothers went to preschool. On the other hand, many more White children of stay-at-home mothers—more than 50 percent of all four-year-olds in this category—attended preschool in the mid-eighties compared to 1970 (Pendleton, 1986). Presumably, these children were not in school because their mothers were working, but rather because their families believed there was an educational benefit to participating in preschool.

FIGURE 1-1
Preprimary School Participation Rates of 4-year-old Children of White Nonworking Women Compared to Participation Rates of 4-year-old Children of Working Women

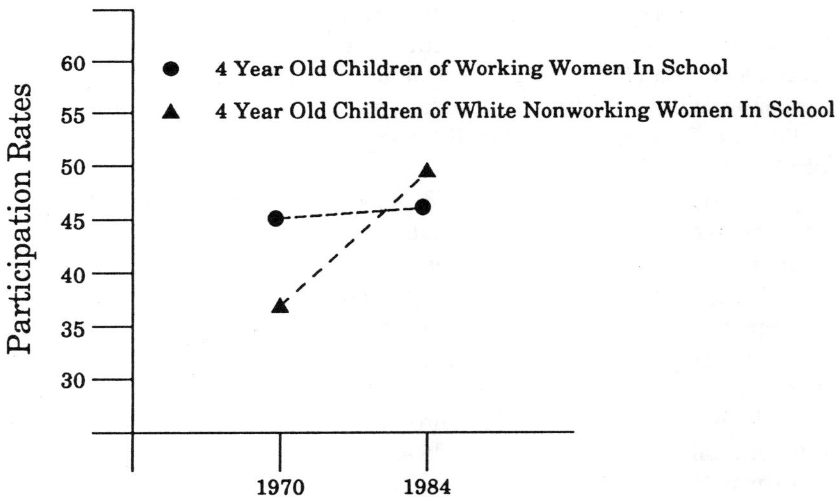

Note: The data are from Pendleton (1986).

In the view of many policymakers today, including Ambach and Edward Koch, former mayor of New York City, there is a disparity of opportunity among four-year-olds that needs redress if equal educational opportunity is to be preserved as a goal of public education (Early Childhood Commission, 1986). The assumption inherent in this point of view is that school programs should offer something different from or beyond that of child care and that this component is beneficial for all children, but especially for the economically disadvantaged.

Several well-reported longitudinal studies of the early Head Start programs have given credibility to the belief that preschool education can change lives. In a fifteen-year study of disadvantaged Black youth, for example, researchers estimated that over the lifetime of the participants there would be an economic benefit of approximately six or seven dollars to every one dollar spent on the Perry Preschool Project (Berrueta-Clement, et al., 1984). Similarly, the national Head Start Evaluation Synthesis and Utilization Project found significant immediate gains in cognitive and emotional development for participating children. While these advantages were not sustained throughout their school careers,[5] participants in the preschool program were more likely to be promoted to the next grade and less likely to require costly special education placement (CSR, 1985).

In the upcoming decades, an increasing proportion of the total school age population will be made up of children who are thought to be more economically disadvantaged and at risk of failure. The problems associated with low-achieving children of poor and minority parents that gave rise to the educational interventions of the 1960s will be exacerbated by the growing numbers of children in poverty (today, for example, 23 percent of all children under the age of six are poor), in single-parent families, and in families whose native language is not English. Demographic trends—the differential birth rate between minority familes and Caucasian families, divorce and other family patterns, immigration, and the wage and economic disparities among these populations—indicate that the public-school clientele of the future will be predominantly "nonmainstream" (Shields & McLaughlin, 1986; Hodgkinson, 1985; National Center for Children in Poverty, 1990).

Given these demographic and social trends, together with the highly publicized results of early intervention studies, one might expect universal agreement on the desirability of publicly funded, school-based, educational programs for four-year olds. Indeed, the American Federation of Teachers has been a longstanding proponent of public school programs for early childhood initiatives, claiming that the public schools are the only national institution with "built-in quality controls" and capability to coordinate and provide continuity between preschool and primary school (Glass, 1986). The New York State School Boards Association (NYSSBA) recently released a position paper that strongly supports public school involvement as a "logical and practical way to increase availability of early educational or child care opportunities." While the NYSSBA does not advocate mandated preschool, it does support full state funding for "prekindergarten programs. . .to reach children all over the state where need is shown" (NYSSBA, 1986).

Early childhood education should be a top national priority and states should consider requiring full-day programs for four-year olds, according to the National Association of Elementary School Principals (NAESP). Unless emphasis is placed on early childhood programs in particular, the NAESP holds that the country may create a "permanent underclass amounting to 25 per cent of our citizens" (Walton, n.d.). The national Committee for Economic Development (1987) and the regional Southern Growth Policies Board (1990) both see publicly funded preschool education for impoverished four-year-olds as an investment strategy that will yield high dividends for the economy by reducing costs for welfare and increasing the productivity of the work force.

While virtually every major professional organization affiliated with public schools has issued statements in favor of universal schooling for four-year-olds (Association for Supervision & Curriculum Development, 1987; New York State United Teachers, 1986; NYSSBA, 1986; NAESP, n.d.), interest groups that represent child care providers and minority children have not generally sought an expanded public school role in the education of preschoolers. In other words, organizations such as the National Association for the Education of Young Children (1985, 1986) and the National Black Child Development Institute (1985) have long advocated more child-care programs and expanded funding and more appropriate oversight at state and federal levels, but not necessarily under the aegis of the public school bureaucracy. At the heart of this issue is the perceived incompatibility of traditional child care with traditional kindergarten or first-grade education as practiced in the public schools.

EARLY CHILDHOOD EDUCATION, LITERACY INSTRUCTION, AND THE PUBLIC SCHOOL

In an historical analysis of ideas shaping early childhood education, Weber (1984) cites the bureaucratization of the public schools as the major force inhibiting any restructuring of primary-grade curriculum. At the time kindergarten programs were incorporated into public schools—in the 1920s—kindergarten teachers believed that they would be able to effect a more child-centered approach throughout the primary grades. Change did occur, Weber states, but in the opposite direction.

Pressured to align their work more closely with that of the rest of the school, Weber says that kindergarten teachers found themselves caught up with the age and grade testing standards of the schools and began to devote more and more attention to preparation for first grade. Whereas the previous goal of kindergarten programs involved the development of attitudes, the new goal—literacy—dominated all other concerns, and reading readiness exercises subsumed ever larger parts of the curriculum (Weber, 1984; Sommerville, 1982).

As Weber sees it, what was important in the early kindergarten programs—the ability to respond to changing notions of how children learn and commitment to the individuality of human growth—was lost with the absorption of kindergarten within the public school system. She believes that preschools have been able to maintain more of a match between the curriculum and the young child's interests and needs, but only because there is not yet a bureaucratic hierarchy to impose its standard. Weber does allow, however, that even preschools have not been "untouched by the American fetish for early literacy. . . [in] the form of parents' anxiety and zeal for their children to have a head start in reading" (Weber, 1984, p. 200).

The Curriculum Issue

Participants in this policy discussion have often dichotomized child care and education, with some educators claiming that traditional child care arrangements lack an educational component, and some child-development specialists cautioning that the typical four-year-old is not ready for the public school primary grade curriculum.

On the one hand, it is not clear what an appropriate "educational component" is or should be for early schooling—be it called preschool, child day care, nursery school, or Head Start. The selection of a curriculum has been the central issue in early childhood education for a long time (Schweinhart, Weikart & Larner, 1986; Spodek, 1986). With the influx of federal money to develop Head Start during the 1960s, researchers created various models of preschool curricula, implemented them in demonstration projects, and tested the effectiveness of these curricular variations by measuring later school achievement.

The goal of the sixties preschool programs was to help disadvantaged children be more successful in school. Early on, measures of school success and, by implication, program effectiveness were based primarily on improved reading and cognitive ability test scores. In the later longitudinal studies published on these data, however, researchers broadly defined success to mean fewer children flunking grades, fewer placements in special education, fewer children dropping out of school, fewer pregnant teens, and fewer delinquents, as well as test scores.

On the other hand, relatively little ambiguity exists about the job of the primary grades: to teach children to read. As former Education Secretary William Bennett proclaimed in *First Lessons* (1986), "the elementary school must assume as its sublime and most solemn responsibility the task of teaching every child in it to read"(p. 21). Historically, few have challenged the appropriateness of this mission, and, in recent years, the importance of early grade success in reading has actually been highlighted. First-grade children who are "behind" their peers in reading are most likely to fail one or two grades in the years ahead, to be assigned to special education classes, and to drop out of school. Girls who consistently score in the bottom quartile of their classes in basic skills are more likely to become pregnant and bear children as teenagers. Poor children are the ones most often caught in the "gridlock" of low achievement and academic failure (McGill-Franzen & Allington, 1991; Edelman, 1990; Slavin, 1989). But clearly, children from families at all income levels who cannot read well will find it very difficult to participate fully in the literate culture of the school and community. The issue—still unresolved—is what should early childhood programs do.

A controversial study conducted by the High/Scope Research Foundation has intensified the debate about what is appropriate learning for preschoolers. In follow-up studies of former preschool participants, High/Scope researchers linked children's participation in particular preschool curricula with their later reported social adjustment or delinquency. Schweinhart, Weikart, and Larner (1986) compared three preschool curriculum models[6] for their social and behavioral effects on the original participants as 15-year-olds. As the authors point out, the highly structured, teacher-directed DISTAR curriculum model was thought to be the most effective way to teach disadvantaged children in the 1960s. Early studies (Weikart, et al., 1978), however, established that children who participated in the other curriculum models—the child-directed traditional nursery-school model and the cooperatively planned High/Scope Perry Preschool model—experienced the same levels of academic growth as children who participated in DISTAR. The 1986 study is an attempt to follow up on the success of these children a decade or so later. According to the High/Scope researchers who conducted the study, children taught by the DISTAR model reported twice the incidence of delinquency and related family and social problems. Participants in the High/Scope and traditional nursery-school groups, according to the study, reported more positive family relations and attitudes toward themselves and others. High/Scope researchers Schweinhart et al. have argued that these results should not be surprising. After all, they said, High/Scope and the traditional nursery-school models included social and behavioral goals for the children, but DISTAR laid claim only to academic goals—a reflection of the confidence that educators at that time had in the benefits of direct instruction in skills presumed to be requisite for reading.

As policymakers examine curriculum choices for the early childhood initiatives of the 1990s, Schweinhart, Weikart and Larner (1986) and other High/Scope researchers have used the results of this controversial study to recommend giving pause to the idea of formal academic schooling for four-year-olds. Not all education researchers, however, agree with the reported ill effects of direct instruction, such as DISTAR, or with their view of what constitutes formal academic learning.

For the past decade, professionals from many different disciplines have been rethinking how best to prepare children for academics and life. Researchers in the field of beginning reading are redefining how children "get ready" to read. Direct teaching of subskills, once thought to be building blocks for book reading in kindergarten and first grade, has lost ground to models that emphasize early experiences with books, playful exploration of written language, and collaborative learning with peers and adults in many different settings. Although research in beginning reading historically has focused on letter and word knowledge in first grade, a recent emphasis on literacy development before entry into formal schooling has provided many insights into what preschool children know about written language and how they come to know it.

What differentiates recent research on beginning literacy development from a past focus on maturation and the idea that lower-level learning must precede higher-level learning, is a characterization of the child who literally from birth is "getting ready to read." According to this view, the child is becoming literate by actively constructing and using symbols within the interactive social context of family, play, school, and community. In order to better represent this shift in perspective, the beginning stage of learning to read is not called "reading readiness" or "early reading and writing" but *emergent* literacy (Clay, 1966; Teale & Sulzby, 1986; Goodman, Altwerger & Marek, 1989) to emphasize that literacy is a developmental process analogous in many respects to oral language learning. Within this concept of literacy development, then, written language learning cannot be confined to the doorstep of the kindergarten or first grade, and a great deal of importance should be attached to the experiences of the three- or four-year-old child (Adams, 1990).

However, while the early childhood educators have been explicit about what they don't want—the curriculum and standardization of the public-school primary grades—those who espouse an expanded public-school role are much less articulate about what learning they want early schooling to accomplish. Ambach (NYS Education Department, 1983), for example, originally built his argument for universal public education for four-year-olds on his perception that the four-year-old of today could already do what is typically taught in the kindergarten and so, he argued, why not move the curriculum down a year, ultimately allowing children to graduate after eleventh grade, at the age of sixteen or seventeen. The focus of the argument seems to have shifted considerably since then, one emphasis being the educational benefits an early start can give to children who are less prepared for school, rather than a general acceleration of the process of schooling.

Gersten, Darch, and Gleason (1988), for example, in their review of the characteristics of academic kindergartens that appeared to promote the later school success of low-income children, note that the relationship between poverty and failure persists in our schools. The authors believe that the separation of academic learning from social development often described by the researchers in the literature on appropriate early childhood education (Schweinhart, Weikart & Larner, 1986; Schweinhart & Weikart, 1988) is a false dichotomy and, if applied to the education of disadvantaged children, would limit what schools might be able to accomplish for these children. Without the economic and educational resources of middle-class parents who provide an academic curriculum at home for their preschoolers, low-income children may depend entirely on teachers and schools to provide them with the resources to achieve comparable academic learning. In the interests of equity, these authors believe that early-childhood education should be "academic."

Lisa Delpit, a former first-grade teacher and McArthur Fellow, notes that the much-maligned DISTAR and its direct teaching of letters of the alphabet may have been considered successful with children of poverty or children of color because it actually taught them new information that they needed to know in order to read and write. Rather than penalize children for what they do not already know from home—what they have never been taught—Delpit says *teach* them (Delpit, 1988).

At the same time, David Elkind, current president of the National Association for the Education of Young Children (NAEYC) and nationally known lecturer and writer, argues emotionally for a nonacademic early childhood experience. Elkind calls the incursion of teacher-initiated academics—particularly reading—into the preschool the "miseducation" of children. In his view, and that shared by many other early childhood educators, such academic efforts are not only misdirected but harmful to the development of young children (Elkind, 1988).

Making good on the promise that every child in America will start elementary school ready to learn to read and write will take more than good intentions and money. Although few would argue with the idea that we need to expand early childhood education to achieve this goal, few would agree on exactly what we would have early childhood education do in order to accomplish it.

ORGANIZATION OF THE BOOK

In this book, I present the findings of a two-part study of early schooling and literacy learning. The first part of the study is an historical review of the literature on this topic, and the second is an analysis of the beliefs and understandings of contemporary policymakers in New York State regarding the issue of public school for four-year-old children, including the meaning of school readiness and the role policymakers assign to literacy learning.

I used purposive sampling to identify not only the contemporary policy participants but also historical documents to be reviewed. As a starting point for identification of contemporary policy participants and policy alternatives, I consulted the reports of *Education Week*, widely circulated journals, and the state government's reports and memos. For purposes of the study, I included state government officials, interest group representatives, career bureaucrats, and academics cited in journalistic reports in my definition of "policy participant." I reviewed the yearbooks of the National Society for the Study of Education, documentary histories, and many additional curriculum, methodology, and theory-based sources. Through thematic analysis of current and historical documents, I tried to ascertain which parameters of school readiness have been prominent at different points in time.

I present the historical review in four chapters. Each of the early chapters describes formal attempts at preschool education. Although the chronology of these innovations overlaps, I treat these preschool attempts separately for purposes of analysis. Chapter 2 ("Early Schooling, Literacy and the Law") describes several early school arrangements, including the infant school, dame school and early reading and writing schools; it covers approximately the late seventeenth through mid-nineteenth centuries. Chapter 3 describes kindergarten from the mid-nineteenth century through mid-1960s ("The Early Kindergarten, Readiness, and Reading"). Chapter 4 ("Child Care, Social Class, and the Government") compares the child care center and nursery school and describes Head Start. In this chapter, I describe the government's differing policy orientations toward special groups of children and cover roughly the period from the early twentieth century through the present time. Chapter 5 ("Development: From Mere Description to a Moral Face") explains current educational thinking on the relationship between early schooling, literacy learning, and child development and provides a summary of the first part of the study, including issues that have been replayed over three centuries.

The second part of the study is an analysis of interviews with individuals who represent important contemporary points of view on early schooling in New York State and whose characterizations of school readiness reflect the perspectives of the social institutions or groups they represent. Throughout data collection, I used analytic techniques (Lincoln & Guba, 1985; Yin, 1984; Glaser & Strauss, 1967) to develop categories of the participants' understandings of the issues surrounding current discussions of public school for four-year-olds. I relate these categories to each other and to issues that have been argued throughout the history of early childhood education. In chapters six through twelve, I report these interview data, interpretations, and additional document analyses, and in the appendix, I more fully explain the procedures and methodology used in the second part of the study.

Contemporary policy participants dichotomize expert knowledge into "program" knowledge and "policy" knowledge. This dichotomy is treated in chapter 6 ("School Readiness Defined: From Mama Robin to the SATs"), as is the participants' understandings of the concept of "school readiness." Chapter 7 presents a thematic analysis of the documents that were identified by program participants as representative of the consensus in the field of early childhood at the time of the study ("The Authorities on Developmentally Appropriate Practice: Dispositions, Language, and Cognitively-Oriented Active Learning"). Chapter 8 ("Readiness for School, but What Counts as 'School'? Education, Socialization, and Habilitation") describes how contemporary policy and program knowledge reflects the bureaucratization of education and the separation of its responsibility from other social services. Issues such as auspice and funding help define what constitutes education, particularly since content or program experts have not been altogether successful in defining socialization as a legitimate educational objective.

Within the broad category of values, all participants shared a single concern—that of securing equal opportunity for children of the poor. This shared value is not new to contemporary discussions but instead was the reason for establishing public primary, or reading and writing, schools in the nineteenth century. However, another value—rationality—is probably an artifact of the contemporary bureaucracy and the interrelated configuration of services provided to young children. Equal opportunity and rationality, or an arrangement of services with the requisite standards, oversight and fiscal support that "makes sense" for the children but does not displace existing structures, are explained in chapter 9 ("Equal Opportunity for the Least of Us and Popular in the Suburbs: Public School for Four-year-olds").

Lastly, the demographics of New York State may be seen as driving public policy toward some kind of response to preschool children. Poverty, educational failure, the problems of working women, and many other social concerns and societal changes are providing "windows" of opportunity for creating new policies. Chapter 10 ("Making the Agenda: Conflicts, Windows, and Labels") develops an explanatory theory of how it all may fit together in New York.

In chapter 11 ("Beginning Reading Materials: Are They Getting Harder?"), I reexamine the role of literacy instruction. As described in chapter 6, present-day policy participants rejected the notion that reading and writing belonged in the preschool curriculum. The early childhood experts I interviewed for this study claimed that the reading curriculum formerly taught in first grade has been shifted down to the kindergarten. Kindergartens were thought to be more academic than in the past, requiring children to have mastered a reading curriculum in kindergarten that used to be taught in first grade. By extension, these program specialists perceived prekindergartens as under pressure to teach what was formerly a kindergarten curriculum. Because the research literature is strangely silent on kindergarten practices, and even less has been written on curriculum practices at the prekindergarten levels, I present an initial review of changes in what might be called the reading "curriculum" itself—the beginning levels of commercial reading materials. Although the focus of this review is the material published by one company, Scott Foresman, these materials have been both widely used and frequently analyzed for change over the past sixty years. Thus, a perceptible shift in either the difficulty of the materials or the age of the children targeted for instruction offers some evidence that may corroborate or undermine the perceptions of the program specialists regarding more reading at earlier ages.

Finally, I synthesize the study in chapter 12 ("The Shared History: Literacy, Young Children and Early Schooling"). Public perceptions of what children should learn and, likewise, public responsibility for early childhood education have changed according to values and beliefs of different historical periods, including the present.

2. EARLY SCHOOLING, LITERACY, AND THE LAW

Agreed that Thomas Fleg, John Whitney, and Joseph Bemus go about the town to see that children were taught to read the English tongue and...some orthodox catechism.... Ordered that Captain Mason and Simon Stone shall go to John Fisk to see if his children be taught to read.

—*Watertown Records*, 1670

ALTHOUGH THE PRESS to teach cognitive skills to younger and younger children is often assumed to be a relatively recent phenomenon related to the "hurried child" syndrome of contemporary life (Elkind, 1988a; Suransky, 1977), it is, instead, an issue that was discussed, even legislated on, more than two centuries ago. How early literacy skills should be taught, by whom, to whom, and at what age are pedagogical and research questions that persist to this day. The actual educational policies that become adopted and the beliefs about children's literacy development that these policies represent are influenced not only by prevailing expert opinion but also by deeply rooted social mores and demographic and economic realities.

In this chapter and in the two that follow,[1] I present in broad strokes an overlapping chronology of formal attempts to educate preschool children: the dame school and the infant school in this chapter, the kindergarten in chapter 3, and the nursery school, child day care center, and Head Start in chapter 4 (see table 2–1). I describe the importance assigned to reading within these programs, particularly the kindergarten, and I identify social and political influences that helped shape what these educational experiments were and what became of them.

TABLE 2–1
Chronology of Early Childhood Education and Influences on Early Literacy Learning

Time Period	*Early Childhood Education*	*Influences*
Late 1600s		Mather (1706)
through	Parents' responsibility	Locke (1693)
mid 1700s	Early dame schools	Pestalozzi (1894)
	First grammar school (1789)	Owen (1823)
Late 1700s	First primary school (1818)	
through	Infant schools (1820–35)	Brigham (1832)
mid 1800s	First day nursery (1840)	
	First kindergarten (1860)	Froebel (1895)
	School entry ages stabilize (1880)	Dewey (1897)
	First public school kindergarten (1880)	Gesell (1912, 1931)
Late 1800s	First nursery school (1920)	Morphett & Washburne (1931)
through	[Progressive reform]	
mid 1900s	First public school nursery schools (1933–46)	Flesch (1957) Chall (1965)
	[Sputnik reform]	Durkin (1959, 1968)
	Head Start (1965)	Hunt (1961)
	[Civil rights reform]	Bloom (1964)
Late 1900s	Kindergarten, nursery school & child day care expansion	Bereiter & Englemann (1966)
through present	[Comprehensive Child Care Act (1971)]	Weikart et al. (1971)
	[Nation "at risk" reform]	Berrueta-Clement et al. (1984)
	First universal public prekindergartens [Giant Step, NYS (1987)]	Elkind (1988)

Within these broad and interrelated topics, I suggest a configuration of values, knowledge, and economic and demographic circumstances that have been realigned during different points in history to produce differing policies toward preschool children and literacy. Knowledge of the past can inform contemporary initiatives for four-year-olds. Knowledge of the issues that have been replayed over the history of American education for preschoolers can offer a useful perspective for studying how preschool education is today achieving a place on the policy agenda.

Literacy and Salvation

In Puritan New England, the reading of the Bible was believed to be inextricably tied to salvation. Given the extremely high infant mortality rate of the time, it is not surprising that they wanted and even forced children to learn to read and write as soon as possible to ensure that children would be saved should they die in infancy (Kaestle and Vinovskis, 1980). Early in the eighteenth century, Cotton Mather advised his congregation that "The Children should learn to read the Holy Scriptures; and as Early as may be" (in Moran & Vinovskis, 1986, p. 30) and "As soon as tis possible, I make the Children learn to write" (*On the Education of Children*, in Cohen, 1974, p. 408). Mid-seventeenth-century law in Massachusetts not only acknowledged the desirability of children learning to read but placed responsibility for literacy and religious training on the family. Such laws authorized magistrates to remove children from families who were derelict in their duty:

> For as much as the good education of the children is of Singular behoof and benefit to any commonwealth, and whereas many parents and masters are too indulgent and negligent of their duty in that kind, it is therefore ordered that the selectmen of every town in the several precincts and quarters where they dwell, shall have a vigilant eye over their brethren and neighbors to see, first, that none of them shall suffer so much barbarism in any of their families as not to endeavor to teach by themselves, or others, their children. . . so much learning as may enable them perfectly to read the English tongue and knowledge of the capital laws, upon penalty of 20 shillings for each neglect therein. (*Laws and Liberties of Massachusetts*, 1648, in Bremner, 1970, p. 40)

A similar law was proposed in Pennsylvania that required all children to "be instructed in reading and writing so that they be able to read the Scriptures, and to write by that time that they attain to twelve years of age." Parents were fined five pounds for each child who did not meet that level of literacy (*Charter to William Penn*, 1682, in Bremner, 1970, p. 101). What is unusual about the Pennsylvania law is that it stipulated an age, and twelve years old was quite late according to first-person accounts of that period. For example, Kaestle (1983) cites a testimonial written in 1690 by a John Barnard to attest to his "reputable" parents' care in instructing him in the Christian religion and "knowledge of letters. By that time I had a little passed my sixth year. . . I had read my Bible through thrice." Widely read in colonial New England, the philosopher John Locke also advocated early literacy in his 1693 work *Some Thoughts Concerning Education*, albeit a child-centered version of reading and writing:

> When he can talk, 'tis time he should begin to learn to read. But give me leave here to inculcate again what is apt to be forgotten, that great care is to be taken that it be never made as a business to him nor he look on it as a task. . .children may be cozened into a knowledge of letters, be taught to read without perceiving it to be anything but a sport, and play themselves into that which others are whipped for. (in Kaestle and Vinovskis, 1980, p. 50)

Historians Carl Kaestle and Maris Vinovskis (1980) note that colonial diarists and letter writers, at least, took Locke's counsel seriously. To illustrate, the authors provide a telling example of one Mrs. Pinckney writing to request a particular toy for her child so that she may "teach him to play himself into learning" according to "Mr. Locke's method." Mrs. Pinckney says she has carefully studied this method, and "Mr. Pinckney (his father) himself has been contriving a sett of toys to teach him letters by the time he can speak. You perceive we begin betimes for he is not yet 4 months old" (p. 309).

Early School Arrangements

Although Puritan New Englanders did not specify precisely at what age children should be taught to read, other than "as fast as ever they can make it" (Cotton Mather, 1741, in Kaestle & Vinovskis, 1980), many colonial families increasingly sent their children to school, and at very young ages, if schools were available. Colonial parents often used the so-called dame schools, where a woman would teach reading and writing in her own home, as well as any sort of free public schools, known as common schools, that may have been established nearby. Between the mid-eighteenth century and mid-nineteenth century most rural four- and five-year-olds were in school (Kaestle, 1983). Lucy Larcom describes a dame school of this era run by her Aunt Hannah:

> I began to go to school when I was about two years old, as other children about us did. The mothers of those large families had to resort to some

> means of keeping their little ones out of mischief, while they attended to their domestic duties. Not much more than that sort of temporary guardianship was expected of the good dame who had us in charge. But I learned my letters in a few days, standing at Aunt Hannah's knee while she pointed them out in the spelling book with a pin, skipping over the *a b ab* into words of one and two syllables, thence taking a flying leap into the New Testament, in which there is concurrent family testimony that I was reading at the age of two years and a half. (in Bremner, 1970, p. 445)

Early district schools were not necessarily an improvement over the dame schools. Many parents simply sent their youngest children along with the older ones, so that forty to sixty children of diverse ages would share an uncomfortable room—too cold for the older ones who had to sit far from the stove and stiflingly hot for the younger ones next to the stove, all sitting on hard backless benches with feet dangling underneath. Apparently the youngest children received very little attention: five minutes twice a day of rote alphabet recitation, according to one account, and otherwise pure boredom and the risk of falling off the high bench and smashing against the floor (Kaestle, 1983). After the youngsters learned the alphabet, they could move on to memorizing one-syllable words and practicing vowel exercises, such as *ab, eb, ib, ob, ub.* It was difficult for the teacher to teach from texts because parents sent their own books to school for their children to use, following what Kaestle (1983) calls a "jealously guarded tradition," and often resulting in as many different texts as there were children.

In urban areas, younger children also accompanied their older siblings to the common school, since between the late-eighteenth century and mid-nineteenth century there were no regulations specifying age of entry. During this time period, however, New England gradually established a wide-ranging system of public and private schools. Massachusetts towns with fifty families, for example, had been required since 1647 to hire a schoolmaster and establish a reading and writing school and, where there were a hundred families, a grammar school. With the establishment of public funding for so-called grammar schools, as in Boston, came the stipulation that entering children must already know how to read and write (*The Laws of the Commonwealth of Massachusetts*, 1780–1800, in Bremner, 1970).

At the same time, there was not yet public funding for the "reading and writing," or primary, schools. Kaestle and Vinovskis (1980) describe the thinking of the members of the Boston School Committee who at first decided that maintaining private schools for children under seven was not "very unequal or burdensome" to the parents. Moreover, the committee felt that "most parents have some leisure and that few among us are unequal to the task of teaching the elements of the letters. It ought never to be forgotten that the office of instruction belongs to parents. . . [and] in the retirement of domestic life, parents have opportunities to impart instruction, and gain an influence over their children which the public teacher does not possess" (Wightman, 1860, in Kaestle and Vinovskis, 1980, p. 52).

However, as Kaestle and Vinovskis point out, Boston officials also realized that the majority of children between four and six years old were, in fact, already enrolled in private schools. The issue was not one of who should be responsible for teaching young children to read but rather who should pay for the schooling. Because private school tuition was ultimately deemed unfair to poor parents, in 1818 Boston established public primary schools for children from four to six years old but purposefully excluded those under four. Children under four continued to attend private primary schools, which enrolled at least 20 percent of all three-year-olds in the city. Outside of Boston, children younger than four were not prohibited from attending the common schools, and they continued to do so in large numbers (Kaestle and Vinovskis, 1980, p. 52).

INFANT SCHOOLS AND SOCIAL REFORM

While efforts to eradicate the effects of poverty through the early education of children of the underclasses would seem to be an idea tied to the compensatory education of the 1960s, historians Carl Kaestle and Maris Vinovskis (1980) and Dean May and Maris Vinovskis (1977) have demonstrated that social reform through early intervention actually originated with the infant school movement of the 1800s. The interesting detail presented in this section comes from these recent histories of the infant school movement and its brief tenure in American education (May and Vinovskis, 1977; Kaestle and Vinovskis, 1980). Contemporary questions of what constitutes appropriate learning for young children and who shall provide it have roots deep in these first early childhood schools.

Originating in England with the reformer Robert Owen, these infant schools were an attempt to socialize poor urban youngsters who were often left to the streets while their parents worked in the factories. British supporters of the infant school were as impressed with the possibilities of abundant labor for industry in the form of working mothers and older siblings as they were with mitigating the problems of an urban underclass. Faced with large groups of infants, some as young as eighteen months old, teachers in the British infant schools seized upon the ideas of Johann Pestalozzi, a Swiss educational reformer, to inform their instructional practices. Although Pestalozzi supported the notion of developmental stages in childhood and early development of cognitive abilities in children, he believed that such stimulation should never be forced upon the child and should take place under the mother's instruction. In general, Pestalozzi and the philosopher Jean-Jacques Rousseau, who greatly influenced Pestalozzi, believed that children should be free to explore and question the natural world, that their experiences should be appropriate for their age, and that their experiences should represent a balance among moral, physical, and cognitive areas. Owen applied Pestalozzi's instructional principles to poor infants in institutional settings, and it was this version of Pestalozzi and the infant school that was first transported to America.

The first infant schools in America were opened in Philadelphia and New York City in the early 1820s, and word of their promise and success rapidly spread through the efforts of William Russell, the first editor of the newly established *American Journal of Education*, and through urban newspapers and women's magazines. Because substantial numbers of toddlers were already enrolled in school in the New England of this time period, the idea of school for two- through four-year-olds was not a radical notion. What excited the educators and social reformers of the day was the content of instruction, supposedly geared to the developmental level of the individual child and not restricted to the "tedious pedagogy" of the common school. Consequently, the new methodology of the infant school held great promise for the moral and intellectual uplifting of impoverished children. In their 5th Annual Report, the ladies of the Infant School Society of the City of Boston optimistically referred to the infant school of 1834 as "a ray of millennial light that reveals a way in which poverty, with all its attendant evils—moral, physical, and intellectual, may be banished from the world" (in May and Vinovskis, 1977, p. 62). Likewise, Russell wrote in his first editorial in the January 1826 issue of *American Journal of Education* that "the establishment of infant schools [was]. . .one of the most important epochs in the history of education," and he promised that his journal would regularly report on the progress of the infant schools. Russell felt there was "no danger of beginning instruction too soon, if it is begun in the right way, and with expectations sufficiently moderate" (in May and Vinovskis, 1977, p. 68).

Reading and the Disease of Precocity

Just as the efficacy of Head Start and the poverty programs of the 1960s became evaluated in terms of cognitive growth, particularly reading achievement, the brief tenure of the infant school in American education was also inextricably tied to the teaching of reading to very young children. Initially, Owen established the infant school to "train children from their earliest infancy in good habits of every description which will of course prevent them from acquiring those of falsehood and deception" (Owen, 1816, *New View of Society,* in May and Vinovskis, 1977, p. 66). Although Owen himself wanted to exclude books altogether from the infant school, others supported teaching young children to read. In 1823, Owen's son wrote that "it has been deemed necessary, in order to meet the wishes of the parents, to commence teaching the children the elements of reading at a very early age" (in Kaestle and Vinovskis, 1980, p. 55).

Although the ladies of the Infant School Society wanted to reform the morality of the children, they were hard pressed to demonstrate moral improvement in toddlers. Because the infant schools were called "schools" and the teachers "instructresses," these first attempts at early childhood education were presumed to teach basic reading and writing, as all other schools did. The idea that the content and methodology were uniquely suited to the development of children at that age was lost on the public at large. Rather, several of the infant schools began holding demonstrations of the reading skills mastered by two- and three-year-olds, something that caught the public's attention and popularized private infant schools among the middle and upper classes. Indeed, the trendy *Ladies Magazine* lamented in 1829 that if infant schools were not soon opened for all children, "at the age for entering primary schools those poor children will assuredly be the *richest* of scholars. And why should a plan which promises so many advantages, independent of merely relieving the mother from her charge, be confined to children of the indigent?" (in May and Vinovskis, 1977, p. 78).

However, just as the infant schools attained rapid prominence because of widely publicized and exaggerated claims of teaching infants and toddlers to read, this association of the infant schools with premature precocity also contributed to their equally rapid demise. As May and Vinovskis (1977) illustrate with Infant School Society proceedings, school records, and journal and editorial comment, virtually all publicity and philanthropic contributions had ceased by 1835, and the remaining infant schools closed their doors within a year.

Kaestle and Vinovskis (1980) identify three sources of opposition to the infant schools. First, what has been called the "cult of domesticity" reemerged in the mid-nineteenth century, emphasizing the importance of the role of the mother in shaping the social, moral, and intellectual development of children, who themselves were being viewed as "innocent" and "pliant." The industrialization of at least urban areas and the separation of the workplace from the home helped to differentiate roles by sex. In the absence of production or "economic work" in the home, a new domestic role may have been created for women, that of training and educating children.

A second source of opposition involved the concern for a balanced program for very young children, one that emphasized their physical as well as intellectual development. While infant schools did provide play in the form of recess, clapping, and marching, they were widely perceived as forcing cognitive development. Ironically, the work of Pestalozzi, which helped ground the infant school movement in "expert" theory, also contributed to its abandonment several years later when his emphasis on the importance of the mother and natural development of the mind and body became more clearly articulated in America.

The philosophy of Pestalozzi that "all instruction of man is only the Art of helping Nature to develop in her own way" (*How Gertrude Teaches Her Children*, in Weber, 1984, p. 29) influenced a spate of hypotheses about maturation written during the 1830s and 1840s. It would resurface in similar forms in the educational literature of the next hundred years. One of the most influential books of the era was physician Amariah Brigham's *Remarks on the Influence of Mental Excitement upon Health*, published in 1832, in which he warns against the evils of precocity in children and "lasting injury" inflicted on body and mind:

> I beseech parents...to pause before they attempt to make prodigies of their own children. Though they may not destroy them by the measures they adopt to effect this purpose, yet they will surely enfeeble their bodies, and greatly dispose them to nervous affections. Early mental excitement will serve only to bring forth beautiful, but premature flowers, which are destined soon to wither away, without producing fruit. (in Kaestle and Vinovskis, 1980, p. 59)

"Precocity" was defined at this time as a "morbid condition" precipitating insanity, imbecility, epilepsy, and premature old age (Kaestle and Vinovskis, 1980). The metaphor of the child as a flower and the deleterious effects of premature reading were extended in another popular book in the domestic literature:

> It is obvious how difficult a task it must be. . .to let their sprightly little darling alone, till the rain and the sunshine opened the bud and prepared the way for mental culture. . .the common idea that if you can teach an infant to read with considerable ease. . .in its third or fourth year, it is. . .so much clear gain, is extremely fallacious. (Humphrey, 1840, in Kaestle and Vinovskis, 1980, p. 60)

The ladies of the Infant School Society, reportedly up to date on fashionable trends in the domestic and child-care areas, withdrew their financial support of the infant schools. However, there was no discernible decline in the numbers of young children enrolled in these schools, even at the height of the educational community's disapproval.

In fact, as Kaestle and Vinovskis (1980) demonstrate with attendance data from Massachusetts, parents did not stop sending children under five to school in spite of the experts' warnings and school prohibitions. In 1840, for example, 40 percent of three-year-olds were still going to public schools, prompting the authors to conclude that parents, rather than school officials, were still in charge of the age of their children's entry into school. Between 1840 and 1875, however, the percentage of three- and four-year-olds in public schools substantially declined. Thus, the authors note, after a "fifty-year campaign by educators against early entrance, many parents acquiesced only reluctantly" (p. 65).

The third and most significant source of opposition to early education and the infant-school movement was the increasing bureaucratization of the public schools. When the infant-school movement was prominent, only urban districts such as Boston were sufficiently bureaucratized to register opposition to the new progressive methodology. And although such districts did oppose infants in school, it was primarily because they did not want to be saddled with public funding for a yet younger group of children. As children under five continued to attend district schools, school bureaucrats who were initially satisfied to warn parents of the "dangers" of precocity, gradually began to regulate minimum entry ages (Kaestle and Vinovskis, 1980, p. 64).

A major reason for school regulations on minimum entry ages was the increasingly "rational" organization of schools according to age grading and other bureaucratic procedures to enhance efficiency. This type of organization further differentiated the school from the family, both structurally and functionally (Kaestle and Vinovskis, 1980, p. 64). Children under five were seen as a disruption and inconvenience to schools, needing nurses rather than teachers, and their presence was viewed as "pernicious:"

> Besides the injury to the young child, a very serious evil results to the schools from admitting children who are sent at an age so tender that no motive can exist for it on the part of the parents except the desire to be relieved from a little care at home. (*Chelmsford Town Report*, 1858, in Kaestle and Vinovskis, 1980, p. 64)

Similarly, the notion of children under five in school was also characterized as "absurd" from every point of view except that of the "majority of parents, who consider that they pay to have children taken out of their way for a given number of hours, and are annoyed by their presence at home" (*Lynn School Report*, 1880, in Kaestle and Vinovskis, 1980, p. 65). The custodial role of the parent, as opposed to the school, was regulated by compulsory attendance or nonattendance, with educators tending to raise the minimum entry age to seven, for children from "proper" families, and five for those less fortunate.

Thus the belief that infants and toddlers could and should learn to read remained unchallenged for the first two centuries of American history, even though responsibility for teaching youngsters shifted from the father to the mother by the early eighteenth century and finally, by mid-nineteenth century, to the school. Formal literacy training of preschoolers fell out of favor by the mid-nineteenth century and did not regain a position of high prominence on the policy agenda until the 1960s. Although toddlers as young as two years old were sent to the early common schools, this practice had become incompatible with the growing standardization and bureaucratization of the later primary schools. But by the turn of the century, the kindergarten movement had become associated with progressive education and, within the next two decades, gained wide public and professional acceptance.

BLACK CHILDREN AND LITERACY: A DIFFERENT HISTORY

About a decade ago, educators Charles Cunningham and Keith Osborn (1979) debunked the myth that Blacks were not involved in early childhood education before enactment of the poverty legislation of the 1960s. According to these researchers, Black Americans have struggled for a long time to educate themselves and their young children. The first Black Americans arrived in the Virginia in 1619 as indentured servants, not as slaves, and these Black indentured servants held the same legal status as similarly indentured White servants. One year after their arrival, Virginia established a public school for "Negroes and Indians." Within the next few decades, however, slavery became more widespread and few formal schools were established for Blacks (Cunningham & Osborn, 1979, pp. 20–21).

Although education was generally "haphazard" for most children prior to the common-school movement of the mid-nineteenth century (Cunningham & Osborn, 1979, p. 20), the initial "free" education laws passed in New York and the New England states applied only to White children whose parents were paupers. Even after the common-school movement took hold and the public began to support free primary schools (primarily in New England and the mid-Atlantic regions), Black children were not permitted to attend these primarily White schools. In the North as well as in the South, formal educational opportunities for Black children were rare. Nineteenth-century historian Morgan Dix (1898, in Bremner, 1970) recalled slave schools in *A History of the Parish of Trinity Church in the City of New York*. Dix preserved the *New York Mercury*'s 1760 announcement of the opening of a "charitable" school for slave children:

> This is to inform the Public, that a Free School is opened near the New-Dutch-Church, for the instruction of 30 Negro Children, from 5 years old and upwards, in Reading, and in the Principles of Christianity, and likewise sewing and knitting; which school is entirely under the Inspection of the Church of England in this City. (Dix, 1898, in Bremner, 1970, p. 336)

All "Persons" who had the "Usefullness and future Welfare of their young Slaves at Heart" were urged to send them to this school, the only cost being firewood for the winter. The same newspaper carried an ad for a "sober Woman of fair Character and Qualifications" to teach the children to read and sew.

There were likewise only a few private schools for Black children. One such school was established in North Carolina by John Chavis, a Princeton-educated, free Black teacher and missionary who educated many prominent white southerners in the early 1800s. Chavis advertised his evening school for Blacks in the *Raleigh Register* in 1808: "The evening school shall commence at an hour by the sun. When the white children leave the house, those of colour will take their places, and continue until ten o'clock" (from Edgar W. Knight, 1930, in Bremner, 1970, p. 520–21). Chavis charged Whites $2.50 per quarter and Blacks S1.50 each quarter.

Cunningham and Osborn (1979) consulted *The Negro Yearbook of 1931–32* to obtain a rough idea of the number of formal schools—free, charitable, and private—established for Blacks during the 240 years between their arrival and the Civil War: There were twenty-four such schools.

Besides "formal" schools, Blacks attended "Sabbath" schools. Based on Bible reading and recitation, such schools were established on southern plantations for the purposes of providing religious instruction and literacy to slaves (Cunningham & Osborn, 1979). The historian Frank Klingberg (1941, in Bremner, 1970) described the advocacy of the Reverend Alexander Garden, a leading Episcopalian minister and educator who ran a Charleston school for slaves for twenty years during the mid-eighteenth century. In 1740, Garden wrote a letter to a fellow official in the Society for the Propagation of the Gospel saying that every plantation owner of at least eighty slaves should send one of his "most capable and best disposed" male slaves away to attend school. The slave should stay at the school "till he be Taught to read the Bible, to say the Church Catechism by heart, and to use the Common Prayer; and who from thenceforth" would be employed by the plantation owner to teach "in that same manner" all the slave children of that plantation and those of any smaller, neighboring plantations (Klingberg, 1941, in Bremner, 1970, p. 335). By the mid-1800s, however, only "oral instruction" was permissible (Cunningham & Osborn, 1979).

Several slave uprisings of the early 1800s, particularly the revolt of Nat Turner in 1831, prompted slave owners to ban literacy for Blacks. Plantation owners feared that literacy would liberate the slaves. Laws were passed throughout the South that forbade teaching Blacks to read and write:

> Any person or persons who shall endeavor or attempt to teach any free person of color, or slave, to spell, read, or write, shall . . . be fined in a sum not less than two hundred and fifty dollars nor more than five hundred dollars. (*Acts Passed at the 13th Annual Session of the General Assembly of the State of Alabama*, 1832, in Bremner, 1970, p. 514)

An 1840 South Carolina statute fined anyone found guilty of the crime of teaching a Black to read. Additionally, if the offender were White, he would be imprisoned; were he a "free person of color" he would be whipped ("not exceeding 50 lashes") (in Bremner, 1970, p. 514). Further, any "assemblages" of slaves, free Blacks, "mulattoes or mestizoes, even in company with white persons" for the purpose of "mental instruction" was expressly forbidden "either before the rising of the sun or after the going down of the same" (*South Carolina Statutes at Large*, 1800, in Bremner, p. 338). Thus, Blacks had to go underground to learn to read and write, creating what became known as the "clandestine" or "midnight" schools, which were operated at great risk by Black teachers and by Whites throughout the South until the end of the Civil War (Cunningham & Osborn, 1979). The reknowned statesman, orator, and writer Frederick Douglass, who was himself a slave, described how he learned to read and write:

> Very soon after I went to live with Mr. and Mrs. Auld, she very kindly commenced to teach me the A, B, C. After I had learned this, she assisted me in learning to spell words of 3 or 4 letters. Just at this point of my progress, Mr. Auld found out what was going on, and at once forbade [her] to instruct me further, telling her, among other things, that it was unlawful, as well as unsafe, to teach a slave to read. To use his own words, further, he said, "If you give a nigger an inch, he will take an ell. A nigger should know nothing but to obey his master—to do as he is told to do. Learning would spoil the best nigger in the world. Now," said he, "if you teach that nigger (speaking of myself) how to read, there would be no keeping him. It would forever unfit him to be a slave." (Douglass, 1825–30, in Bremner, 1970, pp. 516–17)

Douglass described how he was watched very closely after that, but still managed to learn to read by bribing poor white children in his neighborhood to teach him to read ("the more valuable bread of knowledge") in exchange for fresh bread from his master's kitchen. By challenging other White boys that he could write as well as they (and producing a few letters that he had learned from shipyard carpenters, for example *S* for starboard timber), Douglass learned to write. He then refined his writing by laboriously copying the handwriting that he found in discarded copybooks at his master's house.

As Douglass and other former slaves have described in narrative accounts of their lives in bondage, racism and fear on the part of Whites made it well-nigh impossible for Blacks to become literate before the

Civil War. This shocking bit of Black history stands in stark contrast to that period's increasingly more common entitlements to White children, such as the New York law of 1842 that granted education to "all children between the ages of 4 and 16 residing in said city or county" without being "liable to any tax, assessment, or imposition of tuition" (Laws of New York State, 1842, in Bremner, 1970, pp. 463–64). Thus, mid-ninteenth-century slave laws and public records provide mute testimony to the astonishing perseverance and courage of Black children who learned to read during these times—in the North as well as in the South.

3. THE EARLY KINDERGARTEN, READINESS, AND READING

Right feeling is necessary for true thinking; it is only when the heart is joyous that the intellect does its best work. The child depressed by discouragement, burdened with fear, wounded by injustice, or hungry for love, does not thrive either intellectually or morally, and the first aim of the kindergarten is to see that he is happy.

—*Ada Van Stone Harris, 1907*

GIVEN THE STRONG sentiment on the part of school personnel against sending children under the age of seven to school that existed during the middle to late 1800s, it is remarkable that the kindergarten movement for children from two to five would gain such rapid public and professional acceptance by the early twentieth century. The theoretical underpinnings and child-saving objectives of the kindergarten were not much different from those of the short-lived infant school. However, the kindergarten became allied with influential "progressive" educators of the early 1900s—such as John Dewey—who found the kindergarten compatible with their own views of educational reform (May & Vinovskis, 1977, p. 94).

Elizabeth Peabody, teacher and reformer, is usually credited with establishing the first kindergarten in America in 1860 (Kaestle & Vinovskis, 1980). At the turn of the century, only 1 percent of five-year-olds attended kindergarten, and almost half of these children were enrolled in private schools (Spodek, 1982b). Black children also attended kindergartens at this time, but these kindergartens were generally segregated and there were fewer of them (Cunningham & Osborn, 1979). By 1922, 12 percent of all children were in kindergarten; by 1977, this figure reached close to 80 percent (Spodek, 1982b), and currently, all but five states provide free kindergarten to over 90 percent of five-year-olds (NAEYC, 1989). In thirty-nine states and the District of Columbia, all school districts are required by law to provide kindergarten to every family who desires it. Although it has taken well over a century to incorporate the kindergarten into the public school, it is now not only universally available, but in seven states, kindergarten attendance is compulsory for five-year-olds (Robinson, 1987). As Robinson points out, the relatively recent institutionalization of kindergarten and the lowering of the age of compulsory school attendance reflects "the changing nature of society" and its view of early childhood education. Over the last century, the participation rates of White women in the work force and the participation rates of four- and five-year-old children in preprimary school have steadily increased (see figure 3–1).

The evolving definitions of *school* used by the Bureau of the Census also reflect society's changing perceptions of early childhood education. In 1924, the census did not count children under five in school "owing to small numbers and slight educational significance" (U.S. Department of Commerce, Bureau of the Census, 1924). By 1950, the census reported the number of five- and six-year-olds enrolled in kindergarten, but kindergarten children were "not counted as enrolled in school... Nursery schools were not regarded as kindergartens or schools" (U.S. Department of Commerce, Bureau of the Census, 1953). By the time the census published its 1980 criteria for what would count as school, the definition had been expanded significantly:

> [Enrollment] in any type of regular or special school...for at least 2 hours per day...A nursery school is a group or class that is organized to provide education experiences for children during the year preceding kindergarten...The nursery school, as defined here, includes instruction as an important and integral phase of its program of child care. (U.S. Department of Commerce, Bureau of the Census, 1982)

Not only are kindergarten children now counted as going to school by the census, but so are children who attend nursery school. "Essentially custodial care" and "babysitting," on the other hand, are not considered school. A brief history of how kindergarten came to be and how it has become identified with public school may help define contemporary concerns with schooling for four-year-olds.

FIGURE 3–1
Converging Participation Rates of White Women in the Work Force and Children in Preprimary School

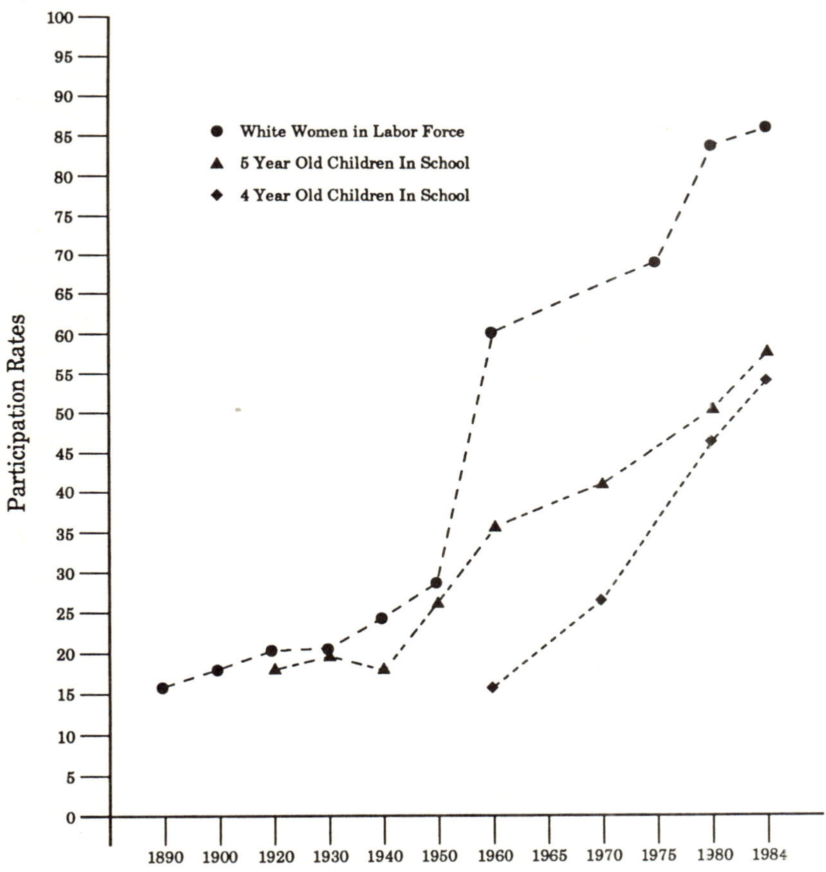

Note: The data on white women in the labor force are from Waite (1981, May); the data on participation rates of 5-year-old children during 1920–1950 are from U.S. Department of Commerce, Bureau of the Census (1953); the data for 5-year-olds from 1960 to the present and participation rates for 4-year-olds are from U.S. Department of Education, Office of Educational Research & Improvement (1987).

Early Kindergartens

Similar to the ill-fated infant school of the 1830s, the kindergarten was developed by Friedrich Froebel in Germany as an educational experience for young children, based on Pestalozzi's principles of child development and mother love. Froebel named his infant school a kindergarten (the children's garden), a most "felicitous" choice, according to May and Vinovskis (1977), because a garden seems a much more appropriate place for a very young child than a school. Unlike the infant school, however, the kindergarten did not enroll children younger than three years old and thus did not conflict with the role of the mother in educating infants. According to one interpretation of his work (Kraus-Boelte, 1907), Froebel cautioned against premature schooling, arguing that the "bridge from cradle to manhood" should be made just as long as possible "by having your child a child as long as possible." Froebel, in fact, believed mothers were the very best teachers and, by extension, motherlike females. However, he also felt that most mothers had neither the leisure nor the strength to carry out his program within an isolated family. But proponents of the early kindergarten were quick to point out that kindergarten was not "invented to relieve indolent or overburdened mothers of troubles and embryo suffering" (Harris, 1907, p. 10). Froebel believed that after the age of three, the child's social and moral development required a "larger company of equals" (Kraus-Boelte, 1907, p. 36).

A second difference between the infant school and the kindergarten was the emphasis on the child's discovery of nature and its underlying unity through prescribed manipulations of objects rather than through the memorization of letters and the reading of books (May & Vinovskis, 1977; Ross, 1976). Games, songs, and finger plays, activities similar to what a mother would do with a child and focusing on the everyday activities of children from small German villages, were substituted for reading and writing.

Contemporary researcher Elizabeth Ross (1976) has discovered many stories about the first kindergarten educators that lend detail to their philosophies. When kindergarten teachers deviated from Froebel's principles as, for example, when teacher Anna Coe espoused the teaching of reading and writing in her "American Kindergarten" exhibition at the 1876 Philadelphia Centennial Exposition, kindergarten leaders swiftly and predictably denounced her methods (Ross, 1976). Peabody, editor of the *Kindergarten Messenger* and columnist for the *New England Journal of Education*, resigned her position on the *Journal* staff over the Coe issue. In her 1877 *Guide to the Kindergarten and Intermediate Class*, Peabody argued that reading should be taught simultaneously with writing, but not until "children are hard upon seven years old" (in Kaestle & Vinovskis, 1980, p. 69). The kindergarten did not challenge the prevailing assumption that early intellectual activity such as reading was inappropriate and even harmful to young children.

As Bernard Spodek, an early childhood educator and writer (1982, 1986) points out, the early kindergartens were not altogether sure exactly what their primary mission was about, although the well-educated and well-to-do founders tirelessly worked to spread this early concept of preschool education. The free or charity kindergartens often combined religious training and social work, whereas those that became affiliated with the public schools tended to inculcate diligence and industry. In practice, however, all early kindergartens represented an attempt at social reform, as did the infant-school movement that preceded them. The goals of the kindergarten program were directed not only at the three- to six-year-old population but also at the education of any younger siblings at home.

A large part of the kindergarten teacher's responsibilities became the education of mothers in progressive child-rearing techniques, usually discussed during home visits and "mothers' meetings." As Ross (1976) indicates, teachers either visited homes or conducted mothers' meetings during the afternoons and held kindergarten classes in the mornings. Out of these mothers' meetings grew a cooperative organization that eventually became the contemporary Parent-Teacher Association. Richard W. Gilder, an early president of the New York Kindergarten Association, addressed the anticipated effects of parent education on immigrant children in a speech entitled "The Kindergarten: An Uplifting Social Influence in the Home and the District." This speech was given at the 1903 National Education Association meeting:

> No one can speak of the kindergarten without including the work of the mothers' meeting and club...the teaching there of games, and of handiwork, along with practical discussions on food, cooking, sleep, play, open air, cleanliness...The first thing learned is, perhaps, cleanliness... health, manners, housework, overstimulating young children...Home visitations...and social work are an integral part of the system, [and] there is a very close bond between the kindergarten and the home; the closest of all is, of course, the child...The social uplift is felt first by the child; second, by the family; and third, by the neighborhood. (National Education Association *Proceedings*, 1903, in Bremner, 1971, pp. 1459–60)

In further discussing the social goals of the kindergarten for the 1880 *Journal of Social Science* "Report from a Department Sub-Committee on Kindergartens," W. T. Harris, the first superintendent to incorporate kindergarten within the public schools, indicated that children of the "vicious and improvident" can be "saved for constructive work in our civilization, instead of drifting into our penal institutions" if they are trained in kindergartens from the age of three (Bremner, 1971, p. 1458). Another group of children who would be saved by the kindergarten were the children of the wealthy, who according to Harris, would otherwise "develop caprice, waste their patrimony, and cost the State large sums to repair their excesses" (p. 1458).

Kindergarten education was also a high priority of the National Association of Colored Women (NACW), established in 1896 "for the purpose of raising to a higher plane—home, moral, and civil life" (Yates, 1905, in Cunningham & Osborn, 1979). Anna Murray, member of the NACW and founder of the first Black kindergarten in Washington, D.C., wrote in a 1900 article in *Southern Workman* that kindergartens were "a way up" for Black children, a way to "remove the cause of the many accusations that have been made against us as a race" (Murray, 1900, in Cunningham & Osborn, 1979, p. 26).

In the 1871 Annual Report of the Board of Directors of the St. Louis Public Schools, Harris again explained the "kindergarten system of culture." As preparation for good citizenship or a "constructive career," Harris proposed a balance between work and play, with the contribution of play preeminent, an interpretation of Froebel that Dewey would also adopt:

> Without work, the child learns to know only his caprice, his arbitrary likes and dislikes, and he is training himself for a tyrant. Without play, he is learning to have no will of his own and no personal interest in anything—he will become a slavish drudge. . . A wise teacher learns more from the play of the child regarding his work at the set tasks. What he does in play is his own throughout, both in contents and form, but in work these are prescribed by custom. (in Bremner, 1971, p. 1454)

Froebel's Gifts and the New Progressives

In addition to their child-saving activities, the early kindergartners, as the teachers were called, were devoted to Froebel's ideals of play and joy and to his well-defined program of instruction. Susan Blow, the initiator and first teacher of public school kindergarten in St. Louis in

1873 and a loyal advocate of strict adherence to Froebel, often said that the most important outcome of kindergarten was to bring each child "personal happiness" (Ross, 1976) or, as Froebel said, "to cultivate the heart" (Kraus-Boelte, 1907). Good teaching practices were those that conformed exactly to Froebel's prescribed gifts, occupations, mother songs, and nature study (Spodek, 1982). Certainly, many of Froebel's traditional materials and activities, albeit with some improvisation, endure to this day, such as circle time with rhythmic finger play and songs and stories, the blocks and pegs and rings of the building corner, the crafts and handiwork of the art area, the flower and vegetable planting, and animal care.

However, by the turn of the century, the voices of religion, idealism, and social reform were mediated by a new notion of expert knowledge gained from the scientific study of people, including children. The kindergartners of the early twentieth century wanted their classrooms to reflect this new scientific knowledge based on the work of John Dewey, G. Stanley Hall, and E. L. Thorndike. Both Dewey and Hall credited the kindergarten movement with laying much of the groundwork for the new "progressive" education (Ross, 1976, p. 68). The kindergarten, said to have been fifty years ahead of its time, was such "a happy place" that primary teachers did not even think of it as school (p. 77). Prominent kindergartners such as Patty Smith and Susan Blow were very much interested in what the progressives had to say about Froebel's educational philosophy, and over the next thirty years, the new psychology somewhat changed the kindergarten, but it also greatly facilitated the assimilation of the kindergarten into the public schools (p. 70).

Although he would alter the rigidity of Froebel's sequence of the gifts and occupations, Dewey himself adopted the term *occupations* to represent his own activities for children, and he praised Froebel for recognizing that children learn a great deal from "creative and productive" work (Ross, 1976, p. 68). Dewey agreed with Froebel's emphasis on cooperation and socialization, and he extended these concepts to the idea of the classroom as an interdependent community. The notion of "learning through doing" and the importance of play in the educational life of the child, concepts espoused by both Dewey and Hall, were attributed to Froebel. Dewey said that Froebel demonstrated how "the spontaneous activities of children, plays, games... previously ignored as trivial, futile and even condemned as positively evil [were] the foundation stones of educational method" (p. 68). In addition to proposing the educational significance of play, Hall claimed that Froebel was the first to recognize the continuity of human development, a "progressive process of becoming," (p. 69) through which each individual recreates "the entire pattern of earlier human development" (p. 68).

In the *6th Yearbook of the National Society for the Scientific Study of Education* (Hill, 1907), part of which deals entirely with the kindergarten, the influence of the new progressivism is already apparent. Prominent kindergarten educator Patty Hill noted that the orthodox Froebelians still adhered to the "rationalistic" or "introspective" psychology instead of the newer interpretation of child development based on genetic psychology. In proposing a more modern use of Froebel's building materials, Hill alluded to the work of the well-known French psychologist Alfred Binet to argue that the formal attributes of objects as displayed in Froebelian fashion were not as important to the child's understanding as the function—the social purposes or personal use of objects. The issue of free form and spontaneity in art instruction was also an area of considerable controversy, but Hill did not mention reading instruction in the kindergarten, presumably because neither the conservatives nor the progressives advocated such instruction. However, the authors of a number of the other articles in the 1907 and 1908 *NSSE Yearbooks* did address the role of the kindergarten relative to the primary school and, in the process, began to articulate the goals of the kindergarten program in school, rather than child-saving, terms.

KINDERGARTEN BECOMES MORE LIKE SCHOOL

In describing the ideal or standard to which the kindergarten is held in the 1907 edition of the NSSE Yearbook, Ada Van Stone Harris, for example, proposed that "quality not quantity; process, not product; culture not acquirement" were foremost and the "true purpose" was to "fit the child to enter upon the relations of life. . .the wish to learn and the power of teaching himself" (Harris, 1907, p. 17). Harriette Mills, another contributor to the 1907 NSSE Yearbook, admonished educators not to introduce the material of the primary school in kindergarten, because "that which is intrinsically best in any particular stage of development is the best possible preparation for the stage that is to come" (Butler, author of the *Meanings of Education*, n.d., in Mills, 1907, p. 109). In addressing what body of knowledge—curriculum, in contemporary language—should comprise the kindergarten program,

Mills said that the kindergarten has no "studies in the narrow use of the term as a basis for instruction and training" (p. 104). The prior experiences of the child become the subject matter of kindergarten, and these experiences may be enriched with literature. In stories, the child can "leave the field of his own personal experience, enter the storehouse of [human] race-experience, from which he may return with a measure for his own life and spirit" (p. 108).

Regarding what she called the "practical" questions about the kindergarten and its relation to the primary school, Mills responded to the issue of promotion and the evaluation of what a child has learned in kindergarten. Criteria for promotion should be based on both behavior and knowledge. The behaviors that the child develops are the "habits of obedience, of cheerfulness, of courtesy, of kindness." In addition, Mills suggested the following description of the "knowledge" gained in kindergarten:

> The child carries into the primary school a partially organized body of experience concerning the common interests of home and nature, with a related body of songs and stories, over which he has some language and esthetic control. His ideas of number and form are concrete rather than abstract. . .thus equipped, the child is ready to begin the conventional control of experience that characterizes the next stage of his development. . .It will be joy enough to read and write about the experiences with which he is familiar. . .Thus, the kindergarten fulfills its mediator office and the separation between home and school is effectually and happily bridged. (Mills, 1907, p. 112)

Reading in the Early Kindergarten

Insofar as reading was emphasized in the primary school, New York City kindergarten supervisor Jennie Merrill (1908), in her contribution to the *7th NSSE Yearbook*, felt obliged to explain the connection between kindergarten and primary school reading instruction. "Oral productions of stories and close attention to phonics belong to the primary rather than the kindergarten age," but the kindergarten student does "play with phonics in imitating the sounds of animals" (p. 14). Further, since Pestalozzi wrote in *Leonard and Gertrude* that before the child can read well, he must speak well, Merrill indicated that reading "in a sense" does begin in kindergarten, although "no written symbols are taught." Instead, an interest in songs, pictures, and stories is cultivated, preparing the child for an interest in books, and "if the kindergartner has done her work well, [she] sends the child forward anxious to learn to read" (p. 15). Harris (1907), also writing on the foundation for reading established in kindergarten, cited the opportunities to observe and experiment with "nature and the occupations of man" as the experiences most likely to give meaning to the child's first books. This interpretation was consistent with Dewey's notion that "learning to read should grow out of [a] motive" or an idea for its usefulness (Dewey, 1897, in Bremner, 1971, p. 1135). Dewey himself did not advocate teaching young children to read, as is obvious in his explanation of the philosophy of education at the university elementary school in Chicago, which was reported in an 1897 article in *University Record:*

> Accordingly, no special effort is made to teach children to read in the sixth year, or even in the seventh, unless the indications are that the child is awakening to his needs in that direction. The premature teaching of reading in the present school system, involves undue strain on the eyes, and the nervous system and takes away time from subjects which have a positive content, and devotes it to a purely formal study which the child can master with much less strain and in shorter time when he is ready for it. (Dewey, 1897, in Bremner, 1971, p. 1137)

Although Dewey lectured and wrote on this topic at the turn of the century, the prohibitions against teaching reading in the kindergarten still held some twenty-five years later. In the *24th Yearbook of the National Society for the Scientific Study of Education*, Guy Whipple (1925) noted the inadvisability of introducing formal reading instruction in kindergarten. Rather, Whipple suggested the wealth of experiences children should have as preparation for reading and described six prerequisites for rapid progress. In addition to many interesting experiences, children should be able to talk about ideas in fluent English sentences, with appropriate vocabulary and accurate pronunciation, and the child should demonstrate an interest in learning to read. Twenty-four years later, Gertrude Whipple (1949), in the *48th Yearbook*, described the characteristics of two different urban kindergarten programs that, in her view, prepared students for reading. These programs—one for "advantaged" children and the other for the "poor"—differed very little from what had been recommended three decades previously. In both schools students spent their first year in a nonreading program, observing, discussing, listening to stories and songs, doing motor and rhythmic activities and gardening, and, perhaps, using a "reading readiness"[1] workbook. For poorer students, whose prior experiences were limited, reading instruction was delayed until the child was "individually ready," which might not have been until the fourth grade.

READINESS AND MATURATION

When the Whipples were writing in the NSSE Yearbooks about good reading programs, the idea of *testing* children to determine when reading instruction should begin was a relatively new idea, as was the whole idea of "readiness."[2] At about the same time that the kindergarten was undergoing a transition from orthodox Froebelian to "progressive," educational theory in general was becoming more "scientific." One of the principal initiators of a scientific inquiry in education was E. L. Thorndike, who wrote in *Educational Psychology* that much is said but nothing is proven in education: "There is a plentiful lack of knowledge while opinions more and more abound. They are often very good of their own kind, but they are not science" (Thorndike, 1903, in Bremner, 1971, p. 1446).

Ross (1976) cites several reasons why the kindergarten was a favorite place for the new educational scientists to begin their investigations. First, educational scientists wanted to prove the efficacy of the kindergarten over primary school, and second, they were interested in studying children who enjoyed "freedom of expression" in the kindergarten (p. 69). G. Stanley Hall compared children who had attended kindergarten with those who had not and entitled the results of his study "The Contents of Children's Minds Upon Entering School" (Ross, 1976). According to a story unearthed by Ross, Hall was so taken with exact measurement that he suggested several of the children be measured over all parts of their bodies, "using caliphers for the diameter of the head and body, tape measures for height and circumference, scales for weight, and special instruments for teeth, eyes, ears, nose and movement" (p. 69).

A third reason for the interest in kindergarten was the large numbers of overaged children in first grade who had failed to learn to read, a problem identified through the new scientific surveys (Holmes, 1927; Durkin, 1970). In published results of a survey by the Reading Readiness Committee of the International Kindergartner's Union (Holmes, 1927), the reason for failure most often cited by first grade teachers was a presumed lack of "mental efficiency," a concept popularized by the mental age gradients of the new intelligence tests. This Committee suggested that promotion to first grade should be contingent on the attainment of a certain level of mental efficiency, and instruction in reading should be postponed until the child was ready.

The notion of being ready or not ready for reading instruction was rooted in the work of Arnold Gesell (*The Normal Child and Primary Education*, 1912, in Bremner, 1971) and his associates, who postulated invariant stages of development that cannot be forced to maturity but rather unfold in a predictable sequence. Although most of his work on maturation involved motor responses and physical development, Gesell noted that "education cannot, by formulating courses of study, force intellectual functions. The laws which govern the growth of mind are as immediate and irresistible in their operation as those which govern the growth of body" (p. 1125). Schools should not be in such a "breathless hurry" to teach reading and writing according to some specified time. Such an approach is "foreign to every impulse of childhood" and the "refuge of tired teachers who need not then be resourceful or companionable" (p. 1124). Gesell asked "what does the 6-year-old child care for print? His fingers are itching for contact with things, and his legs are set for chasing butterflies" (p. 1125).

Gesell's colleagues later published studies of the developmental trends in academic learning, including reading, from birth to the age of five years old (Ilg and Ames, 1950). The use of the maturation concept to explain cognitive learning, particularly reading, was seized upon with much enthusiasm, and the 1920s and 1930s saw the development of a multitude of reading readiness tests. A 1927 editorial by Frances Jenkins in *Childhood Education* captured the optimism with which readiness tests were greeted. Finally, educators believed that they would be able to tell when to begin instruction in reading:

> Fortunately the scientific method points the way toward the solution of this as of other baffling problems. The first steps have been taken. First, the problem has been recognized. Second, a name has been coined for the characteristic which is sought, Reading Readiness, a term not only alliterative but meaningful. Third, tests are in process of development which shall be applicable to any young child. . . So we may look forward to the day when the measure of readiness will rest in objective tests and parent and teacher will both be governed thereby. (in Durkin, 1968, p. 37)

An influential study conducted in the Winnetka, Illinois, public schools by Morphett and Washburne (1931) set a mental age of 6½ years as the optimal age for beginning reading instruction. According to the scientific standards of the day, the Morphett and Washburne study established the level of maturation needed for a child to profit from reading instruction, an interpretation of readiness that was to be accepted as conventional wisdom for the next three decades.

In the *48th NSSE Yearbook* on reading, Gertrude Hildreth (1949) defined readiness in two ways: "maturity for the beginning period in school. . . [and] specific preparation for new learning at any stage. . ." In her discussions on reading, however, Hildreth noted that she would consider only the former. Although Hildreth was actually discussing first-grade reading, her comments on readiness are appropriate here. Hildreth added to Whipple's (1925) list of prerequisites for learning to read. Hildreth believed that children should take intelligence tests, readiness and speech proficiency tests, visual and auditory acuity and perception tests, and motor coordination and social adjustment tests. All of these "traits" are important, she stated, but the most important is a mental age of 6½ years. Echoing some contemporary viewpoints, Hildreth advised teachers to defer instruction in "symbol learning" until such mental maturity is reached. According to Hildreth, "measurement and observation of the traits and capacities of school beginners prove that failure is inevitable if children are given formal word drill prematurely" (p. 58). Regarding the readiness experiences of the kindergarten, Hildreth stated unequivocally that these kindergarten experiences cannot substitute for readiness training in first grade because of the "added months of mental growth" in first graders. She reported that first graders spend from four to ten weeks in experiences that will promote readiness for reading instruction.

READING READINESS RECONSIDERED

During the next two decades (1950–70) the concept of readiness in general and readiness for reading in particular would be redefined. Albert Harris's (1961) article in the *60th Yearbook of the NSSE,* "Reading and Human Development," seems to represent a moderate point of view (for that particular era) on maturation and learning and on chronological age, school entry, and reading readiness. Harris held that chronological age in itself bears no significant relation to learning to read but is "significant because it is a dimension in which both maturation and learning take place; when these are equated, younger children do as well as older ones" (p. 20). Regarding reading readiness, Harris reiterated what he called the "general agreement" that it should be "studied and assessed" but the lack of agreement about whether it can be "built." Harris cited the conflicting points of view represented on the one hand by James Hymes, the influential author of the 1958 work *Before the Child Reads*, who said that "drills and exercises cannot do the job that only growth and maturation and living can do," and on the other hand by considerable research showing the benefits of kindergarten experience and "specific training designed to influence readiness."

In the same yearbook, David Russell (1961) alluded to the developmental stages proposed initially by Gesell (and later by Ilg & Ames, 1950) in order to determine the "psychological sequences" in learning to read. Although Russell did advise that developmental principles cannot be extended "wholesale" to reading, he said that there is a "general relationship" between reading achievement and "patterns of human development" (p. 235). Russell followed the penchant for lists, outlines, and nascent taxonomies that was first recorded in Whipple's 1925 state-of-the-art article on reading (1925) and was much in evidence in the *48th Yearbook*, which was devoted to reading (Hildreth, 1949). Russell divided the reading program into "stages," delineated primarily by grade placement, and enumerated the "skills, habits and attitudes" typically developed within these stages (p. 237). It is interesting to note that the habits, attitudes, and skills he assigned to the prereading and kindergarten period do not differ from the prerequisites of Guy Whipple (1925) and William Gray (1927). For example, the habits, attitudes and skills of speaking clearly; enjoying stories; being helpful within a group; becoming acquainted with school routine; gaining understanding of self and the world through stories; building concepts; associating pictures, objects, and words; and using language certainly were not radical departures from 1925. The addition of auditory and visual discrimination appears related to the widespread use of readiness tests and workbooks since the early 1940s.[3]

Also in the *60th Yearbook* is the first NSSE entry that specifically addressed reading in the preschool years. Entitled "Preschool and Kindergarten Experience" and written by Donald Durrell and Alice Nicholson (1961), this article presented a more aggressive view of what young children might be doing in reading and writing. The authors proposed that the background skills necessary to learn reading and writing needed to be specifically taught. Although they acknowledged that speaking and listening are recognized parts of appropriate child development, whereas reading and writing are not always regarded as such, the authors believed reading and writing should be. Citing Dolores Durkin's 1959 study of children who read early, Durrell and Nicholson felt that it is unrealistic to expect the child to emerge a "full-blown" reader "when he is ready" without teaching him how to do it (p. 262). Regarding the readiness materials and activities of the day, the authors proposed that the language activities do not make children more ready, because they already come to school with a larger vocabulary than they need for beginning reading and, further, the auditory and visual discrimination provided in workbooks may improve attention but not readiness for reading. The authors couched their suggestions for "awakening interest in letters" very carefully because of what they viewed as "objection to providing systematic instruction in letter, sounds and words" (p. 268). At that point in time, Durrell and Nicholson felt that the very words *systematic* and *instruction* were deemed unacceptable in the kindergarten, but the authors believed that more should be done beyond encouraging an interest (p. 268).

READINESS AND LEARNING

In order to more fully explain this changing concept of reading readiness in the fifties and sixties it is necessary to discuss the contributions of several educational psychologists to learning theory. As Edward Tyler (1964) notes in his review on readiness to learn in the *63rd Yearbook*, during the 1930s and for several decades following, influential educators such as Carleton Washburne cautioned against giving the child "something to do for which he has not the necessary ripeness" (Washburne, 1936, in Tyler, 1964, p. 212). In a 1936 *Progressive Education* article entitled "Ripeness," Washburne asked "What's the hurry?" a question that Tyler identifies with the beliefs of educators during the 1930s and 1940s. By contrast, noted Tyler, educators in the 1960s were more apt to ask "What's the delay?" (p. 212). Even in the field of reading readiness, educators had gone beyond thinking that mental age was by itself an adequate criterion for determining when to begin instruction and, as an illustration, Tyler cited Arthur Gates's (1937/1983; Anderson & Gates, 1950) research on the effects of instruction on beginning reading performance. A more "fruitful" approach, in Tyler's view, and one that anticipated the subskill models of reading acquisition of the next decade, was that of "cognitive readiness" or "learning sets." As

Tyler explained it, an assessment of cognitive readiness is "derived from an analysis of the knowledge and skills required for some new cognitive activity [and]...once these components are known, they can be arranged in a hierarchy that proceeds from lower to higher levels of knowledge" (Tyler, 1964, p. 238). Tyler based this approach primarily on the work of Robert Gagne, who demonstrated that success in solving mathematical equations was more dependent on the learner's prior knowledge or "learning sets" relative to the task than on a general ability level (p. 230). Although Tyler allowed that his proposal addressed only educational readiness related to knowledge structure and not other issues such as motivational readiness, other educators were developing hierarchical structures and principles of operant conditioning to apply to children's affective behavior (p. 239).

In a 1964 article entitled "A Hierarchy of Educational Tasks" that appeared in *Exceptional Children*, Frank Hewett outlined an educational program to "establish a point of meaningful contact between teacher and the child" (Hewett, 1964, pp. 3254–3260, in Cohen, 1974). According to Hewett, meaningful contact could only be established when the child is "experiencing gratification in the learning situation and the teacher is in control" (p. 3254). Whereas a normal child will be motivated by grades, approval, and achievement, a child with learning problems needs a "broader educational frame of reference." As Hewett explained it, the teacher of a child with problems needs to find the right type of "gratification," even if it requires candy for each correct response, so that increasing control of the learning situation can be exercised by the teacher, including structure, routine, and definite limits. Hewett's hierarchy ranges from the lowest level of least control for the teacher and maximum gratification for the student, to the fifth level, wherein the child responds to social reinforcement and, finally, to the sixth and seventh levels, during which the child is motivationally ready to take on academic work. In other words, Hewett claims that until the child masters the first five levels the child is not really ready for remedial work. Although academic material may be presented at low readiness levels, the child's educational needs are more basic, and the appropriate balance or "point of contact" between student gratification and teacher control must be initiated.

While other educators were generating taxonomies of behaviors and skills that they believed would enhance the child's readiness to learn, J. McVicker Hunt and Benjamin Bloom began publishing work that would turn attention to the youngest children and, once again, focus on the dimension of time. Bloom argued in *Stability and Change in Human Characteristics* that "marked changes in the environment in the early years can produce greater changes in intelligence than will equally marked changes in the environment at later periods of development" (Bloom, 1964, in Cohen, 1974, p. 3251). Basing his argument on the sequential nature of all of human development, including the stages formulated within Erikson's conflict resolution, Freudian psychoanalytic theory, Piagetian cognitive development and Gesell's maturational theory, Bloom concludes that the earlier developments, those that take place within the early years, are "crucial for all that follow" (p. 3253). J. McVicker Hunt proposed in his 1962 article "The Psychological Basis for Using Pre-School Enrichment As an Antidote for Cultural Deprivation" not only that the early years were important but also that the damage caused by deprivation was also reversible, if it did not continue for too long:

> Presumably, that retardation which occurs during the second year, and even that during the third year, can probably be reversed to a considerable degree by supplying proper circumstances in either a nursery school or a day-care center for children of four and five—but I suspect it would be preferable to start with children at three years of age. (in Cohen, 1974, p. 3246)

While psychologists, educators, and other child development experts were reexamining the preschool years and prior notions of readiness to learn, historical circumstances provided the impetus for governmental involvement in the schools. With the launching of the Russian satellite Sputnik in the 1950s, the movement to turn education away from progressivism and back to fundamentals came to the fore in American education. In addition, the increasing public awareness of urban, particularly minority, poverty brought forth renewed commitment to social reform and to the promise of education as a way to break the cycle of poverty. Arthur Bestor, an outspoken critic of the schools in general and of the tracking and watered-down curriculum of the high school in particular, wrote on the importance of education to all members of a democracy in *The Restoration of Learning*, published in 1955:

> I am not seeking to minimize the difficulty of giving to the children of all the people the intellectual and cultural background that belonged in the past only to those brought up in surroundings of opulence, leisure, and privilege. I am simply asserting that to do this was precisely the task

> which a democratic educational system was created to perform. And I am insisting that the public schools must devote their resources wholeheartedly to this end, for to do otherwise would be to betray the very ideal that created them. (in Bremner, 1974, p. 1761)

Because several educational experiments with very young children in the preceding decades had demonstrated that even two- and three-year-olds could learn to read, such as O. K. Moore's "talking typewriter" and Maria Montessori's "method" preschools, one focus of the fifties and sixties reform was early childhood education. How reading instruction was being taught in schools came under close scrutiny with the publication of Rudolph Flesch's *Why Johnny Can't Read* in 1955 (in Cohen, 1974). In 1959, Mortimer Smith published *A Citizen's Manual For Public Schools.* In this manual, which was sponsored by the Council for Basic Education, an organization founded to strengthen the school's commitment to fundamental skills, Smith noted that many of psychology's "insights" have tended to become "dogmas." Smith said that ideas about "readiness, child development, and individual differences" are areas in which psychological "insights about how learning takes place and about rates of growth. . . sometimes assure the teacher that subject matter and standards are unimportant because pupils will learn when they are 'ready' according to some personal law of growth." Smith went on to say that children are probably "more anxious" to learn reading and writing than theorists allow and that it is appropriate to suggest that "drill in the basic subjects should begin earlier than it does now, and be on a more intensive scale" (Smith, 1959, in Cohen, 1974, p. 3147).

INCREMENTAL CHANGE—READING INSTRUCTION MOVES DOWN

Although the idea that children should not be taught reading until they were mature enough was a dominant pedagogy until the 1960s, a number of educators thought that classroom instruction also could influence readiness to read. As early as 1937, Arthur Gates designed several studies that showed that what was taught in the classroom was as important as mental age in determining whether students successfully learned to read. Because the results of Gates's work did not fit with the prevailing expert assumptions of the time, however, they were largely ignored (Gentile, 1983; Blair & Rupley, 1983). In the mid-1960s Delores Durkin's study of preschool children who learned to read before going to school aroused much interest in the features of the home environment that would promote such precocity and aroused optimism that these features could be incorporated into the classroom.

Durkin herself was a great proponent of early reading. In the 1968 *NSSE Yearbook*, Durkin claimed that there was no research to determine whether preschool reading necessarily injures the child's vision—a common belief to the era. She suggested that such a warning probably did not apply to children who appeared interested and should be interpreted as a caution for parents who would push children who were not interested (p. 58). Regarding the assumption that parents were not appropriately trained to teach preschoolers, Durkin pointed out that teaching children of that age who are interested merely requires "a response to questions or a request for help." If children are bored with first-grade instruction because they already know how to read, Durkin said such boredom "raises questions about 1st grade reading programs, not preschool beginnings in reading." Durkin quoted several proponents of preschool reading to illustrate the optimism and perhaps "wishful thinking" of the 1960s (p. 64), a time she said will surely go down in history as developing "positive and even enthusiastic reactions to preschool reading" (p. 63).

For example, Gates said in 1954, once again ahead of his time, that children could learn to read when they were four years old because they are conversant in oral language at two. In his opinion, learning "to 'read' spoken words and learning to read printed words" were of equivalent difficulty, perceiving one was no easier than perceiving the other, but children learned to speak first because using speech is more convenient for parents than using print (Durkin, 1968, p. 65). John Carroll, in a 1966 article for *Elementary English* also suggested that children may be able to learn to read "naturally" in a way analogous to the way oral language is learned. In 1964, Glenn Doman proffered a widely publicized way to accomplish just that in *How To Teach Your Baby To Read*, claiming that two years old was the perfect age to begin reading and that beyond two years old, teaching a child to read became harder with each passing year. Even Lawrence Kohlberg, sounding a lot like Montessori, advocated teaching reading younger than was the practice. Kohlberg felt that the repetition and tediousness of this low-level sensory-motor task would be more interesting and "challenging fun" for the younger child, but there was nothing inherent in "the cognitive structure of the reading task which involves any high challenge to the older child" (Kohlberg, in Durkin, 1968, p. 67). Durkin concluded that there was no reason for the "start of reading and 6-years-old to go together" other than "an educational system that continues to use a chronological age of 6 as the criterion for starting school and, consequently, for beginning reading" (p. 67).

One area of school life that should be closely examined, according to Durkin, was the function of the kindergarten year and the desirability of reading instruction. Not only whether reading should be taught then should be examined but also how to best teach it. "Otherwise," Durkin said, "if objections to kindergarten reading are heard, it would be difficult to know whether they stemmed from stereotyped concepts of instruction or from factual descriptions of children living in the 1960s" (p. 70). At that point in time—the late 1960s—Durkin could find no consensus in the practices of school personnel. Some first-grade classrooms still clung to the notion of maturation and routinely prescribed a readiness program for all students, while there were kindergarten classrooms with workbooks, whole class repetition, and drill.

The Association for Childhood Education International opposed reading instruction in the kindergarten and regularly ran articles in *Childhood Education* affirming the kindergarten year as a time for the child's social and emotional development (Durkin, 1968). Finally, in a text entitled *School Readiness*, Ilg and Ames (1964) restated the developmental view held by Gesell.

Thus, the earliest kindergartens had no reading instruction, and the notion of maturational readiness at six years old insulated the kindergarten from the pressure to teach reading at younger ages. However, with more children attending kindergartens and a philosophical return to the basics in the 1950s, kindergarten gradually began to look more like "school," and reading instruction—or what has been called "reading readiness"—gradually moved down to the kindergarten from the first grade.

4. CHILD CARE, SOCIAL CLASS, AND THE GOVERNMENT

[T]he day care lobby is a very vocal group of very middle-class women. . . [who] speak for certain day care providers and. . . are very dedicated, [but] poor people's needs as they would see them don't often get heard because there's no vehicle for that. . . And sometimes when I listen to some of our people and some of the day care people I feel that we're being paternalistic—the notion that government should license and approve everything. You know, shouldn't that be the parent's job? [We assume] that she can't make a good choice for her job. . . On the other hand, lots of kids are put in day care situations that aren't up to standard and lots of parents, both middle-class and poor, don't know that. So it's a dilemma around quality and who decides quality. . . What one person might think [for example], the criticisms that I have about my daughter's experience, I'm sure that 80% of the mothers of her peers think the program is just great. We've got different values. . . I don't see clear answers. . . That's a family/government/class issue that we're all going to have to struggle with as policy-makers and as individuals involved in [preschool] services. . . and it's one that we barely acknowledge let alone know how to work out.

—A policy expert in New York State government

SINCE MOST four-year-olds who are enrolled in an early childhood program today are in what is commonly called child day care, nursery school, or Head Start, I present a brief history of the origins of these programs and their relationship to the public schools. Publicly sponsored nursery schools were established and prospered during periods of national crisis. When these crises subsided, so too did the public support for free nursery schools, and their numbers subsequently declined. Head Start, an educational innovation that was also established during a period of national concern, has managed to survive periods of eroded public support. In the 1990s, with renewed public support, Head Start is expanding.

Day nurseries, as child day care centers were originally called, had their beginnings prior to the Civil War. The first ones were founded in Boston around 1840 for the "unfortunate" children of widows or of the working wives of absent sailors (Scarr, 1983, p. 3). During the waves of immigration that followed this period, settlement houses such as Jane Addam's Hull House also began to provide day nurseries for poor working mothers whose children would otherwise have been uncared for. Even though these day nurseries were established not to take the place of the family but instead to provide support to poor working mothers, they did not represent mainstream American values. The American ideal was the educated mother who had gone to college to "learn how to be a better mother." This attitude was typified by President Theodore Roosevelt's comment that the "hand that rocks the cradle rules the world" at the 1909 White House Conference on Children (Scarr, 1983, p. 3).[1] The beneficiaries of such charity apparently accepted assistance reluctantly. As impoverished or deserted women, they had nowhere else to turn (Cohen, 1985). Day nurseries, and the child day care centers that evolved from the day nurseries, thus became associated with settlement houses, welfare, disadvantage, and working mothers (Scarr, 1983, p. 3). Perceived as help for working mothers in the late nineteeth century, child day care came to be seen as a last resort for the "pathological" and needy family. By the 1920s child day care had became clearly associated with social work and the welfare system (Steinfels, 1973).

On the other hand, nursery schools had much more respectable and later origins, primarily as "laboratories" housed in universities as part of the growing science of child study, home economics, and parent education (Scarr, 1983). In 1920, there were only three nursery schools in existence; in 1924 there were twenty-five; and by 1930, more than two hundred (Goodykoontz, Davis & Gabbard, 1948, p. 44). Lawrence Frank, director of child study for the Laura Spelman Rockefeller Memorial, funded many such university programs in the mid-1920s, including those at Iowa, Georgia, Minnesota, Yale and Columbia's Teachers College. Through the philanthropic investments of the Rockefeller Memorial and Frank's interests in the field, the infrastructure for the new profession of child study was created, including the establishment of the *Child Development* research journal and *Parents Magazine* (Cravens, 1985). The nursery school became an extension of the middle-class family. The child did not attend nursery school so that mother could work but rather because such experience would benefit the child. Like the kindergarten, the nursery school became associated with the educational system (Scarr, 1983, p. 3).

Nursery schools for Black children followed a similar path. With the enactment of the Second Morrill Land Grant in 1890, a number of Black colleges also were able to expand their studies of domestic arts and child development (Cunningham & Osborn, 1979, p. 25). In 1929 teacher-educator Phyllis Jones Tilly opened the first laboratory nursery school at the all-Black Hampton Institute in Virginia, and in 1930 Pearlie Reed opened a second nursery school at Spelman College. Flemmie Kittrell, the first Black recipient of a doctorate in early childhood education, established a similar program at Bennett College and used Rockefeller Foundation support to provide scholarships for students interested in teaching nursery-school children. According to Kittrell, Dorothy Howard established the first private nursery school for Black children in Washington, D.C., in 1927 (Cunningham & Osborn, 1979, p. 26). Kittrell said that, for more than fifty years, the school served the children of Washington's Black professionals—"Howard University professors. . . ministers, lawyers" (p. 26).

EARLY PUBLIC NURSERY SCHOOLS

Unlike the kindergarten movement, the day nursery and the nursery school had rather slow beginnings in terms of both enrollment numbers and the level of public involvement. What accelerated the development of both the day nursery and the nursery school was federal intervention to alleviate extraordinary social conditions brought about first by the Great Depression and, ten years later, by the entry of the United States into World War II. During the depression years between 1933 and 1937, the federal government funded the Works Progress Administration (WPA) nursery schools, a program designed to extend nursery education to low-income families and provide jobs for unemployed teachers and other unemployed workers. According to the 1939 study, *Educational Activities of the Works Progress Administration,* conducted by the U.S. Advisory Committee on Education, the number of nursery schools grew from three hundred, all privately operated, in 1932 to approximately two thousand schools in 1937, fifteen hundred of them under the purview of the WPA. Two-thirds of the WPA nursery schools were housed in public schools. The rest were either affiliated with university and normal school training centers or run by community agencies. The committee was optimistic that the nursery school would "come to be looked upon as an essential part of the State school system" after the states recouped financially from the depression (U.S. Advisory Committee on Education, 1939, in Bremner, 1974, p. 1597). The WPA nursery schools were intended for children from two to four years old. By 1937, they had enrolled about forty thousand students and apparently had long waiting lists. They also had a clear educational mission:

> The emergency nursery school is not intended as a convenience for the relief of parents; it is not a creche but an educational institution, including in its routine proper nutrition, health service, supervised play, and training in good habits of personal care and behavior. (U.S. Advisory Committee on Education, 1939, in Bremner, 1974, p. 1597)

Thus described, the emergency nursery school was clearly aligned with the educational system but was also conceived of as a temporary measure: funding support was to end when large-scale unemployment ended. However, just as the emergency nursery-school program was scheduled to be phased out, the United States entered World War II, setting in motion another set of social problems. As Ruby Takanishi (1977) pointed out, even with a critical lack of workers to meet the needs of the war industry, the government affirmed the responsibility of mothers to care for their children:

> The first responsibility for women with young children, in war as in peace, is to give suitable care in their own homes to their children. In order that established family life may not be unnecessarily disruptive, special efforts to secure in industry women with young children should be deferred until full use has been made of all other sources of labor supply. (U.S. Department of Labor, 1943, in Takanishi 1977, p. 144)

Nevertheless, in 1943 the Lanham Act was passed, a federal emergency proposal to provide child-care services in communities where large numbers of women were needed to work in defense-related industries (Takanishi, 1977, p. 142).

Although the Lanham centers provided child care as well as an educational program, the programs were not limited to low-income families, nor were they called "day care" but instead, "nursery education":

> There is fairly common acceptance of the point of view that such services as have been provided are *educational* services, that what goes on in a good nursery school is the sort of curriculum that is appropriate to the learning activities of boys and girls of two, three, or four years of age. A nursery school is, therefore, not an institution for "day care," a term generally used by social workers to denote care of children outside their own homes. . . As such [the nursery school] is appropriately a responsibility of public education and should be provided in the same way as are school facilities for other groups. . . [T]here is a somewhat vague but nevertheless determined opinion that the federal government [also] has a stake in services for young children. (Goodykoontz, Davis & Gabbard, 1948, p. 62)

In spite of widespread use, the Lanham Act was clearly a temporary measure, authorized to end when the war ended. Thus, although the federal government had provided funding for preschool programs for over a decade, increasing "nursery" school enrollment to around seventy thousand children, all federal support terminated in 1946. No state except California continued its child-care centers, even though between 1942 and 1945 seventeen states lowered the age of entry into public schools to *below* six years old and ten authorized state and local funds for child-care programs (Goodykoontz, Davis & Gabbard, 1948, pp. 46–47).

Proponents of preschool education had been hopeful that "nursery" education would follow the same path as the kindergarten to become part of the public-school establishment. Goodykoontz, Davis & Gabbard (1948) noted that the incorporation of the kindergarten had progressed in a similar fashion, with states first granting localities permission to start kindergartens and then moving to authorize state money for this purpose. Nursery schools and child-care centers that were affiliated with the public schools all but disappeared in 1946, so that at the time the *46th Yearbook of the NSSE* on early childhood education was published, professionals who supported these preschools had identified a number of issues that were troublesome to the public and were formulating their arguments for keeping nursery education a public responsibility.

OBJECTIONS TO PUBLIC SUPPORT

Questions concerning whether public support for preschools was appropriate focused on a number of by now familiar issues. In a 1949 speech to the World Organization of Early Childhood Education, George Stoddard, then president of the University of Illinois, said that the resistance to preschools began "like war" in the "minds of male administrators" (Takanishi, 1977, pp. 155–156). Stoddard identified the cost of preschool programs as an additional "blockage" to preschool education. According to Stoddard, when the *Nation's Schools* magazine randomly surveyed school administrators on their support for child-care services in 1945, the administrators were about evenly divided on whether the public schools or welfare should be in charge of such services, but they clearly thought parents should be responsible for paying for them, not the public schools (Takanishi, 1977, p. 156). Goodykoontz, Davis & Gabbard (1948, p. 59) also believed that the rapid demise of the Lanham centers was in part a function of the way they were funded. Even though the Lanham centers were housed in the public schools, fiscal control was vested in local agencies or committees separate from the schools, and because full employment was a factor in the establishment of the centers, the schools felt little responsibility toward these centers and would not have been able to afford the high levels of staffing anyway.

Another objection was the familiar notion that the institutionalized care of young children should be administered by the welfare system, not the public schools. The authors responded to this objection by saying that the idea of continuous human growth makes it impossible to differentiate "care" from "education" (Goodykoonz, Davis & Gabbard, 1948, p. 54).

Two more points often raised in opposition to nursery education of this era were that children that young were not ready for formal education and that the role of the mother was being usurped to the detriment of the child. As proponents of preschool, Goodykoontz, Davis & Gabbard, (1948) argued that when professionals follow a "hands-off" policy until the child is six years old, the "haphazard education at home often leaves him unable to make the most of the later educational opportunities which are offered" (p. 51). Regarding the responsibility of the parents for the education and care of preschoolers, the authors remarked:

> It is a great physical and psychological strain for both child and mother to spend the whole twenty-four hours of every day together. The release of this strain, for even a few hours each day which nursery school or kindergarten provides, has been found beneficial to both child and mother. Instead of taking responsibility away from the home and encouraging the mother to shirk, the respite offered by nursery schools and kindergartens more often has been found to increase the parent's desire to fulfill his obligations with more competence. (p. 52)

Educator Roma Gans (1948) claimed that the role of the preschool as "supplemental" to the family would be responsive to the changing roles of women, in this case, the return to the home to be with their young children. With employment high and the "lean years" behind them, Gans noted that many women desired the "dual role of homemaking and motherhood" (p. 11). However, the author emphasized that nursery schools are essential for all children because all children need experiences with groups, starting at three years old (p. 10).

THE CURRICULUM OF HABIT FORMATION

Following a similar argument, Engleman and Nash (1948) bemoaned the fact that "some parents and many taxpayers. . .consider the nursery school merely as a place to *play*" (p. 363). The authors explained that many qualities that are highly valued in American society have their roots in the child's early years and are encouraged through play and appropriate developmental activities. Examples of such qualities are "spirit of cooperation and fair play, independence, courage and self-confidence and resourcefulness" (p. 363). Because they believed that such attitudes could be developed only in group interactions, under the "guidance" of professionals, the authors recommended "extending the age for entering school downward" (p. 365). Although Engleman and Nash did not specifically exclude lower-income children from their analysis, they clearly were extending the potential benefits of preschool to more affluent families.

Levinger and Murphy (1948) noted that the emotional stress caused by divorce, illness, and so on, also fell upon middle-class families and that less than "half" of the preschoolers in America grew up in a "loving and comfortable home" where they could be socialized into "taking it on the chin, hold your own, be a good sport" and other important habits (p. 18). Increasing numbers of only children, without the opportunities for "give and take," were also mentioned as beneficiaries of group-centered preschool education (*U.S. Office of Education Bulletin*, 1932, in Engleman & Nash, 1948, p. 365). Further, the nursery school would be used to facilitate parent education. Unlike "the teacher, doctor, accountant or engineer" who are trained for their work, parents are not trained for parenthood and are "unaware of developmental needs of children" (Engleman & Nash, 1948, p. 369).

NO FORMAL TEACHING

The only danger perceived by Engleman and Nash (1948, p. 366) was trying to modify a "formal kindergarten curriculum" for a younger child, a tendency that they thought was more likely to occur when preschool programs became affiliated with the public schools. Gans also emphasized that there was a "dichotomy clearly marked between the *play* years and *formal learning* years." Research with children from six to twelve has focused on learning to read, the author explained, and child development research has usually ended with the five-year-old, so there exists a sharp difference between preschool and primary programs in point of view, goals, and even the language used to describe the children's work (Gans, 1948, p. 12). In descriptions of a day in nursery school, kindergarten, and first grade by Fuller, et al. (1948, pp. 107–113), no reading or story time was mentioned during the nursery school observations, and the only literacy activity during the kindergarten morning was a visit to the school library, where the librarian read the group a story.

Anderson (1948) noted that curriculum for the preschool child should be conceptualized as "guided experiences" in which content is "minimized" and "stress placed on adjustment and modes of attack on problems. It is not what the child learns in formal terms which is important but what he gains from experiences in the way of self-control, emotional balance, initiative, interest, and enthusiasm for the material in question" (p. 91). Regarding readiness, which he defined as related to both experiences and maturation, Anderson held that preparation for reading was "facilitated" by the child's having had experiences that he will read about (p. 91).

In a related chapter of the *46th NSSE Yearbook*, the predictive value of reading readiness tests was addressed by Kawin (1948). Although he agreed that readiness tests are a more useful indicator than mental age, Kawin asserted that inner maturation or readiness cannot be separated from experiences, and for a child who has not had the environmental background, "time alone will be inadequate to make him ready to read" (p. 311).

In spite of efforts by preschool professionals to build an educational rationale for "nursery education" by stressing the development of appropriate social habits and despite the extension of the benefits of preschool to more middle class families, financial support of public nursery schools was abruptly ended at the end of World War II. Private preschools continued to operate, however, and, in fact, today they are flourishing.

HEAD START—EDUCATIONAL INNOVATION AND SOCIAL REFORM

During the 1950s and 1960s the pressure for more attention to the basics, the concern with poverty, and the promise of early childhood education combined to open the door for government investment in preschool training for poor children. In 1965, President Johnson included a $120 million budget recommendation for preschool education in his "Special Message to the Congress Toward Full Educational Opportunity."[1] Project Head Start, a program to "assist young children who have not reached the age of compulsory school attendance (PL–89–794)" was thus inaugurated. As a rationale, President Johnson stated that the "slum" child is behind before he starts school, with "tests show[ing] that he is usually a year behind by the time he reaches third grade—and up to three years behind *if* he reaches eighth grade" (in Bremner, 1974, p. 1800).

Speaking to the Congressional Committee on Labor and Public Welfare, Sargent Shriver, director of the Office of Economic Opportunity, explained what Head Start was not. Head Start was not an ordinary preschool, which, he said, had been around since the Germans invented the kindergarten in the nineteenth century, nor was Head Start a "kindergarten or a government-paid-for babysitting service adorned with crayons, stuffed animals and picture books. . . Head Start is in reality a microcosm of community action" (in Bremner, 1974, p. 1820). Shriver believed that the government needed a "multiplicity of systems that [would] attack the multiplicity of poverty causes." He identified the five components of Head Start: medical services, social services, psychological services, volunteers, and last, school readiness (Hearings on S. 3164, Amendments to the Economic Opportunity Act of 1964, 1966, in Bremner, 1974, p. 1820).

Even though Head Start may have been developed as a multifaceted program, it was the mission to promote school readiness that generated the most interest. An article appearing in *American Education* in 1965 was typical of descriptions of how Head Start benefitted "slum children." Mackintosh and Lewis, the article's authors, described how a ghetto child of four years old finally said the word *soup* after nearly a year in school without speaking. They called the incident a "near miracle" but one that was taking place more often as Head Start programs were becoming more common. The authors felt these children were not ready for school, not even for kindergarten; they apparently communicated with gestures, sounds, and a few "street" words, did not provide their own names, could not label common objects, and had no experience with pictures or books. Before Head Start, according to the authors, the "lag" was so immense that for these children the "efforts of the average school were fruitless" (in Bremner, 1974, p. 1817). Head Start was so popular that Shriver remarked that the House of Representatives committee recommended more money for the program than the Office of Economic Opportunity wanted. Frances Keppel, then U.S. Commissioner of Education, recommended that the public schools provide preschool education for all disadvantaged children and kindergarten for all children, remarking that "our greatest possibility lies in early childhood education" (Mackintosh & Lewis, 1965, in Bremner, 1974, p. 1819).

As noted in chapter 1, various curriculum models[2] of Head Start were put into place in an effort to discover which methods of instruction produced the most cognitive and achievement gains among preschoolers. These curriculum models were evaluated for their effectiveness and compared with each other.

Many such studies were published in the literature of the seventies and eighties, and some longitudinal evaluations continue to the present day. Of all the Head Start projects that were established as models, the most famous is the Perry Preschool Project in Ypsilanti, Michigan. This project spawned the High/Scope curriculum (Hohmann et al., 1979) and the longitudinal studies that suggested the long-term economic benefits of this type of program (Schweinhart, Weikart & Larner, 1986; Weikart et al., 1978; Farnworth, Schweinhart & Berrueta-Clement, 1985). The High/Scope longitudinal studies have shaped the direction of contemporary preschool education and the beliefs of early childhood educators today. Because the Perry Preschool Project has been so influential, I examine the literature on this project and the curriculum associated with it in much greater depth in chapter 7.

For the present discussion, however, I must emphasize that all of the national evaluations of Head Start have shown a disappointing return on the government's investment in early childhood education. Early gains in achievement were not maintained at the time of the first national evaluation, prompting Richard Nixon, then president, to remark that Head Start's contribution may have been to raise to the public agenda the fact that poor children are already "deficient" when they begin school and that "our schools as they now exist are unable to overcome this deficiency" (Nixon, 1969, in Bremner, 1974, p. 1824). Lois-ellin Datta, author of *A Report on Evaluation Studies of Project Head Start*, pointed out the narrow scope of most Head Start evaluations, which focused almost entirely on cognitive growth and academic achievement (Datta, 1969, in Bremner, 1974, p. 1825). Still other proponents made this argument:

> No public school system has ever before been abolished because it could not teach children to read and write. Yet compensatory programs, aimed at the very children who are going to be losers in the regular school program are in just this situation. The programs are being asked to succeed in a shorter time than that which the regular school systems have had... [Evaluation] should be tempered by the realization of the magnitude of the task with which they are confronted and the short time they have been coping with the task. (McDill, McDill, & Spreche, 1969, in Bremner, 1974, p. 1827).

Although Head Start had been in existence then ten years, no long-term academic gains had yet been demonstrated, nor have such gains ever been demonstrated in a national evaluation, even after twenty years of authorization (CSR, 1985). In spite of its demonstrated inability to deliver sustained achievement gains, Head Start is the only government-sponsored preschool program to survive. In the present political climate and bolstered by the publicity given the economic benefits of the Perry Preschool Project, Head Start is thriving, with a good chance that the program itself will expand to serve all eligible children before the end of the next decade (Edelman, 1990). As discussed earlier, two other examples of government-subsidized preschool, which were developed for noneducational purposes, did not survive. The child care programs initiated during the depression and war years enjoyed only the briefest government support.

CONTEMPORARY CHILD DAY CARE

Among educational professionals in particular, the "tainted" associations of day care with social welfare have persisted to contemporary times. A case in point is former New York State Education Commissioner Ambach's observation that middle-class children are mostly in preschool education programs, not day care (Ambach, 1985, p. 7). However, early childhood specialist Bettye Caldwell (1986) holds that even though child day care was not considered a legitimate concern of child development twenty years ago, today it is "conceptually indistinguishable" from other types of early childhood programs (p. 38).

Approximately 25 percent of the eight million children of working mothers are enrolled in child day care centers; the remaining 75 percent are cared for in their own or another's home (U.S. Department of Commerce, Bureau of the Census, 1987). Of the children who attend child day care, only 3 percent are in programs affiliated in some way with the public school (Harrison & Magri, 1985). The part-time nursery schools, typically offering a two-hour program once or twice a week, are not practical for working mothers and remain convenient only for middle-class mothers who stay at home.

In 1948, sentiment was clearly running against child day care in favor of more nursery schools. Increased availability of nursery schools, it was hoped at the time, "would lessen the need for 'day care' agencies" (Goodykoontz, Davis & Gabbard, 1948). By 1982, sentiments had changed. Demographic trends showing increased participation in the labor force by women from all socioeconomic levels and a dramatic surge in child-care enrollment prompted Caldwell and Freyer (1982) to wonder whether there was a future for part-time preschool. Likewise, Mitchell (1987) asked whether the creation of more part-time programs—even for "targeted" children such as those served by Head Start—is "good policy," given the child-care needs of working families today. Research questions that in the past have focused on whether child day care was harmful to children are now starting to address what characteristics of a child-care program are good for children. As child-care moves from being a "nontraditional alternative" for children's care to "the modal early childhood environment," Caldwell and Freyer (1982) note that there is "virtually no curriculum research in day care."

CHILD DAY CARE AND THE PUBLIC SCHOOLS

Bettye M. Caldwell (1981), former director of the Children's Center of Syracuse University and now director of the University of Arkansas

Kramer Project, explained that her research with young children and schools lies in "boundary areas lacking any undisputed natural divider to demarcate clear regions of influence and authority" (p. 121). Caldwell (1986) characterized the relations between public schools and child day care as "natural enemies—natural allies" (p. 34). Caldwell (1981) noted that child day care has historically been the "poor relation" of early childhood education, carrying the double burden of having originated in the social welfare system and being commonly perceived as custodial rather than educational care for children of working mothers (p. 121). The importance of the early years was established by the research of the sixties, which finally legitimized the educational function of child care. According to Caldwell (1981), child day care was transformed from a "pariah into a prodigy." Several decades of research on the effects of early intervention on later cognitive performance were initiated in this era, and several centers, for example, the Frank Porter Graham Child Development Center at the University of North Carolina at Chapel Hill (Ramey, 1985; Viadero, 1990), continue to specialize in this work. But however much interest there was at the university and research level on early intervention, the institutions of child care and the public schools continued to seek two very different identities for themselves, with child day care claiming the "care and protection of children" and schools claiming "education" (Caldwell, 1986, p. 38). As Caldwell pointed out, this distinction does not differentiate the functions that child day care and the schools actually provide since health and nutrition "care" are given in the schools and "teaching" takes place in child day care (Caldwell, 1986, p. 38). Although not necessarily agreeing with Caldwell's idea that schooling and child care perform similar functions, Edward Zigler (1987), himself a founder of Head Start and long-time advocate of quality care for children, recently proposed that the public school is an ideal *building* for administering and housing both day care and education services. Zigler believed, however, that such services should be differentially funded and staffed. He would include a "developmentally appropriate educational component" for three- and four-year-olds, but these programs would be "primarily places for recreation and socialization" (p. 35).

STATE RESPONSIBILITY IN EARLY CHILDHOOD STILL QUESTIONED

The extent to which "child care" actually "teaches" children may be crucial in determining whether government perceives a legitimate interest in child care. Contemporary working parents may look to public institutions for the care of their young children much as colonial families did before the age of school entry was regulated, and while the public schools appear more responsive and eager to extend schooling downward now than at the turn of the century, Congress and the state legislatures are not completely convinced that preschool is the responsibility of government. Even though in 1989 the National Conference of State Legislatures identified child care and early childhood education as high-priority human services issues, there are clearly at least two points of view on the nature of early childhood education and the responsibility of state government towards children under five years old (Harrison & Magri, 1985).

On the one hand, Philip Warner, then chair of Indiana's education committee, does not believe child care is a state responsibility (Harrison & Magri, 1985, p. 15). Echoing this sentiment, Anne Lindeman, State Senator from Arizona at that time, questioned whether schools should be in the "baby-sitting business" and suggested that if children "aren't getting the right preparation at home," perhaps parent education is the answer (Harrison & Magri, 1985, p. 13). Lindeman said that each state should explore which agency would be best suited for parent education. Harrison and Magri (1985) note once again that child care is often thought of as the purview of social service, not the public schools. In response to arguments such as Lindeman's, Gwen Morgan of Wheelock College, explained that the public schools have always "served a dual purpose. . .Parents have always relied on the fact that their children were responsibly and reliably cared for during these hours." In this respect then, Morgan held that "schools *are* a form of child care" (Harrison & Magri, 1985, p. 13). New York Assemblywoman May Newburger also insisted that child care today is not something that state legislatures can consider a frill or fringe; it is instead a "necessity" (p. 15).

The federal government has had minimal involvement with preschool education. Thus, exceptions to this federal laissez faire stance are important. Past participation by the federal government may help define the parameters of early schooling or literacy development that appear to legitimate public responsibility in this issue.

FEDERAL INVOLVEMENT IN PRESCHOOL—DEFINING THE PUBLIC INTEREST

Federal involvement in preschool education is noteworthy because there has been so little of it over the course of public schooling in America and because a similar configuration of issues becomes apparent whenever there has been a federal investment. Two descriptions of past federal involvement in preschool education may help determine what policymakers view as important public concerns in contemporary discussions of preschool education. In an analysis of the Works Progress Administration nursery schools, the Lanham Act centers, and Head Start, Takanishi (1977) identified four common themes in each of these federally funded programs. First, all of these programs were established during a time of crisis in response to economic, political, and social concerns, and they were planned to be temporary (p. 141). These programs ended when the crisis was over, except for Head Start, which was supposed to facilitate a permanent resolution of the problem. Second, special groups of children, most often the unfortunate or "unlucky" ones, were targeted to receive federal aid, not the general population of children (p. 142). Third, each of these programs was conceived as a way to effect social reform. Fourth, each program recognized and supported the family as the chief agent of child socialization and early education (p. 143). According to Takanishi, all three of these federal initiatives had an economic rationale unrelated to the welfare of children (p. 158). The WPA nursery schools employed large numbers of out-of-work teachers and provided teacher training for other unemployed workers (p. 146). Not only did the Lanham Act centers continue to employ these people, but they also enabled women with children to keep the defense industries going during the war years (p. 147). In spite of the fact that many women expressed an interest in continuing to work after the war ended (p. 155), the government abruptly ended all financial support for these centers when there was no longer a compelling economic reason for maintaining them (p. 148). Even though Head Start was perceived as a children's program, it was attached to the Economic Opportunity Act. One of Head Start's stated goals was community development through the employment of poor and untrained adults, so that involvement of professional educators in the programs was often curtailed when resources were limited (p. 142).

In an analysis on why the child care initiatives of the 1970s failed to materialize, McCathren (1981) noted several of the same themes described by Takanishi. Additionally, McCathren presented the differing agendas that needed to be satisfied for a child-care coalition to support legislation that was developed in the 1970s. As the author suggests, an analysis of why such legislation failed goes far in explaining what advocates need to succeed with future initiatives.

Three child-development or child-care bills were surveyed: the Comprehensive Child Development Act of 1971, the Child and Family Services Act of 1975, and the Child Care Act of 1979. In general, McCathren noted a dichotomy between the way government responds to the child-care and development needs of the poor, and the needs of the "nonpoor." Child care for the poor is essentially social reform, tied to community employment and the job training of welfare mothers. If health and educational benefits are attached, the purpose is to "break the welfare cycle" (p. 103). For the nonpoor, however, McCathren claimed there is no such substantive involvement by government in child care. The subsidy of prekindergarten is tolerated only because it is perceived as "education" rather than "child care" and because it is controlled through local boards of education (p. 103). The income tax credit for child care is acceptable because parents may select an option from among the alternatives available or marketed within their communities. The government eschews any substantive policy content involving child care and the nonpoor, according to McCathren (p. 104).

The history of the Comprehensive Child Development Act of 1971, as told by McCathren, suggests that many members of the coalition in support of child care legislation had to compromise their positions. Those who viewed it as a vehicle for community organization and further enhancement of minority civil rights had to compromise their position substantially. Those who wanted the bill to focus on compensatory education for children already behind their more advantaged peers also saw their narrow objectives substantially enlarged. Ultimately, the bill included the full range of health and social services for children, based on an assumption that the quality of the care vested in the child rather than more cognitive training would best serve the "whole child" (p. 107). Further, the bill acknowledged that children are entitled to develop to their full potential and that child development services should be available as "a matter of right" (p. 112). Although the coalition established by lobbyists Marian Wright Edleman and Robert Warren and Congressmen Mondale and Brademas pushed the bill through both Houses of Congress with little discussion, President Nixon's veto emphasized that several of the bill's provisions conflicted with deep-rooted American values.

As McCathren indicated, the bill was widely perceived as encroachment of government on parental prerogatives and responsibilities. Virtually all the services listed in the bill were activities that parents were expected to perform in caring for their children, and opponents feared that parents would assume less responsibility for these duties with such substantial government presence in child care (pp. 114–115). Another objection was the involvement of "experts" in setting the standard for child care and in defining what each child's "potential" might be (p. 115). A third objection was the fear that the rights of children as articulated in this bill would override the rights of parents and school authorities, particularly since the language of the bill referred to the use of "advocates" for children (p. 116). McCathren viewed the above objections as legitimate although unintended interpretations of the 1971 legislation. According to McCathren, President Nixon's veto message went beyond these objections and expressed several political values that were replayed in subsequent attempts to enact child care legislation (p. 118).

For example, McCathren read Nixon's veto message as a series of implicit declarations. The first declaration was that "the poor deserve 'workfare' with compulsory custodial child care, not voluntary, expensive developmental child care. . .Mainstream American family values are not relevant to [the poor]" (p. 119). Child care for the poor, according to McCathren, is viewed as a necessary cost to reduce welfare and provide industry with a cheap source of labor. A second declaration was that the middle class should have child care subsidies that support parental prerogatives as well as the private sector market, thereby giving "the most benefit" to those with the most income and power (p. 119). And third, Nixon's veto was interpreted by supporters of the bill as "protection of local elites," those who had been accustomed to complete control over an area such as child day care where government "incursions [may] threaten to bring to the fore mores, values, or opinions unacceptable to the local elite" (p. 119).

In 1975, the same coalition of child-care advocates cleaned up the 1971 bill but, in McCathren's opinion, did not pay enough attention to Nixon's implicit "declarations." The bill itself was called the Child and Family Services Act of 1975, and all language from the 1971 bill that was thought to "undermine the family" was eliminated. In the new statement of findings and purposes that preceded the bill itself, the family was emphasized rather than the rights of children:

> "[T]he family is the primary and the most fundamental influence on children. . . [and] child and family service programs must build upon and strengthen the role of the family and must be provided on a voluntary basis only to children whose parents. . . request such services, with a view toward offering families the options they believe are most appropriate for their particular needs. (*Statement of Findings and Purposes, S. 626,* 1975, in McCathren, 1981, p.123)

All offending phrases were replaced. For example, the phrase "child and family services" was used instead of "child development." However, the 1975 bill did not pass, primarily because, unlike the 1971 bill, it lacked the support of organized labor.

After the 1971 presidential veto of child-care legislation, the American Federation of Teachers became actively involved in negotiations over the form and substance of new initiatives. While supporting the concept of "universal early childhood education," Albert Shanker insisted that "the responsibility for the enlarged program should be borne by the public schools" (*New York Times*, September 8, 1974, in McCathren, 1981, p. 141). Because the proposed bill did not urge public school responsibility for the child-care program, and indeed did not want AFT-sponsored programs, the teachers' union blocked labor's support of the legislation. The contention over public school involvement turned out to be moot, however, because the American public reacted with such an unprecedented outpouring of letters to Congress denouncing the bill that it was, in McCathren's words, "soundly defeated" (p. 125).

In 1979, during Walter Mondale's vice-presidency, Senator Cranston developed yet another child-care bill based on a series of public hearings in California and Washington, D.C. The 1979 bill was unlike previous legislation in that there was no community involvement, no welfare reform, and no educational or child-development component. Cranston's bill was designed with a very limited goal: to create a modest system of child care not limited to low-income parents. However, no strong coalition developed to support the proposed bill, and Cranston cancelled all further hearings on it.

For future success at legislating child care, McCathren (1981) suggested that the "debate must be recast" from "should parents or others care for children" to "should government respond to that phenomenon [of working parents]" (p. 131). McCathren suggested several scenarios that could provide a compelling reason for government to consider child care legislation or, as McCathren said, "the larger philosophic and value questions into which the child care debate may be transformed" (p. 132). Because the country has made value shifts in the past and because unforeseen social or political circumstances could emerge, McCathren indicated that predictions were difficult to make, but "the success of any new categorical child care initiative is dependent on broad acceptance of a new theory or rationale for federal involvement" (p. 133). Two possibilities were suggested by McCathren: first, equality for women similar to that enjoyed by women in European countries could become a "national goal" and, second, "a heightened interest in the competence of children" could provide a rationale for "an increased government presence in child care":

> As the dependency rate increases (the ratio of nonworking-age to working-age members in the society) and the social and economic costs of unproductive citizens rise, there may be a renewed effort to assure the development of each child to a higher level of competence than is now accepted. The public education function could be extended down to include at least 3- to 5-year-olds, although public schools need not be the only or even the central institution relied upon. This is occurring rapidly in this country now as the enrollment in preschools, nursery schools, and kindergartens reflects. (p. 132)

McCathren's words presaged much of the rationale for the spate of child care legislation introduced by the 101st Congress. At least three recent bills authorizing federal funds for child care or early childhood programs have been seriously considered by Congress. Each of these bills cited the increasing numbers of working parents and the social and economic benefits of developing competence in children through high-quality early childhood programs as reasons for authorizing federal initiatives for child care.

As the 101st Congress considered these possibly historic initiatives into federal child-care subsidies, the bills with the best prognosis were the Early Childhood Education and Development Act (H.R. 3) and the Act for Better Child Care Services (S. 5). These bills were introduced by Congressman Hawkins and Senator Kennedy, respectively, and were supported by a broad coalition of advocates for children and for public education, including the Children's Defense Fund, whose president—Marian Wright Edelman—was also a major lobbyist for the ill-fated Comprehensive Child Development Act of 1971. She has worked tirelessly to promote child care legislation since that time.

During the summer of 1989 the Act for Better Child Care Services (S. 5), also known as the ABC bill, was passed by the Senate, and, in the spring of 1990, the Early Childhood Education and Development Act, also known as the Hawkins bill, passed the House. The language of both of these bills clearly demonstrated that the child-care lobby has learned—since the veto of the Comprehensive Child Development Act of 1971—how to describe the federal interest in subsidized child care. Thus the very first purpose identified in the memoranda accompanying both these bills was "to build on and to strengthen the role of the family by seeking to ensure that parents are not forced by lack of available programs or financial resources to place a child in an unsafe or unhealthy child care facility or arrangement" (Hawkins, 1989, p. 2; Kennedy, 1989, p. 3). Other stated purposes were to "improve the productivity of parents in the labor force by lessening the stresses" associated with inadequate child care and "to strengthen the competitiveness of the United States by providing young children with a sound early childhood development experience" (Hawkins, 1989, p. 3; Kennedy, 1989, p. 3).

Although there was congressional support for the concept of child-care assistance for low-income families and the expansion of early childhood programs for working families, there was and continues to be much dissention over the distribution and jurisdiction of the funds. *Education Daily* reporter David Schumacher compared the House and Senate versions of such legislation in a Special Supplement to the newsletter (June, 1990). The House bill (H.R. 3) would authorize over $27 billion in block grants to the states over a five-year period, whereas the Senate bill (S. 5) would authorize over $17 billion for direct payments to service providers over a four-year period. Both bills would authorize these funds for a variety of child-care services including school-based child care and an expansion of Head Start to year-round, full-workday operations, but the Senate bill allows the states more discretion in dispersing funds (pp. 1–2). It is expected that the issue of how to finance child-care assistance and how to determine child-care jurisdiction will continue to be obstacles that the House and Senate conferees must negotiate before any major child-care legislation passes both houses of Congress (Edelman, 1990, p. 2).

Other legislation before the 101st Congress focused primarily on early childhood educational programs for four-year-olds whose families are poor. In the House, the Hawkins bill (H.R. 3) carried a provision (Title II) that would amend the Elementary and Secondary Education Act so that public schools could fund early childhood education for four-year-olds through the provisions of this act. Also in Congress, the House passed a bill (H.R. 4151), sponsored by Congressman Kildee, to authorize $6 billion in Head Start appropriations so that all eligible children will be served by 1994. Similar legislation was pending in the Senate. Smart Start (S. 123) was a bill before the Senate that reiterated the findings and purposes of the House bills; it proposed that high-quality early child development programs can "increase the literacy rate, the graduation rate, the employment rate, and the rate of enrollment in higher education" as well as "decrease the incidence of cognitive, learning, and emotional handicaps, teenage pregnancy, welfare dependency, and incidence of arrest and juvenile delinquency" (Kennedy, 1989, p. 2). The Smart Start bill also indicated that fewer than one-third of the children of poverty participate in such child-development programs, and "the less income and education parents have, the less likely their children are to be enrolled in early childhood development programs." The first purpose of Smart Start was to make such early childhood programs "widely available, especially to low-income children" (Kennedy, 1989, p. 4).

THE EDUCATION MARKET AND THE MIDDLE CLASS

For middle-class families, the private sector has moved in to fill the "need" for child care (Edmondson, 1986, p. 29). The rate of enrollment in early childhood education programs has tripled since 1965, and most of this growth has been in private programs. Only 11 percent of children enrolled in grades kindergarten through twelve are in private schools, but more than 66 percent of the nation's preschoolers attend private schools.[3]

Although smaller numbers of families are having children, more upper-income families are choosing private schools, according to *American Demographics* editor Brad Edmondson (1986, p. 54). This trend is particularly apparent for preschools where "earlier and more comprehensive educational programs" are very popular (p. 28). Kinder-Care, a private, for-profit child-care corporation, said that it does very little market research because it is too busy keeping up with current demand. Towns apparently contact Kinder-Care and invite the company to build; Kinder-Care selects building sites based on income and educational levels of the community and the proportion of working parents (Edmondson, 1986, p. 29). Karen Anderson, vice president of Gymboree, another purveyor of education for the three- to five-year-old, claims its clients are "trendsetters...[who] believe in shaping a child's development. These are the same people who believe in preschool programs, Montessori education, and Lamaze classes" (Edmondson, 1986, p. 52). According to market researchers, education and nutrition are the two "hottest selling items in the kid's market today" and public schools in affluent areas, such as Stamford, Connecticut, have had to offer parents extended day and preschool services in order to compete with the private schools in the area (Edmondson, 1986, p. 51).

But not only preschools are prospering. Children's books and workbooks are also enjoying an unprecedented boom, with sales increasing by about 20 percent a year since 1983. This trend clearly pleases the president of the Association of Booksellers for Children, who tells her clients that "children can benefit from being around books from the moment of birth" (Edmondson, 1986, p. 51). Sales of children's books are a one billion dollar business (Association of American Publishers, 1990). Random House, according to Edmondson, has a line of workbooks for middle-class parents to buy for their preschoolers. Using special paper, a light pen, and a speaker embedded in the book, children practice letter and shape recognition. A special tone tells the child whether the answer is right or wrong (p. 51). *Publishers Weekly* attributed the growing market in children's books to well-educated and working parents who are actively involved in their children's education (*Education Week*, Apr. 8, 1987). Baby boomer parents view learning to read as something their children should master "the earlier, . . . the better" and they believe that teaching their children to read is a "parental responsibility," according to Tom Engelhardt, former editor at Pantheon publishing house and an authority on children's culture (Engelhardt, 1991, p. 57).

Buying books and private preschool lessons are obvious material advantages that middle-class parents can provide for their children. Nonetheless, it is the talk about the books and the uses of literacy in their everyday lives that provide the most powerful advantage to middle-class children. As researchers are beginning to document, families, peers, and communities teach children important lessons about written language long before they ever reach kindergarten or first grade.

5. DEVELOPMENT: FROM MERE DESCRIPTION TO A MORAL FACE

> *Theories of development, by their stipulations about human growth, also create rules and institutions that are just as compelling as mortgage companies: delinquency, truancy, ''milestones of growth,'' national standards. . . It is. . . congruence [with values that prevail in the culture] that gives developmental theories—proposed initially as mere descriptions —a moral face.*
>
> —*Jerome Bruner, Actual Minds, Possible Worlds*

HOWEVER MUCH THE early childhood professionals protested the incursion of the elementary school into the kindergarten during the 1960s and 1970s, recent statements by the National Association for the Education of Young Children (NAEYC) (1985; 1986) on developmentally appropriate instruction suggest that reading instruction may be a *fait accompli* in the kindergarten of the 1990s. The following NAEYC guidelines represent a marked change in attitude from that of some early childhood professionals a few decades ago:

> [D]uring kindergarten most children are physically and cognitively ready for exposure to written language. However, a range of developmental ability and interest is to be expected in any group. In a group of 20 5-year-olds, a few are able to read the picture books in the library corner and will gladly persist until they have completed the whole book; some are able to read the language experience story the class dictated following their field trip to the dairy; others are able to recognize the words under pictures posted around the room in each learning center, like the block area, the dramatic play center, and the science corner; many children are just beginning to identify words that begin with the same letter as their name; some children show little interest in written language. The variety

> and complexity of language experiences provided by the teacher for this group should reflect both age-appropriate and individually appropriate planning (1985, p. 3).

These activities are very similar to what Durkin suggested in 1968 (and also in Durkin, 1970; 1974–75) as imaginative ways to incorporate reading into the routines of the kindergarten, as is the caveat about adjusting instruction to the interests of five-year old children. However, the NAEYC did not issue its draft policy paper to revisit the issue of reading instruction in the kindergarten per se but rather to "clearly articulate" a definition of what is appropriate for four- and five-year-olds in schools. According to the cover statement sent to afflilate groups along with the draft position statement, the position paper represents the work of a commission created by the NAEYC governing board in response to "requests and concerns" of the membership on appropriate education for four- and five-year-olds and "reflects the consensus of the early childhood profession"(Cover statement, NAEYC, 1985). Although early childhood programs have changed "dramatically"—public schools are assuming a larger role, children are entering programs at a younger age, the length of the program day is increasing, and there is much more pressure to teach academic skills—the NAEYC stated, "there has been no comparable evidence of change in what young children need for optimal development of how they learn." The NAEYC noted that program changes have been for "social, economic and political" reasons, and "not responsive" to the needs of young children, which have not changed (1985, p. 1).

The quality of the care, according to the NAEYC, is not affected by the length of the program day or whether sponsorship is public or private. What is important is that the instruction be *developmentally appropriate*. In its policy draft,[1] the NAEYC clearly defines "developmentally appropriate" in terms of the "milestones of human development":

> All domains of development—physical, emotional, social, and cognitive—can be described in terms of predictable, age-related sequences of growth and change. Developmentally appropriate program practice reflects the body of age-related knowledge about children's readiness and expected acquisition of skills and abilities. . .Children need years of play experiences with real objects and events to enable them to understand the meaning of symbols such as stories and pictures, letters and numbers. . .As children develop during the first 4 years, their conceptual and language abilities gradually develop to allow understanding of more complex concepts

> presented in stories and pictures. Commercially prepared workbooks, worksheets, coloring books, and adult-made models of art products for children to copy are *not* appropriate for young children, especially those younger than 6. Although children beyond the age of 5 show increasing abilities to learn through written, spoken and other adult-initiated activities, the child's active involvement with concrete, real-life experiences continues to be a key to motivated, successful learning. (NAEYC, 1985, pp. 2, 4).

The curriculum guidelines list appropriate materials: sand, water, blocks, puzzles, games, small toys, dramatic play props, science equipment, "a changing selection of books and records; supplies of paper, markers and material for creative expression," and gym equipment (NAEYC, 1985, p. 5).

An even stronger statement was issued by Brenda Krause-Eheart (Krause-Eheart, Learitt & Steinkamp, 1985), director of the Developmental Child Care Program at the University of Illinois. She restates the position that teaching reading and writing to four-year-olds is a "short-sighted" practice that not only does not develop the ability "to learn how to learn" but "may make future learning more difficult." Instead of "formal instruction and workbooks," which she says are clearly inappropriate, *"child-directed play must be the curriculum"* (p. 1).

One reason, perhaps, that NAEYC and others have vigorously restated their positions on what they believe is appropriate care for four-year-olds is the potential encroachment of the public schools into early childhood education. Having seen the almost total assimilation of the kindergarten into the bureaucracy of the public school, bringing with it the introduction of age-grading, standardized assessments and reading instruction, early childhood professionals clearly do not want this to happen to the preschool.

The most recent educational incursion into early childhood was Head Start, which was initiated in the 1960s, a period of social and educational reform that gave rise to the idea of academic intervention at the preschool level. From the child development point of view, this academic emphasis, rather than a "concern with the overall adjustment of the child" has been attributed to post-Sputnik rhetoric and "a facile and overstated environmentalism" that supposed rather meager intervention could effect dramatic growth in intellectual levels (Zigler, 1984, p. xi). More recently, the instruction of academic skills in the preschool and kindergarten continues to be repudiated in much of the early childhood literature.[2]

TITANS OF DEVELOPMENTAL THEORY: JEAN PIAGET AND LEV VYGOTSKY

Obviously, the interaction between instruction and development is complex. An uncontested definition of the "truth" of the relationship does not exist. In his recent book, *Actual Minds, Possible Worlds*, American cognitive psychologist Jerome Bruner (1986) wrote that if we believe that it is possible that "man *can* learn from experience, we arrange our conduct and our institutions in such a way that is is *necessary* that he learn from experience" (p. 138). Bruner calls Jean Piaget and Lev Vygotsky two "modern titans of developmental theory" (p. 136) whose work has helped to create the rules and institutions through which the culture—our contemporary culture—defines what constitutes human development and what provides opportunities for human growth (Bruner, 1986).

Although both Piaget and Vygotsky wrote in the earlier part of this century—and in Piaget's case, voluminously throughout his long professional career—their work was not widely accessible to American educators until much later. Piaget wrote *The Language and Thought of the Child* in 1923, and although it was translated into English soon after, his ideas did not influence American educators until the 1960s and 1970s. Indeed, Piaget, who was originally trained as a biologist, was not concerned with ways to move development forward. Instead, Piaget believed that growth would occur naturally as the child acted upon his environment. As Bruner (and others) have emphasized, *learning was invention* for Piaget, and each child invented the world anew.

Through clinical interviews with children and carefully documented observations, Piaget demonstrated the internal logic of the child's thinking, although different from that of the adult. Piaget hypothesized qualitative changes or stages as new ways of thinking over time transformed the old. How to speed up this cognitive process was for Piaget, the "American question." The legacy of Piaget—what Bruner (1986) believes will ultimately find its way into the "canons of our culture"—is a profound respect for the logic of the child's mind. If the culture comes to believe that "to invent is to learn," then as Bruner points out, perhaps to teach is more than "simply to transmit, to fill a vacuum" (p. 141).

One of Piaget's students in the 1950s, Eleanor Duckworth (1972), explains that the essence of cognitive development for children is not moving through Piagetian stages at a great clip, but rather, "the having of wonderful ideas" (p. 218). Because there is not a straightforward path from Piagetian theory to educational applications, Duckworth believes that the best use of such theory is *not* in making decisions about what children ought to be able or not able to do at different ages. Rather, children have wonderful ideas because they know something well, because they have personal intentions for working through their ideas, and because they have their wonderful ideas affirmed. Being able to have wonderful ideas is dependent upon the child's experiences— "knowing enough about things is one prerequisite to having wonderful ideas" (p. 231).

Later students of Piagetian theory, such as Donaldson (1978) and Harste, Woodward & Burke (1984), empirically demonstrated the wisdom of Duckworth's reflections. Children, even preschool children, are more accomplished deductive thinkers and language users than Piaget would have predicted. When children are given tasks that are embedded in their own experiences, tasks that have purposes meaningful to them and that they can recognize as meaningful to others, their performance is not so egocentric as Piaget had claimed (Donaldson, 1978, p. 17). Many researchers today suspect that Piaget was wrong to subordinate language to thinking and to isolate learning from context (Harste, Woodward & Burke, 1984). In their view, even the language of the research experiment shapes children's understanding of the tasks and influences the outcomes of these measures. With different levels and kinds of experiences, children's performance on tasks also changes qualitatively, so that thinking cannot be pulled apart from language or experience or human intentions (Harste, Woodward & Burke, 1984, p. 101).

In the case of written-language development, children do not proceed randomly, nor do they proceed in a fixed linear sequence. There are no age-related milestones in becoming literate as there are in physical development (McLane & McNamee, 1990, p. 38). There is no one way for every child to learn to write and read (Sulzby, 1986, p. 53). Instead, and this is the contribution of Piaget to our knowledge of literacy learning, children observe and act upon their environment; they solve the problem of writing and reading just as they solve other problems: by inventing their own operational rules, testing their rules, and revising them when the rules no longer appear to work.

But reading the work of Piaget and his many followers often conjures up a mental image of a child working on his own to render the world meaningful. In *Actual Minds, Possible Worlds*, Bruner (1986) observed that in the 1970s he himself wrote some "very insistent articles about the importance of discovery learning—learning on one's own" (p. 127). Yet in the years since then, Bruner has come to understand that "most learning in most settings is a communal activity, a sharing of the culture" (p. 127). This understanding of the human mind as a "product of culture" as well as a "product of nature" is the "inspiration" of Lev Vygotsky (p. 78).

Literacy, for example, seems to emerge naturally when children participate in an environment where meaningful literacy activities take place, where their questions are answered, and where their responses are valued. As children use their literacy—as they practice being members of this literate community—their written language use more closely resembles that of the adult community. Or, as Vygotsky (1978) put it, "children grow into the intellectual life of those around them" (p. 88).

Although Lev Vygotsky wrote his major works in the late 1920s and early 1930s, his work was not translated into English until *Thought and Language* was published in 1962 and *Mind in Society* appeared in 1978. Unlike Piaget, Vygotsky assigned a major role to speech in the development of thinking. Vygotsky believed that speech helped the child regulate his thought—"solve practical problems"—and that, ultimately, language was the medium through which the tools of the culture such as literacy, literature, and counting would be shared across generations. Through the medium of language, adults assist children to accomplish tasks that the child could not do on his own. The difference between what the child can accomplish independently and what he can do in collaboration with an adult or more capable peer is called the child's "zone of proximal development." Vygotsky considered the zone of proximal or potential development an "index of the child's readiness for further development" (Stone, 1985, p. 132). Vygotsky believed that tomorrow the child will be able to do independently what he could only do with assistance today. Although Vygotsky did not explain this process precisely, he did suggest that the acquisition of oral language provides an analogue for how such interpsychological collaboration—or the "borrowing of consciousness"—between child and tutor might work (Bruner, 1986, p. 76). Bruner helped to flesh out the process by describing the features of the mother-child dyadic interactions around picturebook reading that he and his colleagues have studied extensively (1986, p. 77 and see, for example, Ninio & Bruner, 1978).

As Bruner (1986) explained it, the mother establishes the routine and the format for these interactions; the mother—as tutor—"raises the ante" each time the child masters a new element of the dialogue, always staying "on the growing edge of the child's competence" (p. 77). Snow (1983) demonstrated the similarities between these patterns of interactions between mother and child in oral language acquisition and those of written language acquisition. Of course, the language of the school, between teacher and child and between children, can provide the social support to cross the zone of proximal development as well. Cazden and Clay (1990) describe how teachers who are informed and sensitive observers of children's beginning reading development can "recover" those who are faltering. By providing the right kind of assistance, teachers enable children who are experiencing difficulty in learning to read to become "self-improving systems," capable of monitoring and reflecting on their own strategies and knowledge. In her descriptions of preschoolers' conversations around the writing table in a child-center, Rowe (1989) suggests that even the interactions of three- and four-year-olds can provide the cultural support needed to construct shared meanings about the purposes and forms of literacy activities and to nudge young children into the reciprocal roles of author and audience.

For Vygotsky, "instruction" was defined as the guidance that adults give to children at home and at school (Wertsch, 1985, pp. 70–74). Unlike Piaget, who believed that children's thinking passed through invariant stages whether or not the child received any instruction, Vygotsky believed that instruction could not only influence development but also transform it (Wertsch, 1985, p. 72). Further, Vygotsky said that "instruction is good only when it proceeds ahead of development. Then it awakens and rouses to life an entire set of functions which are in the stage of maturing, which lie in the zone of proximal development. It is in this way that instruction plays an extremely important role in development" (Wertsch, 1985, p. 71). At first, these more mature functions are possible only in collaboration with adults or capable peers, but they eventually come under the child's control. Vygotsky was clearly speaking of very young children as well as school-aged children. He said, "Instruction and development do not meet for the first time at school age; rather, they are in fact connected with each other from the very first day of a child's life" (Wertsch, 1985, p. 71). What becomes of the child's development then is dependent to a great degree on the opportunities for instruction within the child's culture.

Bruner (1986) claims that Vygotsky is a "growth theorist" whose ideas for "raising consciousness" have great potential for "liberation ideology"—far more potential than even those of Freire or Illitch (p. 141). Indeed, Leont'ev (cited in Wertsch, 1985), one of Vygotsky's students, suggested that the difference between American and Soviet psychology is that "American researchers are constantly seeking to discover how the child came to be what he is" whereas Soviet psychologists are "striving to discover. . . how he can become what he not yet is" (p. 67).

SOCIAL CLASS AND LITERACY DEVELOPMENT

Although children from middle-class families do better as a group in beginning reading than do children from poorer families, the reasons for their advantage are not altogether clear. Recent ethnographic studies of literacy development among children from Black and working-class communities and middle-class mainstream communities (Heath, 1983) have provided some hypotheses about why this might be. As Heath has pointed out, written language is not used for the same purposes across these various community cultures. Without explicitly evaluating the "literateness" of the Black and working-class cultures, Heath has suggested that the mainstream middle-class community presents children with language use that more closely matches that of the school (p. 350). Noticeably present in the middle-class community and missing in the others was ritual story reading to the preschool child, particularly bedtime stories (p. 350). While other types of print reading were available to children in the nonmainstream culture, story reading has assumed particular significance as cognitive "scaffolding" (Snow, 1983, p. 170) that enables the child to understand and participate in increasingly complex and decontextualized language, (p. 187). Parents in Heath's middle-class community do not think they are "formally" teaching literacy skills to their preschoolers, but rather that they are doing what seems natural. Other studies of early readers (Durkin, 1974–75), writers (Bissex, 1984), or family literacy (Taylor, 1983) also suggest that parents do not usually perceive themselves as "teaching" reading to their children but as responding to their children's inquiries. While representing a departure from a model of learning to read proposed in the 1950s and 1960s and perhaps still prevalent in commercial readiness materials, the print-laden environment of the middle-class home as a natural context for reading to develop is very much in tune with the contemporary idea of emergent literacy.

Nonetheless, how much of the literacy that emerges among middle-class children is really untutored is not clear, nor is the distinction that educators as well as some researchers make between "formal" and "informal" learning. Ferreiro (1984), for example, noted that Mexican middle-class and poorer children demonstrated comparable developmental awareness of what writing represents early on, but "in subsequent years, [poorer children] were deprived of formal instruction in literacy as a result of social factors," (p. 205). In summarizing the results of the University of Victoria Symposium on Children's Response to a Literate Environment, Goelman (1984) recalls that the participants could not agree on the meaning of "formal" instruction, although several thought that it was probably not necessary for literacy to develop.

Regarding the question of whether literacy could be taught in the schools, Hillel Goelman says that there was some argument in favor of "valuable, meaningful, noncoercive literacy learning [taking] place in schools through informal education" (p. 212). As an example of such "informal" education Goelman cited a statement generated earlier by Frank Smith in 1984 that "literacy is acquired through collaborative experience rather than through explanation and precepts." Certainly the middle-class nursery schools described by Cochran-Smith (1983) and Schieffelin and Cochran-Smith (1984) are examples of collaborative experience or "informal" education. No reading and writing were explicitly taught, but children initiated and participated daily in many literacy events embedded within the social routines of life at the preschool and in their community. How to make this informal education or collaborative experience accessible to children without such community support and to what extent story reading and other middle-class accouterments are necessary to develop literacy were not resolved.

Although the ideas associated with promoting reading among preschoolers have taken a more developmental turn—"emergent literacy" as opposed to "building readiness"—the belief, or perhaps the hope, persists that parents and teachers (or competent peers) can intervene early in the lives of children to accelerate literacy development. In her review of home factors that influence "print-development" Hiebert (1986) explains that children do not learn about print "via osmosis from a print-saturated environment" but rather through interactions with parents who focus attention on different dimensions of print, depending on their own notion of what was appropriate and important (p. 151). Such parents clearly wanted their children to learn these things, and many believed it was their responsibility to teach letters and sounds before their children went to school. These findings are certainly consistent with Adam's (1990) hypothesis that middle-class children come to school having had thousands of hours of individual tutoring by parents who read regularly with their children and "guide" their ideas about print (p. 85).

Olson (1984) suggested that the key to the notion of a literate environment may be in how parents differentiate what may be taught from what is merely learned. According to this view, subcultures differ in how they regard and use language: oral societies do not regard language as an object—it is not formal and cannot be taught—whereas literate communities regard language as a "body of knowledge" and teach it as such. Even though children do not need to be "taught" how to talk, Olson claimed that middle-class or literate parents teach them to speak "in a manner appropriated from the practice of teaching them to read ("See! Jumping!")," (p. 188) but Heath's working-class Black parents do not ("No use me telling him [the names of things]. . . he just gotta learn.") (p. 187). Although this type of orientation may have little to do with how well children learn to speak, Olson said it may have "everything to do with literacy" in that it provides children with a metalanguage for thinking about the meaning and structure of language (p. 189). Further, Olson suggested that the metalanguage taught to children as they learn to talk is an "oral language antecedent" of literacy. Thus, in explaining the literate competencies Olson was proposing that the answer lies not only in the "mental activities of children" but also in the "tutorial practices" of teachers and parents, the literacy-related activities of home and school. Olson stated that the acquisition of literacy may be thought of as a developmental process, typically the psychologist's point of view, and increasingly, as "cultural-historical" transmission (p. 185).

How educable the beginnings of literacy may be within this more complex description is subject to much debate, even among the experts. Already intervention studies (Morrow, 1988; Mason et al., 1989) are starting to reflect some dimensions of emergent literacy descriptions, and researchers are beginning to explore how children's play contributes to literate behavior (Johnston & Fleming, 1986; Paley, 1990; Nourot, Henry & Scales, 1990; Pellegrini et al., 1990). Whether these activities are considered "educational" may determine to a large extent who pays for and supports literacy development in early childhood programs.

SUMMARY

The myriad issues raised in contemporary discussions of public school for four-year-olds are not new. What constitutes appropriate state or government interest in very young children has been an issue since colonial America. It appears that early on families endorsed a custodial or child care role for the common schools, because they sent children as young as two years old off to school with older siblings. Later, with increasing differentiation between the roles of the school and the family brought about by industrialization and bureaucratization, the school staked out an education function and relegated child care to the family, primarily the mother.

At crucial points in history when social conditions were dramatically changed—by unemployment or war, for example—government temporarily supported child care in the public schools. It remains to be seen whether the demographic changes in the role of women over the last several decades and consequent care of dependent children outside the family constitute enough of a social change for government to support universal child care. For special groups of children, government has assumed some responsibility for their welfare when parents are unable to fulfill their obligations, as in the case of children living in poverty. Rarely has government—in the form of public schools—assumed either an educational or a custodial role for children under the age of five. When expert knowledge and social conditions converged during the 1960s to demonstrate that poverty deprived children of appropriate educational experiences as well as adequate care and that the effects of educational deprivation could be reversed, government assumed an educational role and intervened in the lives of three- to five-year-olds.

Because these early-intervention programs have not generally provided the "head start" in educational performance that was originally expected, government is less sanguine about the outcome of compensatory programs and, perhaps, less sure of a public responsibility in early childhood education. Certainly there is less consensus on what may be accomplished. Indeed, in later evaluations of the Head Start program, the social and community outcomes were emphasized more than in previous studies. In the early evaluations, children's later reading achievement was one of the primary criteria on which the efficacy of Head Start was evaluated.

Of course, the connections between early childhood experiences and literacy are not completely known, and expert opinion has not pointed consistently in one direction. Some professionals in the field of early childhood education may cling to a maturational or developmental hypothesis whereas others are more likely to take a Vygotskian perspective and point to the benefits of instruction. As differences in language use and literacy development across cultural groups are becoming more apparent in the research literature, the questions of what is teachable and what is learned become more complex.

6. SCHOOL READINESS DEFINED: FROM MAMA ROBIN TO THE SATs

The whole issue of school readiness is like. . . layers upon layers of different views. . . and everyone has a different definition of what school readiness means.

—An advocate for schools

I don't know if our standards are going up. They may be, but I don't know that they are. And clearly, kids who. . . don't get read to, who don't have experiences that are beneficial for four-year-olds, have less to build on.

—A policy expert in New York State government

LOCATING THE ISSUE of public school for four-year-olds in contemporary state politics helps provide a context for understanding the statements of policy participants in this and subsequent chapters. Therefore, before describing the results of the interviews conducted for the study, I present a brief account of the status and recent history of the issue of public school for four-year-olds in New York State politics.

NEW YORK STATE: THE DECADE OF THE CHILD

In the state of New York, public school for four-year-olds has become an agenda item, originally through the efforts of Gordon Ambach, former education commissioner, and the New York State Board of Regents, who have repeatedly proposed legislation to make public school universally available to children between the ages of four and six. In addition, Governor Cuomo (1987) declared in his State of the

State message that his personal goal was to make preschool education available for all disadvantaged children in the state of New York:

> And that we set as our goal the provision of early childhood education to every disadvantaged four-year-old child in the state (p. 11).

Among the initiatives proposed in the Executive Budget was early childhood education with both an education and a child care component. Although the Legislature substantially increased funding for both day care and prekindergarten programs, the legislature did not fund the Governor's initiative for coordinated child care and education (LEG1). Instead, the Legislature allocated a half-million dollars for the New York State Council on Children and Families to study the proposal and develop recommendations for legislation in the area of early childhood education for the following fiscal year. The Council convened a committee of key statewide policy figures in early childhood education and related child-care fields in order to commence study of how child care and education might be coordinated for preschool children in New York State (LEG1). Three surveys were commissioned by the Council, and the results of this research were presented at the Legislative Symposium on Early Childhood Programs (February 3, 1988), jointly sponsored by the New York State Assembly and Senate with grants from the National Conference of State Legislatures, the Carnegie Foundation, and the Business Council of New York State.

One year after the initial gubernatorial proposal to fund education for disadvantaged children, Governor Cuomo recommended in his State of the State message (1988) that prekindergarten be available to all four-year-olds in New York State. This proposal for universal prekindergarten was considered the cornerstone of the Governor's declared support for children and families ("Decade of the Child", 1988). The year following the Governor's initial proposal to make education and "wrap-around" child care available to all disadvantaged children was a period of intense political activity on the early childhood issue, and it was during this period that I conducted interviews of the participants in this process.

THE INTERVIEWS

Using the roster of agencies or organizations that were included in the NYS Council on Children and Families' coordinating activities during the summer and fall of 1987 (LEG1), I identified and interviewed policy analysts[1] about their perceptions of public school for four-year-olds and children's readiness for schooling. Participants were selected to represent particular statewide perspectives—program or curriculum viewpoints, fiscal and budgetary concerns, legislative or executive office perspectives, and interest-group advocacy—on public school for four-year-olds (see appendix for participants' identifying codes and professional affiliations). All participants were themselves members of the New York State Council on Children and Families' statewide coordinating committee established by the legislature and organized by the governor's office, or were nominated by members of this committee as people responsible for analyzing this issue (LEG5).

The interview questions (see appendix) were designed to explore what individual policy participants viewed as the important parts of the issue of public school for four-year-olds and any ways this issue may have been reconceptualized over time. How these policymakers defined school readiness and their perceptions of changing standards for school entry were probed. I asked policy participants to describe what outcomes of public schooling for four-year-olds would be beneficial, which problems or issues are yet unresolved, and what ideas or which people have been influential in shaping their thinking on public school for four-year-olds. There was no formal question on literacy, nor was there one on the role of literacy in early schooling. The questions were designed to be broad, to allow those who are publicly identified with public school for four-year-olds to define the dimensions of the issue. I felt that literacy-related concerns would emerge from the more general questions, presenting a natural opportunity to probe this topic.

Policy participants told the story of this issue from their own perspectives—perspectives that were influenced not only by their particular jobs and the information they are privy to but also by their encounters with preschool through their own children's experiences or experiences of children they have known. As these policy participants spoke about what was important, they characterized the issue in the language of their profession and identified components of the issue to which they must attend. Each encounter with these policy participants informed subsequent encounters. Whereas the first few interviews were more open ended—an exploration of how participants were currently defining the role of public schools in the education of four-year-olds—the last served mainly to verify the categories of perceptions described by members of the policy community who were interviewed previously. Participants' responses to my questions helped me refine the categories that emerged from my analysis of the history of past attempts to school young children. However, expert knowledge, social values, and political, demographic, and economic conditions continue to be viable categories to use in describing the influences on public policy toward the education of young children. These categories appeared again as contemporary participants' perceptions of public responsibility and child development were compared and contrasted with those of earlier decades.

EXPERT KNOWLEDGE DICHOTOMIZED: POLICY VERSUS PROGRAM EXPERTISE

For analysts in budget positions, legislative and executive office staff for education or human services issues, and advocacy or interest-group lobbyists, there appeared to be a clear demarcation between types of expert knowledge—with policy formulation on the one hand, and program or curriculum knowledge on the other.[2] One respondent explained that he himself was not an educator but "would define myself in the realm of looking at these issues as a politician. . .Sometimes I feel like a pontificator, I stand up here and talk about education policy, and what should go on in a classroom, and I've never taught in my life. . .I would view myself as a political and not a professional educator by any stretch of the imagination."(LEG3–12).

When asked what outcomes of public school for four-year-olds might be considered beneficial, another respondent reported that she did not "know of any. . .I don't know enough about that. . .It's funny, because questions like that are beginning to delve into the difference between people who in a sense make laws, and people who do the work. You have to know that if you are somebody who's going to be a. . .teacher trainer or who's going to set up a program" (LEG2–34–35).

Likewise, the issue of whether public schools should provide four-year-olds with education and what such schooling should accomplish was not viewed as a "fiscal concern because it is more a programmatic issue." But budget analysts pointed out that they understand that these are issues for "those people who are deciding" (EX4). Once program decisions are made, budget analysts "go by what the experts have indicated. Whatever they determine is the best way to evaluate. . .We're just saying from the fiscal point of view, we would like to make sure that the program people can tell us that the money we're spending is getting the intended results" (EX4,5–51).

No policy participant cited himself or herself as an expert on literacy acquisition per se, although the majority expressed opinions on reading and writing development, and only three—two affiliated with the administration of state-funded preschool programs and one with a university-based research project on early childhood—considered themselves experts on early childhood curricula, in the sense that they would advise the participants in other areas of state government on developmentally appropriate programs.

Who are considered the experts or where does expert knowledge come from? Budget analysts, for example, do not consider themselves experts in the issues addressed in this study but instead consult with statewide administrators of preschool programs, advocacy group leaders, and program specialists in early childhood education and social services agencies. What concerns the fiscal staff are "the numbers" not the program:

> [W]e don't profess to have expertise in this area. We try to become as knowledgeable as we can on the issue. But we look at the numbers. When we need program input, we have some people in the field. . .who have been very strong advocates for the existing experimental pre-K program. . . [and] very gracious in terms of assisting us and bringing in a number of people who run pre-K programs in other areas throughout the state, to meet with us and brief us, and we can bounce ideas off of them. And the education department has its own early childhood education specialists, and we've been able to meet with them too. Social services has. . .someone who deals with the day care aspects, and the whole child care advocacy group out there as well. We've seen them in action, but we have not met with them because we deal with the education component of it. (EX4–33)

However, several of the above sources of expertise—the advocates for children and early childhood professionals—do not consider program issues to be particular strengths. One said, for example, that the "education [component] is not mine" (IG3–4). Yet another wanted to make clear that her expertise was in the political process:

> Again, I want to stress. . .I'm a political person, and I'm a policy person, and one of the things I do constantly in my work, is that I look to other people for answers. You know I would never negotiate regulations or curriculum or anything without getting people who know that stuff to

> specifically say this is what we think is important, and then I'll carry their message to other people. But I'm not trained as an early childhood person. I don't know the first thing about—I mean I'm learning myself about early childhood development from being in this job. (IG4–30)

Similarly, legislative policy analysts see "constituency groups" as the source of their information on program issues such as public school for four-year-olds. "Constituents" are defined as field-based providers of educational services and those who represent these providers. In the view of one analyst, it is his job to hold hearings on educational issues of public concern so that interested groups can voice their preferences:

> I would say basically we always have a formula...in dealing with any particular issue, and that formula starts from the premise that we're not the experts, that the experts are out in the field, and you've got to create the forums for those people to express themselves and give you specific recommendations...[W]e've got to get a better sense of where the providers themselves and those groups that represent the disabled community...and those people who are running experimental pre-K programs and day-care programs, how they think that this fit should take place...I see the constituency groups as having a major voice and major say in the direction that we go in. (LEG3–25,8,26)

Finally, parents were cited as the group responsible for making the decision about whether four-year-olds should go to school:

> Again, that's not an issue that we have to deal with in the budget, but I think that question came up when Commissioner Ambach was pushing for the opportunities being provided for all four-year-olds, and he himself said that readiness is an important factor. That if a parent—because again, he was not talking compulsors, that if a parent determined that a child simply isn't ready for this experience, well, then it doesn't make sense to them...(EX4–36) It's less of our fiscal concern...but we understand that it is an issue for those people who are deciding, and I think the parents are the first people who should decide whether their child is ready for that. (EX4–37)

Thus, expertise in defining school readiness is vested not in the policy participants but rather in the early childhood program specialists in the State Education Department; in the associates in the Council on Children and Families; in the constituency groups who represent the interests of schools, teachers, and child care providers; and in the parents of children who may be eligible to attend preschool programs.

FROM MAMA ROBIN TO THE SAT: THE POLICY PERSPECTIVE ON SCHOOL READINESS AND LITERACY

While some policy participants do not view themselves as experts, they do hold views on what constitutes school readiness and the role of literacy in programs for preschoolers (see table 6–1). As might be expected, these views ranged considerably in sophistication. From the idea that school readiness is "like Mama Robin knowing when to push a certain chick from the nest" (EX4-37) to preparing children for the "challenges ahead" such as the "job market. . .to be able to read when they go through the school system" and to score better on the "languishing" SAT scores, these policy participants did not hold to a singular view of what school readiness might mean.

TABLE 6–1
Policy Participants Definitions of School Readiness

How much is a first grader supposed to know when they come to school? I think that [they] need to come to school with a certain experiential background that allows them to be ready to learn. . . so that they know what an apple is when they have to learn to try to read what the word *apple* is, or that they have some sense of the world that allows them to imagine when they begin to read what another person's experiences are. . . but they shouldn't come to first grade knowing how to say their alphabet and. . .why should they? (IG4–37–38)

We recognize that some children have different levels of preparedness, readiness, whatever, for that type of environment, and I think it's like Mama Robin knowing when to push a certain chick from the nest. (EX4–37)

I don't know if our standards are going up. They may be, but I don't know that they are. And clearly, kids who don't have the kinds of opportunity, don't have stimulation, don't get read to, who don't have experiences that are beneficial for 4-year-olds, have less to build on. (EX1–26)

It's tied into the whole notion that parents really feel like their kids have to go to school, that they have to learn to read and write, and they have to do dittos. . .My family encouraged me to learn. . .to question. Those are the things

(*continued*)

that matter, not that you come home with a piece of paper, that you copied all your letter As. And I think that parents are discouraging that kind of interactive learning because they think their children are supposed to be able to recite their "ABCs" by the time they're a year old. What's more, I find my friends who work in special ed are telling me that they're seeing more and more kids referred as learning disabled who aren't learning disabled at all. They're just not learning as quick as [someone] would like them to learn. . . I'm very concerned about this whole notion. . . I hear day care people say to me that it's a problem for them, that they're pushed so much by parents and by school districts that want the kids to be ready to sit at little desks, and write on their little pieces of paper, that they're finding it hurting their desire to not do that. . . I mean parents ask them. . . shouldn't the kid have homework. . . when they're really little. . . I think that's really dangerous. . . It comes from this whole sort of yuppy success. . . I have to have a successful kid philosophy. (IG4–36)

Where do you help a [disadvantaged] kid come up to the same skill level that a middle class 5- or 6-year-old has? There are also people who get really angry at that and say, what the hell do you expect from a 5-year old anyway? How can you possibly be educationally disadvantaged. . . the first day you walk into school. (LEG2–42)

[M]y definition of school readiness is indeed to have children ready to increase [skills] to be ready for the job market, to pursue post secondary studies, but indeed to have them [ready] when they go through the school system to be able to read, write and whether good or bad, to raise SAT scores, that have been languishing over the last several years, and I think the idea of getting children into an environment that starts preparing them for those types of challenges ahead, . . . the idea of getting them in at age four is something I think that we obviously have to take a look at, and that's how I relate to something called school readiness. (LEG3–13)

I'm not as close to the educational side of this issue, and what the establishment thinks about it [but] clearly there's been change in terms of more focus on what's appropriate for 4-year-olds. . . and important material rejecting this notion of teaching kids too early, pushing them too fast, and. . . that has implications for. . . school experiences. . . The content of those experiences has to be rethought so we don't get into this craziness of teaching 3- and 4-year-olds how to write and thinking we've done something because they write a year earlier or they can read words. . . [W]hat you try to teach them or do with them at four is help them deal with structure, learn to interact. . . basic stuff like colors and shapes but not this notion that we're going to teach them all to read at four. (EX1–4,5,8,9).

For example, the idea of being behind in school before the child even starts was thought to be outrageously unfair ("What the hell do you expect from a five- or six-year-old anyway?" (LEG2-42)). Being "educationally disadvantaged" on the "first day you walk into school" (LEG2-42) was dismissed by two analysts, who questioned "how much...a first grader is supposed to know when they come to school." Two policy professionals attributed this "pushing" of children to a "yuppie philosophy" that presumes part of the parent's success is "having a successful kid" who can "recite their ABCs by the time they're a year old" (IG4–35; LEG2–43). But another analyst believed children "who don't get read to, who don't have experiences that are beneficial" have "less to build on," regardless of whether standards for school entry were going up or not (EX1–26). Another analyst used his experiences with his own child to gauge what kind of preschool and home background children might need to participate successfully in school:

> I know in my own case my daughter is in the third day of first grade and she can read...not every word in the sentence, but she can get through...certain storybooks. That is [because]...of two years in nursery school, a year of kindergarten and a mother and father who...read with her...[who] attach a great deal of importance to schooling...Youngsters who come from families where they don't have those three years already...[whose] family doesn't have the money to pay for those things...[they're] right behind the starting line from the beginning. (EX2–7)

Even though the importance of literacy, or the role of literacy, in preschool programs was not directly addressed in the interview format, the topic of *reading* was always initiated by the policy participants. Reading and writing for four-year-olds was soundly rejected by the policy participants as something children should learn to do in preschool. Children were seen as needing "a certain experiential background that allows them to be ready to learn...so that they know what an apple is when they have to learn to try to read what the word *apple* is." Children were seen as needing "a sense of the world that allows them to imagine when they begin to read what another person's experiences are...but they shouldn't come to first grade knowing how to say their alphabet...and why should they?" Four-year-olds were thought to need some "basics" like colors and shapes and how "to deal with structure" (EX1–8,9) but not "this craziness" of teaching them to write and "thinking we've done something because they can write a year earlier or can read words" (EX1–5).

DEVELOPMENTALLY APPROPRIATE AND NO READING: LITERACY AND LEARNING FROM THE PROGRAM PERSPECTIVE

Program professionals pointedly and unanimously denounced any attempts to teach four-year-olds to read and write. It is not surprising then that the statements of policy professionals—who rely on this source of expert knowledge—reflected similar sentiments. These early childhood professionals, whether affiliated with the advocacy groups, state level administration of early childhood education, or the university, uniformly rejected the idea of formal instruction not only in preschool programs but also in kindergarten. As may be seen from their responses to interview questions (see table 6–2), teaching children to read and write at four and five years of age is clearly anathema to what these program experts call a "developmental" curriculum. Instruction in reading and writing is tantamount to academic or formal schooling and definitely not acceptable practice, according to theories of child development espoused by the program experts in this study.

TABLE 6–2
Program Experts' Definitions of School Readiness

[T]here is a whole body of literature in this area. . .that emphasizes the importance of developmental readiness, that incorporates both cognitive domain and the affective domain as well. And certainly there's a body of literature in research that more recently is based on the insistence that kids not be put in school in formal learning situations until they are fully able to cope with it. . .Academic research. . .reported in the early childhood journals, certainly the Perry Preschool program is one that is oftentimes cited. (IG1–25)

[P]art that I didn't mention before is the idea that the kids can be given the tools and the dispositions to learn later on, but not necessarily have drilled into them certain factual knowledge. . .maybe that's part of the term *readiness*. . .I remember the screening test my own kids went through. . . [it] had some kind of test of basic physical coordination. . .That kind of thing (IG1–26–27).

I remember the research that I've seen from past years that deals with the kids who have entered school earlier and tend to get held back. And I've heard districts [are] coming up with innovative arrangements whereby kindergarten has been broken out into a two year period. [T]hey assess it at a halfway point and see whether or not they think their kids are going to be able to make it, and if not, they put them into some kind of special intensive remediation. There

(*continued*)

is a lot of innovative stuff out there because of the fact that there is the demand to get the kids into school earlier. Get them started earlier. (IG1–33–34).

The most popular interpretation of school readiness. . .is how to get those children ready to do the work of our rigorous kindergartens? What do you do [for example] with a child [who transfers into the program] when we're already on *K* and he hasn't done *A,B,C,D,E,F,G,H,I,J*? What good is it talking to a person [who worries about that] to say that there is no value in 4-year-olds learning the letters of the alphabet, or 5-year-olds?. . .In this state right now, they are flunking kindergarten children right and left. . .Somebody from [a local district] came in the other day, and 28% of the kindergarteners failed, and I told him he ought to be ashamed of himself. . .If I had a 5-year-old right now, I'd keep that child out of school (IG5–46).

They're doing the wrong things in kindergarten. . .[T]he fact of the matter is the development of children is still by and large the same as it was twenty years ago. Reports [to] home from kindergarten teachers say that this child needs more work on the numeral 8, or the kid has, for lack of better terminology, dyslexia, or certain other neurological things. [But] nothing is wrong, just not old enough. It's turned into the kids being ready for the schools, instead of the schools being ready for the children. . .We need to look at the NAEYC statement on acceptable practices for 3- , 4- and 5-year-old children. (IG5–47–48)

[T]here needs to be a connection between concepts and the concrete, so. . .a standard child development class would look at outstanding people such as Piaget and Erikson. . .(EX3–27) and diversity [in child development curriculum] is very important. . .in terms or what is available for children to play with or learn from. . .(EX3–28) You would want a reading corner where children can go to books freely. You would want to be reading to children. . .[But] many 4-year-olds don't have the muscle development to hold a pencil and so one of the fears is that you're going to start to make demands on kids to do things before they are physiologically ready, that is, before they're developmentally ready. . .(EX3–29) If you want to look to guidelines that there is a great deal of consensus on. . .the NAEYC accreditation process, I think there is more consensus on quality than people assume. The other thing I will tell you, is there are different grasps that children can use at different ages. And you will see some 4-year-olds who have never been exposed to crayons or magic markers [and who] will grasp a crayon the way a 2-year-old will grasp a crayon. They will probably go through the stages much quicker, but if you were going to put a pencil in their hand. . .there's no way that [they] have control when you do that. If you look at the scribbling of a 2-year-old, that's what you get [with the 4-year-old]. . .[W]hat I worry about with a rigid curriculum is setting kids up for earlier failure. (EX3–30)

(continued)

TABLE 6–2 *(continued)*

I would have you go to the NAEYC standards. . .as a good place to go to look at. . .concerns about the trends that we see in kindergarten. We have required more and more formal reading readiness in terms of work group activities and pencil activities, and at younger ages. In fact, you will see in some states, a movement to set up transitional classrooms between kindergarten and first grade. Very often I think that's an indication that some of the things that are being done in kindergarten are not starting right where the kids are. . .We put little kids in situations all the time and make them feel bad that they can't do something. . .[W]hat we know about early childhood gives us a lot of proven information about how to make the schools more in tune with families and children. What I often feel has happened is that the structure of schools has impinged on early childhood programs until. . .these programs for 4-year-olds [feel] they must prepare children for school success in kindergarten and must have the children achieving certain things by the time they leave. And to give you an example, sometimes it's felt a child needs to have accomplished a number of things before they get to kindergarten, things that kindergarten used to concentrate on. (EX3–31,32)

Children at age four need a lot of concrete materials. . .they need a lot of open-ended materials. . .they need a lot of experiences [like] sand and water play, and loads and loads of stories that's available which make the statement that reading is important. . .Armed with rich experiences and language and concrete and open-ended materials, [the] child is also developing physically. So, by the time that he is able to cope with abstract notions, around seven or eight, he's got all the concrete experience in back of him to bring to his reading, to bring to his math, in other words, the formal academics. . .The idea of universal pre-K for all turned—after a long time and a lot of criticism from a lot of people all over the United States—into the notion that it was not to be made an early kindergarten with formal academics, nor was kindergarten to be made a little first grade. . .This is misinterpreted all over the place (IG5–9). Kindergarten, by this time, has so much of its work as first grade. It's all developmentally cockeyed and crazy and inappropriate. (IG5–8)

One of the problems is that they did away with a nursery through three certification about twenty years ago, and we're reaping the results of that with people who have never had a course on child development. When you talk about child development, they don't understand what you mean. . .That it isn't just a simple progression because growth. . .is highly individual from one child to the next. And a child who may have a 190 IQ may not have eye-hand coordination. He may not have binocular vision. He may not have sufficient neurological development. . .His mind, in other words, can handle things more quickly than the mechanics of writing and reading and all this stuff. You know

(continued)

TABLE 6–2 *(continued)*

how a child who is very bright can sit and stumble over words in reading, when he can hear a story that is far more complicated. . . So you don't saddle an immature child with the mechanics of things before he's ready. But you feed him rich experiences through talking with him and letting him look at things, and working with these materials while his development is proceeding. (IG5–9–11)

[Lillian Katz] said that children who have had that kind of [structure like DISTAR] were not creative thinkers, and as they grew older they had more difficulty with their peers and other adults. Part of it is the right-or-wrong-answer syndrome. That child has the possibility of growing up seeking answers from other people instead of discovering them for himself. . .Those people who developed DISTAR were not educators, number one. . .I have any number of friends who have kids at the second grade level who have gone through DISTAR and come to second grade not being able to read. (IG5–12).

The whole issue of school readiness is like. . .layers upon layers of different views. . .and everyone has a different definition of what school readiness means. . .So, twenty years ago. . .what you had to know, what you had to be able to do to go to kindergarten was different than what you have to be able to do [now]. . .[K]indergarten teachers who have taught for a long time say that it feels to them like it shifted to what you used to know when you got out of kindergarten is now what you're supposed to know when you start kindergarten. . .[T]he objectives for first grade are now the ones for kindergarten—what is expected in kindergarten. . .[but]. . .the developmental level. . .the kids haven't changed a whole lot. (IG2–28,29)

As they explained their ideas of what "developmentally appropriate" instruction should look like, these program experts invoked the research of David Weikart at the Perry Preschool Project, Lillian Katz's philosophy of early childhood learning, Jean Piaget's stages of cognitive development, Erik Erikson's eight ages of man's social and emotional growth, and the National Association for the Education of Young Children's (NAEYC) guidelines for appropriate curriculum practices. One statewide administrator of early childhood programs (IG–5) said it was almost impossible to bridge the communication gap between her and teachers with academic leanings. This program expert was not sure how to get across "that there is no value in four or five-year-olds. . . learning the letters of the alphabet" if a teacher is worried about children missing instruction in specific letters because of late enrollments or transfers (IG5–46). "Getting children ready to do the work of our rigorous kindergartens" is the "most popular interpretation of school readiness" (46) according to this program expert, who believes that kindergartens today are "doing the wrong things," that much of kindergarten is first-grade-level work, and that it is all "developmentally cockeyed and crazy and inappropriate" (8). In her view, children are failing kindergarten in record numbers and others are being labelled dyslexic when, in reality, they are simply not old enough. To illustrate, this program expert said that a child "with a 190 IQ may not have eye-hand coordination. . . [or] binocular vision. . . [or] neurological development. His mind, in other words, can handle things more quickly than the mechanics of writing and reading. . . A child who is very bright can sit and stumble over words in reading when he can hear a story that is far more complicated" (10). What such immature children need are "experiences. . . talking. . . look[ing] at things and working with. . . materials" (10). Regarding reading instruction in particular, this program expert felt that "around seven or eight" the child "is able to cope with abstract notions [because] he's got all the concrete experience in back of him to bring to his reading, to bring to his math. . . the formal academics." Experiences that she felt would prepare the child for formal academics were "sand and water play and loads and loads of stories. . . which make the statement that reading is important. . . rich language and concrete and open-ended materials." By contrast, children who have had instruction in programs like DISTAR have "problems with their peers and other adults. . . [because] they grow up seeking answers from other people instead of discovering them for himself" (12).

A second early childhood program expert (EX3) expressed similar views on what constitutes a "developmentally appropriate curriculum" and the place of reading and writing. She agreed that a "reading corner where children can go to books freely. . . and reading to children" should be included, but cautioned against introducing things to children before they were "physiologically ready, that is, developmentally ready." As an example, this program expert alluded to the often immature muscle development of four-year-olds, which might preclude being able to hold a pencil for writing or drawing (29). Additionally, many four-year-olds may not have had exposure to crayons or markers and may grasp them like a two-year-old, producing "the scribbling of a two-year-old" and thus setting them up for early failure (30). This program expert also implicated the kindergarten in "not starting where the kids are" (31) and expecting children to have "accomplished a number of things before they get to kindergarten—things the kindergarten used to concentrate on" (32). She repeated the claim made by the statewide administrator that children have not changed over the last twenty years, but more is being expected of them. More formal "reading readiness in terms of workbook activities and pencil activities" (31) is being initiated at younger ages, more transition rooms are being established, and children are being made to feel "bad that they can't do something" (32). In her view, "the structure of the schools has impinged on early childhood programs" in a negative way, yet the field of early childhood education could provide "proven information about how to make the schools more in tune with families and children" (32).

The leader of an advocacy group representing local schools (IG1) also referred to educational research, particularly the Perry Preschool Project, which, he said, emphasizes the importance of "developmental readiness," incorporating the "cognitive domain and the affective domain," and not putting children into school "in formal learning situations until they are fully able to cope with it" (25). Such children can be given the "tools and the dispositions to learn later on" but not "have drilled into them certain kinds of factual knowledge" (26). He mused that this could be "part of the term *readiness*" and cited the screening his own child had for preschool, which included physical coordination as a measure of development (27).

In his view, districts have been able to provide "innovative arrangements" for children who are not ready. Making kindergarten a two-year program, assessing children at the "halfway point to see whether or not they. . .are going to make it, and if not, provid[ing] special intensive remediation" are some of the "innovations" born of the "demand to get the kids into school earlier" (34).

Despite the rejection of formal academics by program experts, at least two research and curriculum sources cited by these professionals have extended their definition of "developmentally appropriate" practices to include written language learning. It is interesting to note how the language of program experts echoes that of the authorities they cite, particularly Lillian Katz. Yet, in several instances the extemporaneous remarks of these statewide program experts belie a misunderstanding or incomplete understanding of the points these research and curriculum authorities have made in either the documents provided by the program experts or referred to in the commentary by the program experts. In the next section of the present study, research studies or curriculum reports that were identified by the program experts as relevant to their own philosophy of developmentally appropriate practice in early childhood education are summarized. The thematic content of these papers is analyzed for congruence with the program experts' beliefs and for the role assigned by these acknowledged early childhood authorities to written language learning in preschool programs.

7. THE AUTHORITIES ON DEVELOPMENTALLY APPROPRIATE PRACTICE: DISPOSITIONS, LANGUAGE, AND COGNITIVELY ORIENTED ACTIVE LEARNING

> *I really think that there is more consensus on quality than people assume. . . I would have you go to the NAEYC accreditation standards [because] this is an area where there has been a great deal of consensus. . . [W]e see child care connected to it, it's connected to nursery schools, and NAEYC also has a membership from public school teachers who are working with four-year-olds.*
>
> —*An early childhood expert in New York State government*

MANY OF THE POLICY participants interviewed for the study cited the early childhood educator Lillian Katz, the Perry Preschool Project in Ypsilanti, Michigan, and the curriculum guidelines published by the National Association for the Education of Young Children (NAEYC) as the most powerful influences on their own thinking about appropriate practices for four-year-olds. In this chapter, I explain what these oft-cited national authorities have written about schooling for four-year-olds and, in particular, what they say about reading and writing in the preschool. Throughout my analysis of the writings authored by the national authorities, I looked for beliefs that these experts seemed to hold in common with the policy participants interviewed for my study. Likewise, I looked for ways that local perspectives might diverge from those of the national authorities. Of course, any interpretation is my own, based on my own readings of the texts and interviews as well as my own understanding of the issues involved.

A NARROW VIEW OF LITERACY: THE INFLUENTIAL PHILOSOPHY OF LILLIAN KATZ

Lillian Katz, director of the ERIC Clearinghouse on Elementary and Early Childhood Education, University of Illinois at Urbana-Champaign, and editor of *Current Topics in Early Childhood Education*, was mentioned by name on one occasion, and her labels for different kinds of learning and/or the goals of such learning were mentioned by each of the program experts. In a keynote address at the New York State Education Department Conference on Early Childhood Education held at Kingsborough Community College in April, 1986, Katz discussed important issues before the profession. In an edited transcript of this speech provided by a New York State program expert, Katz differentiated among "knowledge," "skills," and "dispositions or habits of mind" (p. 2). In terms of young children, Katz considered the "names of things, stories, songs. . .telling them how things grow, where they are made, and where they come from" all part of the knowledge teachers wish to impart (p. 1). As far as reading was concerned, Katz viewed "decoding" as a reading "skill" as opposed to a "disposition to be a reader." Dispositions cannot be learned from "exercise books or from instruction" but instead from "being around people who have them." Rather than being "taught. . .it's useful to think of dispositions as being strengthened or weakened" (Katz, 1986, p. 3).

Katz emphasized that there are "risks" in introducing academic content too early. Academic content appears synonymous with the notion of a "formal curriculum," which Katz defined as "introducing a group of children to the same task" (p. 5). By children, Katz meant those five to seven years olds or younger. The younger the child, the more informal the "treatment" or teaching should be, she believed. "Informal" in this sense means that a variety of materials and methods are employed (p. 5). As a reference on this point, Katz cited a 1980 lecture by Durkin entitled "Is Kindergarten Reading Instruction Really Desirable?" but she did not explain how her comments related to Durkin.

According to Katz, when the same task is given to all children, a third already know how to do it, a third will learn it (p. 6) and a third will become "psychological dropouts" because they did not understand it (p. 7). Such academic work usually involves teaching children to read. As Katz emphasized in this statewide address to early childhood educators:

> When we talk about academic work for young children, what we usually mean treats the term quite loosely. *We mean reading*. When we read to children, we don't have to worry about the length of words, or the familiarity of words. If there is a new word, we can always explain it or put (it) in context. But when we want children to read themselves, we have to select from a pool defined by a readability index. The principle here is that the younger the child that you want to read, or want to learn to read, the smaller the range of words that can be used, and the smaller the range of words, the less meaningful the materials are. You've probably seen absolutely inane material with (a) selection of 15 words. Whereas, in fact, the younger children are in learning to read, the more important it is that the materials be meaningful. After all, reading is about meaning. (p. 7)

Katz reiterated that the "major risk" of teaching academic work to children too soon is that even though we may teach children "basic skills," the disposition to use these basic skills is "damaged." Although it may seem to those "not familiar with young children" that preschoolers and kindergartners are willing to do academic work, by the end of second grade "we have used up the good will of these children with trivial, meaningless tasks" (p. 8). Developmental psychology has demonstrated, according to Katz, that children learn best from interaction. As an aside, she noted that "at least writing is an active activity. If you ask a four-year-old to write, [the child] will make a long scribble for a long word and a short scribble for a short word," something Katz viewed as a "sort of preparation for doing more formal writing" (pp. 9–10).

In the area of language, Katz seemed to restrict her comments to spoken language only and cautioned teachers not to interrogate children with questions like "What color is your shirt?" but to let them ask questions in small groups concerned with a context (p. 11).

The last concern raised by Katz was the development of social competence in children, the ability to maintain peer relationships. If a child is isolated or neglected by peers in childhood, Katz pointed out that such a child is likely to become a high-school dropout (p. 4). It is the teacher's role to break the recursive "cycle of incompetence. . .to be right there on the sidelines and move in" (p. 16). A child is not seen as able to change patterns of social interaction without assistance from the teacher, who "has to stay on top of it until he gets it right" (p. 16).

Finally, Katz closed her speech with the observation that teachers are caught in a "cycle of blame" for what she termed "education for the next life" (p. 17). Teachers feel they have to prepare children for first grade, parents feel they want their children to be successful in the academic instruction of the school, and administrators and policymakers feel accountable for test results to the community at large. Leadership is necessary to break this cycle and, in her view, to bring informal approaches to children's learning.

In a June 1987 Special Section of the *Wingspread Journal*, the Katz speech appears again, apparently delivered for a program on early childhood education held in Racine, Wisconsin, sometime during the 1986–87 school year. The presentation by Katz entitled "What Should Young Children Be Doing?" was edited by the vice president of the Johnson Foundation for publication as an article. This later version of the Kingsborough address is interesting for its elaboration of several points made in the earlier address.

For example, Katz again pointed out that children should be engaged in interactive rather than passive experiences. As an illustration, Katz noted that it is better to introduce writing to children before reading and that a "weakness" of typical academic work geared down to younger children is that it reduces the amount of time available for "interactive processes" (Special Section, p. 1). There is no "compelling evidence" to support the introduction of academic work to young children and there are reasons to believe that such early introduction is "counterproductive." Although kindergartners and preschoolers may appear happy doing worksheets and reading flashcards, Katz claims that is not reason enough to do it. In her view, "academic" curricula—and remember, Katz is talking about reading—use a single approach, emphasizing workbooks, drill and practice. Such academic work, according to Katz, typically employs a "general positive feedback" strategy that "works very well to induce young children to keep working at disembedded, decontextualized, and often trivial tasks." Although such academic work—phonics or workbooks—might seem harmless or even beneficial in the short term, Katz proposed that "longitudinal studies" suggest otherwise (Special Section, p. 2).

According to Katz, the choice of curricula for early childhood education is not between academic work, socialization or "spontaneous play," as many people believe. What the research indicates, in her view, is instead an "intellectually oriented approach in which children interact in small groups as they work together on a variety of projects which help them make sense of their own experience."[1] These projects should also strengthen their dispositions to observe, experiment, inquire, and reconstruct aspects of their environment (Special Section, p. 3).

The advantages of the "project" learning proposed by Katz over workbooks and other forms of "passive" learning are very much akin to the arguments for hands-on and "active" experimentation made by the early childhood professionals interviewed for the study. Similarly, both Katz and some of the local early childhood professionals view reading very narrowly: as a passive rather than an active process, as directed by the teacher rather than under the control of the child, and as imparting trivalized knowledge rather than the construction of meaning and the creation of stories. Although phonics and flashcards were rejected by Katz and by the program professionals, there was no acknowledgement of a broader conception of literacy learning, that is, the idea that literacy learning is embedded in the social and cultural lives of children.[2] Reading, according to this narrow view, is tantamount to drill and skill phonics, flashcards and workbooks.

PERRY PRESCHOOL PROJECT

The only research cited by both policy professionals and program experts alike was the Perry Preschool Project, an early intervention program for high-risk preschoolers from the small industrial city of Ypsilanti, Michigan. The research project began in 1962 and continued for five more years under the direction of David Weikart. At that time, Weikart noted (Hohmann, Banet & Weikart, 1979, p. xi), preschoolers were targeted for intervention not because anything was known about teaching them but rather because the school system was unresponsive to the needs of poor children, and preschool was seen as outside the control of regular educators. Longitudinal followup of the original 123 children who were three- and four-year-olds at the time of the project has demonstrated to the policy community that early intervention is cost effective in terms of reduced retention rates, fewer referrals to special education, lower rates of delinquency and higher high school completion rates among these children at age nineteen than among similarly high-risk children who did not attend preschool (Virginia Adams, in Homann, Banet & Weikart, 1979, p. 285).[3]

Less often cited among members of the policy community, but very much explicit in the comments by program experts on developmentally appropriate curricula are the results of another earlier study conducted by researchers associated with the Perry Preschool Project and High/Scope Research Foundation. The purpose of the earlier study was to determine which of three curriculum "treatments" is best for high-risk youngsters.[4] Researchers followed 41 of the original participants to try to answer this question. Early results of the curriculum project suggested that there was no advantage to any one curricular approach, that all three approaches were equally significant in raising the test scores of children in the early grades (Weikart et al., 1978).

However, as these children were followed into adulthood, the High/Scope researchers suggested that "child-initiated" curricula were better predictors of social adjustment for these teenagers than was the "teacher-directed" approach (Schweinhart, Weikart & Larner, 1986, p. 43). These researchers cited increased incidence of delinquency and familial problems associated with children who had participated in the direct-instruction preschool curricula, commonly called the "DISTAR" model, to support their assertion that such teaching is not the most appropriate model for preschool. Further, these researchers suggested that such "direct-instruction" curricula may have long-term deleterious effects on children, an assertion that is very much contested by proponents of explicit instruction (p. 42).

Although all three curricula approaches were equally effective in developing academic skills among high-risk children who participated in these programs as preschoolers, researchers associated with the High/Scope Research Foundation and the Perry Preschool Project did not feel that academic competence per se made the difference later in the lives of these children. Farnworth, Schweinhart, and Berrueta-Clement (1985) tested this idea. According to their results (pp. 457–461), improved academic competence does not directly influence children's attachment to school or alienation from school, but rather indirectly, by enabling such students to avoid placement in special education, in particular, and to avoid retention in grade, both conditions that are highly correlated with dropping out of school.[5]

Even though the results of all of the above Perry Preschool Project studies have been widely promulgated by the High/Scope Educational Research Foundation, which has also conducted and published these studies, the cost-benefit analysis was the finding most often cited by policy professionals as the rationale for making preschool education available to disadvantaged four-year-olds in New York State. Particularly persuasive was the reported reduction of the dropout rate among the Ypsilanti youngsters who participated in the early intervention program. It was assumed that such intervention in New York State would similarly reduce the high dropout rate among poor and minority youngsters there. Several policy and program professionals cited New York State's own evaluation (NYSED, 1986) of its Experimental Pre-K program as further substantiating the long-term educational benefits of public school for four-year-olds. They appeared to equate the findings of the New York State evaluation and those of the Perry Preschool Project even though these studies differed significantly in the reported benefits. In the Perry Preschool Project, the reduction in the proportion of children placed in special education services contributed substantially both to the social bonding of participants to the school culture, thereby increasing the holding power of the schools, and to the increased benefits of preschool relative to the initial cost outlays. For participants in New York State Experimental Pre-K, there "were no statistically significant differences between the former Pre-K students and the control group in the proportion of students receiving special education services for children with handicapping conditions" (NYSED, 1986, p. 2). Both New York State Experimental Pre-K students and those in Ypsilanti scored higher on school achievement tests than those without preschool and were less often retained in grade. Furthermore, in both locations, children who were the most disadvantaged tended to benefit the most from preschool experiences.

While policy professionals tended to emphasize the benefits of preschool for four-year-olds relative to the costs, program experts tended to emphasize the notion of *developmental appropriateness* that was "proven" by the Perry Preschool Project studies on curricula approaches. They identified DISTAR by name as being inappropriate for young children and, by extension, they seemed to construe all academic work related to reading as formal instruction employing either "direct" teaching, "abstract verbal symbolism," or "workbooks." Any instruction in reading or writing was considered inappropriate by early childhood professionals in New York State. However, an examination of Weikart's "cognitively oriented" curriculum, both the 1971 and 1979 editions which were developed for and used by the Perry Preschool staff, helps explain some of the ideas about language and Piagetian theory that appear in the program experts' explanations of what is developmentally appropriate for preschoolers, particularly as it relates to literacy.

References to literacy development in the 1971 edition of *The Cognitively Oriented Curriculum* (Weikart, et al., 1971) are few but very much to the point. On the second page of the preface, the authors present an extended example of what their curriculum is not:

> [I]n a recent classroom visit to an ancient ghetto school, I observed a large group of kindergarten children seated in a cluster about the knees of their

> teacher. (The classroom's full-time paraprofessional was cleaning tables in the back of the room.) Each child held a picture of a dog, Zip, a character in a weekly science paper "designed" for young children. The teacher talked about the picture in which Zip was getting a bath. After five minutes of general discussion, she asked if any of the children had dogs at home. About five raised their hands. Then one boy wanted to talk about something else, which the teacher permitted for a few minutes. When she returned to the picture she asked again who had a dog at home. This time five different children raised their hands. As we left, the teacher commented that she had five more minutes allotted to Zip and his bath. This traditional style of classroom discussion with its high level of symbolic material and lack of object relevance to the children is viewed as inappropriate. There is nothing wrong in having a discussion about a dog being given a bath if it's part of some goal and the children have had the necessary experience with dogs beforehand. But there's not much point in talking about Zip just because the science paper arrived containing that particular picture. The object of classroom teaching is not passing time but nurturing the development of each individual (p. ix).

This strongly worded rejection of the kindergarten teacher's methods arose from the authors' understanding of Piaget, who is quoted in their text as saying that "concepts cannot be taught verbally," so teachers must use methodology "founded on activity" (p. IX). Words are characterized as "representation at the sign level," where "arbitrary symbols bearing no resemblance to an actual object or event" are encountered. The use of signs such as words depends on the "attribution of socially shared meanings" (p. 28). In *The Cognitively Oriented Curriculum*, the authors noted that "reading and writing, the representation of objects and events by a configuration of letters, are not attempted" but "in providing adequate experience with representation of real objects and events at the earlier levels [of representation], a foundation is laid which provides the child with meaningful and vivid mental pictures to which the written word can later be attached. It is hoped that this foundation will support the child when he encounters reading and writing in the regular school setting" (Weikart, et al., 1971, pp. 29–30). Books are the seventeenth suggestion (out of nineteen) for materials to be available in the quiet area of a preschool classroom. The authors suggested that the books be "realistic to abstract" and "coordinate with the other materials in the classroom: i.e., animal books, books on vehicles, etc." (p. 43). Parents were encouraged to obtain inexpensive children's books, even if the children did not care for them properly, in order to provide the child with opportunities to "handle" and "live with books" (p. 82).

Language—meaning spoken language—in *The Cognitively Oriented Curriculum* was not to be taught directly, or "depended upon to teach concepts, but rather to accompany the experiences that build concepts." Further, language used by the teacher to stimulate, expand, and question was to be adapted to the child's "level." Spontaneous language would "evolve" as the child interpreted and represented his own experiences (pp. 56–57). Everything the authors had to say about "language learning" was said in just 4 (out of 182) pages of the 1971 edition.

By contrast, 23 pages (out of 336) were devoted to key experiences for developing language in the 1979 edition, and there were 7 more pages for suggestions on reading and writing in particular. In the foreword to the new edition, *Young Children in Action*, Hohmann, Banet, and Weikart (1979) discussed the changes in the cognitively oriented curriculum that evolved through what they called "collaborative" staff work. When the Perry Preschool Project was first established, little in the way of early childhood curricula met the scholastic needs of the children, without being "restricted to training in specific skills and without focusing on rote learning and memorization." Cooperative nursery school curricula, in the authors' minds, were simply exercises in "free play," and other prevailing philosophies seemed to suggest that the preschool should provide social and emotional support only. A decision to focus on "general cognitive development" represented a "reaction to the alternatives" rather than any real conviction about the form an early childhood curriculum should take (p. xiii). The authors explained that the first year of the project looked very much like an organized kindergarten rather than a nursery school, in that traditional curricula were emphasized, sequenced learning was very much in evidence, and the goal was "defined as preparing the children for school" (p. xiv).

According to Hohmann et al. (1979), J. McVicker Hunt's 1963 work *Intelligence and Experience* and his treatment of Jean Piaget's developmental theory introduced the Perry Preschool staff to the theoretical framework they had been looking for. The Piagetian stages of cognitive development allowed them to reorient themselves away from "preacademic activities" and toward a developmental view of the child. The notion of "representation" was a way to link preschool experiences to "traditional academic exercises in reading and mathematics" (p. xiv). During the last phase of the curriculum development, after a decade of experience with young children, the staff came to acknowledge the "child as 'constructor' of knowledge" and the teacher's role as that of "support for independent learning" (p. xv). In Hohmann et al.'s words, the teacher "helps children consolidate their abilities in developmentally appropriate ways, through direct and representational experience, *without trying to accelerate their development or push them along to the next level*. . . Each child is recognized as an individual who builds his or her own knowledge through initiatives shared with supportive adults. Which is to say, each child is active" (p. xvi). The second edition (1979) of the open-framework curriculum—*Young Children in Action*—was written during this last phase of curriculum development.

While acknowledging the limitations—or at least the unresolved controversies surrounding the developmental stages proposed by Piaget—the authors of the 1979 edition nonetheless held that Piagetian theory is the most useful fit between psychology and early childhood curriculum. According to the authors, Bruner and Noam Chomsky as well as Piaget have contributed much toward describing development but offer "little information on the specific determinants of developmental change of the sort that can be translated into educational practice" (p. 2). Logical insights emerge in "predictable developmental sequences that resist acceleration through adult intervention," rendering didactic teaching developmentally invalid. This viewpoint assumes that teaching verbal labels will not teach the concept; it is only after the child masters the concept that teaching verbal labels makes sense. Action, not language, is the way children learn logical and physical relations (p. 4). In the open-framework classroom, language is not something teachers have to teach but is instead integrated into the school day (p. 12) with the teacher becoming an instigator of developmentally appropriate activities.

Further, the authors pointed out that language, at least in terms of grammar, also develops in predictable stages and, like cognitive development, cannot be inhibited or accelerated. What appears amenable to environmental control is the "richness and scope, rather than the pace, of development in any sphere" (p. 149). Nonetheless, the 1979 edition not only extended the space—and presumably the importance—allocated to language but also broadened the definition to include written language as well as oral (see table 7–1 for a comparison of the language in the two editions of High/Scope materials).

In addition to *talking* with children about relevant experiences and encouraging children to express their feelings in words, the authors recommended that teachers *write down* children's own words and *read* these words back to them (p. 187). Teachers were encouraged to respond to children's interest in "letters, sounds and words. . . and to follow up

TABLE 7–1

Change in Understandings of Developmentally Appropriate Literacy Experiences for Preprimary Education in Professional Materials Published by High/Scope Foundation and National Association for the Education of Young Children.

National Association for the Education of Young Children's Position on Developmentally Appropriate Literacy Practices—Changes In the Language From 1985 to 1986

Earlier		Later
Children learn best when they create their own concepts through first-hand meaningful experiences with materials and people. These experiences should match the child's *readiness and development*. . . Children need years of play experiences with real objects and events to enable them to understand the meaning of *symbols such as pictures and stories*. . . [italics added] (NAEYC, 1985)	→	Learning in young children is the result of *interaction* between the child's thoughts and experiences with materials, ideas, and people. These experiences should match the child *developing abilities*. . . *Pictures and stories should be used frequently* to build upon children's real experiences. . . *Some 4-year-olds and most 5's display a growing interest in the functional aspects of written language, such as recognizing meaningful words and trying to write their own names.* [italics added] (NAEYC, 1986)

High/Scope Curriculum Text For Early Childhood Teachers—Changes In Language On Literacy Activities From 1971–1979

Earlier		Later
[R]eading and writing, the representation of objects and events by a configuration of letters, are not attempted [in the preschool, but]. . . in providing adequate experience with representation of real objects and events at the earlier levels [of representation], a foundation is laid which provides the child with meaningful and vivid mental pictures to which the written word can later be attached. . . [T]his foundation will support the child when he encounters reading and writing in the regular school setting. (Weikart et al., 1971)	→	[The preschool teacher should respond] to interest in letters, sounds and words. . . and follow up on [these] pre-reading and pre-writing processes. . . by taking dictation. . . [and] assisting children to recognize and write their own names. . . [and] whenever there is an opportunity, encouraging children to look at books and "read." (Hohmann et al., 1979)

on [these] pre-reading and pre-writing processes" (p. 165). In "taking dictation"—whether for children's plans, labels, notes, stories, captions, recipes, or whatever—the teacher demonstrates the "representation" or mapping of the spoken language into written language and the "child becomes confident that his or her language works and that his or her ideas are important" (p. 164). Hearing his own language read back provides the child with a sense of empowerment—that he or she is a "maker of stories" (p. 188).

Another suggestion was to provide experiences playing with or "having fun" with language. Although Ruth Weir's (1962) work was not cited, the authors alluded to "nap talk" as indication of how infants and older children try out new combinations of sounds, sentences, songs, and stories in a playful, repetitive way (p. 166). In order to promote this language play, the authors recommended a number of strategies for teachers: reading to children "whenever there is an opportunity [but]. . .*at least once a week or at least occasionally at small-group time*" (p. 167); encouraging children to look at books or "read" (the authors' quotes); telling stories; using rhymes, singing songs and chants and improvising new rhymes along with the children; and, if possible, collecting children's dictated work in "song books" or illustrated story books (pp. 166–67; 187). When reading back children's own stories, teachers were advised to point to each word as they read it, although no rationale for this behavior was established in the manual. Teachers were also advised to have children make up the words for wordless picture books. Besides simply rereading the children's dictation, the manual suggested that teachers make covers, bindings, and titles; gather and number pages; and talk about the parts of a book (p. 188). Children were to be encouraged to read their books to the group so that others would want to create their own books. Finally, the authors told teachers to assist the children in recognizing and writing their own names, including the arrangement of alphabet letters and copying or tracing an adult model (p. 189).

The apparent shift in attitude from 1971 to 1979 toward reading and writing was not explained in the introduction to the second edition of the open-framework curriculum, nor was it addressed in the brief history of how the 1979 curriculum evolved. In view of the striking differences in how literacy learning is treated in the two editions, it is puzzling that no attempt was made to resolve the issue of how written language development came to be seen as appropriate for preschoolers. It is also not clear from the bibliographic references (after the sections on both representing and language in the second edition) who in particular might have been responsible for the form that literacy development theory ultimately took, a form that appears consistent with the research on emergent literacy almost a decade after *Young Children in Action* was published. The only bibliographic reference on reading and writing is a 1977 publication of the High/Scope Foundation entitled "The Cognitively Oriented Curriculum—Writing and Reading" (No. 6) and written by Oon Bee Hsu. It appears to be referenced as appropriate for elementary children. Notations following this publication describe it as "a plan for developing writing and reading abilities in elementary-age children." Such abilities are founded on the belief that

1. writing and reading are best learned together;
2. the child's initiation into literacy is a matter of his discovering the connection between spoken and written language;
3. the child discovers this connection when his own experiences are the content for his first attempts at writing and reading. (p. 190)

Thus, the actual content of literacy activities in the Perry Preschool curriculum is in sharp contrast to the views on reading and writing espoused by program professionals in New York State. Although they often cited the Perry Preschool Project as one arbiter of what constitutes effective and "developmentally appropriate" practices, the project's reading and writing recommendations appear to be at odds with many of the beliefs expressed by local program professionals.

NATIONAL ASSOCIATION FOR THE EDUCATION OF YOUNG CHILDREN

The governing board of NAEYC, the professional organization for child-care, nursery school, and kindergarten teachers, created a commission to develop guidelines for appropriate education for four- and five-year-old children in July, 1984 (The Commission on Appropriate Education for Four- and Five-Year-Olds). NAEYC then issued a draft policy statement in November 1985 on "developmentally appropriate practice in early childhood programs." After soliciting the reactions from professionals in the field, NAEYC then revised the statement. The revised version was published in the September 1986 issue of *Young Children*. Since all of the New York State early education professionals cited NAEYC guidelines as *the* determinants of what they would concur were "developmentally appropriate" practices in the education of four-year-olds, it is imperative to identify NAEYC's position on literacy learning. Of particular interest is how the NAEYC position paper changed from the first widely promulgated draft in 1985 to the published version in 1986 (see table 7–1).

First, these versions differ in subtle but important ways in how they defined "developmentally appropriate." Both versions suggested that appropriateness is determined by both age and individual characteristics. However, the initial version presented a strictly maturational view of development: "milestones" such as "first step, first word, first independent solution to a problem and first understanding" of object permanence. All developmental "domains. . .can be described in terms of predictable, age-related sequences of growth and change." Further, appropriate practice is that which "reflects age-related knowledge about children's readiness and expected acquisition of skills and abilities" (NAEYC, 1985, p. 2). The implications for individual children rest on the "match" between the educational experiences provided and the "child's readiness and development." As an example of the variation in "individual development," the draft of the position paper described the range of "development and interest" in written language among a typical group of five-year-old kindergarten children. To paraphrase, some children can be expected to be able to "read the picture books" and others will be able to "read the language experience story the class dictated" and still others will be able to read captions under pictures. Some children in this hypothetical example will recognize "words that begin with the same letter as their name" but others will not be interested in written language at all. After presenting a description of such variation, the NAEYC says that "the variety and complexity of language experiences provided by the teacher for this group should reflect both age-appropriate and individually appropriate planning" (1985, p. 3).

In the published version, the kindergarten teacher was to be a "resource" to be called upon as the children required. If the children were to request a label or other written words during the course of their play, for example, an "emergency" sign for a hospital built of blocks, the teacher would assist them (NAEYC, 1986, p. 5).

The revised definition of "developmental appropriateness" also appears to take a softer stance on maturation: "Knowledge of typical development of children within the age span served by the program provides a framework from which teachers prepare the learning environment and plan appropriate experiences." Gone are the references to matching experiences with "readiness." Instead, the revised definition suggests that "experiences should match the child's developing abilities, while also challenging the child's interest and understanding" (1986, p. 5).

The revised statement on appropriate curriculum experiences appears to take a more expansive view of literacy and the teacher's role in the process of learning, while maintaining the broad framework described in the original document. For example, in the original, "stories and pictures" were included in the list of the "symbols" that a four-year-old needed "many years of play with real objects and events to. . .understand" (NAEYC, 1985, p. 4). In the revised version, stories and pictures were deleted from this list of inappropriate symbolic learning but "letters and numbers" remained. Stories and pictures should be used "frequently," said the new version, "to build upon children's real experiences" (NAEYC, 1986, p. 7). The revised curriculum guidelines retained the admonition that for children younger than six, "workbooks, worksheets, and coloring books" were not appropriate, although children older than five were considered to be able to follow "adult-directed teaching strategies" (1986, p. 7). In the section on appropriate curriculum specific to the four- and five-year-old child, the revised version added a whole section on developing literacy (although it is not referred to as "literacy") that was not included in the original. "Some" four-year-olds and "most" five-year-olds were characterized as showing increasing interest "in the function aspects of written language, such as recognizing meaningful words and trying to write their own names." However, experiences "designed solely to teach the alphabet, phonics, and penmanship are much less appropriate. . .than providing a print-rich environment that stimulates the development of language and literacy skills in a meaningful context" (1986, p. 9).

Story and poetry reading was also added to the revised document's section on adult-initiated activities that foster communication. Whereas in the original, listening activities were not viewed as appropriate before the "third or fourth year onward," when children could be expected to "listen as well as talk in meaningful conversational exchange" (NAEYC, 1985, p. 10) the new version suggested that children as young as two might listen to "an absorbing story" (NAEYC, 1986, p. 13). However, both the original and revised versions declared that children must be eight years old before they are really able to learn about "other, more distant people" (1985, p. 6; 1986, p. 9). Although children in the first, second and third grades "can learn from the symbolic [or, in the original version, "vicarious"(1985, p. 6)] experiences of reading books and listening to stories. . .their understanding of what they read is based on their ability to relate the written word to their own experiences" (1986, p. 9).

In addition to these changes in the body of the NAEYC Position Statement on Developmentally Appropriate Practice from the draft to the version ultimately published, the published version also included contrasting lists of "appropriate" versus "inappropriate" practices for four- and five-year-old children. Besides the restatements of the inappropriateness of "sitting passively" and "listening" (1986, p. 23), the list devoted a separate section to what was referred to—for the first time in the document—as "language and literacy development" (1986, p. 24). Appropriate practice in literacy development was defined as providing children with "many opportunities to see how reading and writing are useful before they are instructed in letter names, sounds, and word identification. . . [L]istening to and reading stories and poems. . . field trips, seeing. . . print in use, experimenting with writing by drawing, copying, and inventing their own spelling" were all deemed "appropriate" practice. On the other hand, activities that isolate skill development, such as "recognizing single letters, reciting the alphabet, singing the alphabet song, coloring within predefined lines, or being instructed in correct formation of letters on a printed line" were deemed inappropriate (1986, p. 24).

Although the NAEYC now appears to be interpreting some aspects of literacy learning as developmentally appropriate for four-year-olds, New York State program professionals seemed largely unaware of this shift. New York program expertise thus reflected a more narrow view of both development and appropriate written language learning.

NATIONAL ASSOCIATION OF EARLY CHILDHOOD SPECIALISTS IN STATE DEPARTMENTS OF EDUCATION

Besides the National Association for the Education of Young Children, another professional organization that represents state-level early childhood specialists' perspective, NAECS/SDE, issued a position statement in 1987 that focused on kindergarten practices in elementary education. I have included the NAECS/SDE position statement because this is the professional organization that represents state early childhood specialists such as those interviewed for the study. The issues included in this paper are also the issues discussed by program specialists in New York State.

According to NAECS/SDE, certain kindergarten practices, though "well-intentioned," do not further the interests of children (p. 1). In particular, the association does not want teachers to "yield to pressure for acceleration of narrowly-focused academic curricula" that is virtually indistinguishable from academic curricula of the early elementary grades. It is a misconception, in their view, that children are "smarter" now than in prior years. Overzealous parents who "expect children to read in kindergarten" have contributed to the problem faced by teachers. "Abstract curriculum materials. . .routinely tied to tightly sequenced. . . grade level lists of expectations for skill acquisitions" have replaced "rich creative experiences" in kindergarten. The association noted that children who are "ready to learn to read are more likely to advance as far as they are able in active-learning classrooms" rather than in the academic type (p. 4). This point of view was restated by program professionals in New York State.

However, program experts in New York were not sensitive to a second problem identified by the NAECS/SDE: Children who may benefit the most from kindergarten are being denied entry to school because they are not "ready" for the academic curriculum. The "gift of time" ironically denies these children opportunities and actually increases the variation in age, size, ability, and backgrounds among kindergarten children to which teachers must respond (p. 5). Related to this issue is that of screening or sorting children with invalid and unreliable "readiness" assessment. Because of such testing, large numbers of children are perceived as failing school before they even begin (p. 8). In response to this problem, the association rejected "developmental" or "readiness" kindergartens and transition rooms as another form of retention (p. 10). Retention was viewed as having deleterious effects on children and no educational benefits (p. 7). An overreliance on the maturational point of view was seen as the culprit:

> The notion that children unfold on an immutable timetable, however appealing, cannot be overgeneralized to intellectual, social, linguistic and emotional development. A responsive, success-oriented kindergarten curriculum and teacher are bound to have a powerful effect on young children's learning. Children come to school as competent, naturally motivated learners. One of the school's critical responsibilities is to ensure that these characteristics are maintained and strengthened, not destroyed. . .The issue is not whether we keep children with age-

> mates. . .It is whether we can continue to uphold practices and programs predicated on failure. Failure by any name does not foster success. . . Limited Federal, state and local resources are being used inappropriately as a result of well-intentioned but misdirected policies. (NAECS/SDE, 1987, p. 11).

The analysis of the readiness issue provided by the NAECS/SDE introduces an element of complexity to the definition of developmental appropriateness that the state program experts did not address. In fact, the NAECS/SDE rejects the simpler explanation of physiological maturation that New York program professionals apparently still subscribe to. Not only is "maturation" not viable as a proxy for school readiness but early intervention, in the sense of keeping children "back" or "in transition" is perceived as harmful, not beneficial, to their development (p. 10). Yet the transcribed interviews suggest that some New York program professionals—at least at the time of this study—subscribed to a view of developmental readiness that is being questioned by the NAECS/SDE.

8. READINESS FOR SCHOOL, BUT WHAT COUNTS AS "SCHOOL"? EDUCATION, SOCIALIZATION, AND HABILITATION

When you're dealing with twenty-one-year-olds you can clearly differentiate between education, room, and board. . . [W]hen you're dealing with those younger age groups. . . there's [the] issue as to what is education, what is habilitation, what is socialization. . . [B]oth federal. . . [government and]. . . state government are trying to sort those things out now. . . as to what is education responsibility and who should finance it.

—A policy and budget expert in New York State government

EARLY CHILDHOOD AND policy professionals in New York State and nationally visible early childhood authorities who have rejected the notion that preschool children be taught reading and writing—what early childhood professionals call "formal academics"—have difficulty explaining how preschool "educates" the child. Learning to read and write has traditionally been considered the *raison d' être* for primary school, at least the part of school that is publicly funded. This viewpoint is particularly troublesome for initiatives to make public school for four-year-olds universally available, thus encompassing children from middle- and upper-middle-class families as well as disadvantaged and handicapped children.

As I discussed in chapter 4, publicly funded, particularly federally funded, preschool for disadvantaged children has been seen as a legitimate government concern. It rests on the assumption that parents in poverty cannot provide appropriate resources to their children and that such disadvantage contributes to social and welfare problems. In such cases, government is seen as having a legitimate function in providing such resources to children when families cannot.

In the case of handicapped children, New York State policy professionals have described preschool intervention as habilitative rather than educational. Thus, preschool is considered more of a medical benefit than a school service. Providing public school to children younger than the age of entitlement (in New York State, age six) whether those services are construed to be child care or education or medical services, has not been done outside of narrowly described definitions of eligibility for special programs like Head Start and the Experimental Pre-K or the judgements of family court in the case of handicapped children. If government or public assistance is not required because of either poverty or other extraordinary conditions, then the care of children younger than school entry age has been considered by the public to be child care and not the type of service typically assumed by government (McCathren, 1981). Public policy has deemed child care to be the parents' responsibility.

In New York State, as elsewhere, however, early childhood educators have taken the position that child care—whatever its form in specific programs—is indeed education.[1] But the goals of early childhood programs have typically been couched in terms such as "socialization" or "social and emotional support," and to many minds, these are different from so-called educational goals. When the possibility of government funding was proposed by Governor Cuomo (1987, p. 75) for full-day early childhood programs, part of which would be "child care" and part "education," providers of both child day care and preschool programs scrambled to show that their type of program was both care and education and therefore eligible for funds.

Each of the interviewed participants addressed this conflict. New York's early childhood professionals did not want to make any distinction between child day care and school programs for four-year-olds. All of early childhood is a "distinct field," with children on a "pre-verbal level" (IG5–20). Part of the problem, according to the program specialists, is that at this time there is no early childhood certification.[2] It is not considered "a legitimate profession. . . so if you're dealing with. . . threes and fours the notion is you're just playing around with these little kids" (IG5–20). In the view of one advocate, the teachers union (which she thought was either "Public Employees Federation or Civil Service Employees Association") is responsible for the demise of early childhood certification in New York State because it wanted a way to be able to "shuffle people around when there were layoffs" (IG4–17).

She continued to say that a very "different teaching style" with an "emphasis on play" was required for early childhood education, a style that made traditional teachers uncomfortable.

For many policy professionals, however, the educational component of child care services and the curriculum of pre-K programs remains poorly defined and not well articulated in terms of the more common goals of schooling. According to one policy analyst, it was unclear "how much of a quotable curriculum there is or how much of an established program as suggested by the professionals exists." Although "an established program" may be available, she was concerned that such "knowledge...isn't widespread...[among] the public...and professionals...and may not be as available as learning to be a...10th-grade science teacher" (LEG2–17).

An advocate for local boards of education said that he himself did not know about "methods and strategies" for use with children, but he did know that successful preschools have "systematic traits, characteristics, and qualities" and they "tend to emphasize...children getting along in a social situation...[and] relating to adults...and [they] provide a nurturing...caring environment." Regarding "educational content," he did not "know that much about the different curricula that are offered" (IG1–12).

The leadership for quality child care cited the problems of even middle-class parents in finding child care that is stimulating in an educational sense, as well as safe and caring. Because such parents provide many resources in their middle-class homes, "the educational component" is not so much an issue. Middle-class parents put children in school settings so that they can have socializing experiences with their peers, but families with limited resources need "more [education] from schooling" (IG4–26).

What defines the educational component of child care services was also not clear to budget analysts. Distinguishing between socialization and education was difficult, they said. Perhaps "playing with blocks with letters on them" is education, ventured one budget analyst, or perhaps socialization is a "component" of all education, mused another. Although they thought "there should be a difference" between Head Start and nursery schools on the one hand and child day care centers on the other, these analysts said that "no one has made it clear what the differences are." From an "auditing perspective," these analysts would very much prefer "absolute consistency...[with] each program out of a cookie cutter...[exactly] the same." They would prefer that each program be separate and definable so that auditors could say "Oops, that's different, it must be wrong" (EX6–58).

Program experts in the field of early childhood disagreed. One program expert noted that "a good Head Start program, a good pre-K program and a good day care program should be indistinguishable" since there is "really no such thing as custodial care." Providing play with blocks is an example used by this program expert. She said that "to the untrained eye," children would look like they "were playing with chunks of wood, [but] to a trained eye, you are working on socialization, . . . language, . . . and math concepts" (EX3–15). She believes that there is a problem in "our culture by what we call education" and a general lack of understanding that a child learns from the moment he is born, not with "the alphabet." Reading itself is "far more complicated than the alphabet," and children who memorize the alphabet may have "no idea what it means" (EX3–13). Another program expert restated that "good programs for children should look absolutely the same" and none of them, in her view, have " formal academics for four-year-olds" (IG5–34).

The advocate for child care programs expanded on this notion: "Education doesn't mean you do dittos. Education means when he plays with the ball, the person says, 'This is red. This is round. What else is round?'. . . [and] a 'babysitter' isn't someone [who is going] to 'watch my kid'. . .you 'watch' television. . .you don't 'watch' children." According to this advocate, "most people in the general public. . .don't see that a babysitter is someone who should be providing an educational environment for your child." Likewise, the general public expects too much from young children in a school setting. Parents say their child "doesn't bring home enough dittos" so they "don't think they are learning anything [whereas]. . .when they're that age everything they do is learning. . .Play is what kids are supposed to do [and] play is learning. . .For God's sake, children [at that age] learn when they sleep" (IG4–22, 23).

Related to the public perception of the differences between the care of children and the education of children are the perceptions described by one analyst that child day care is "custodial," that it is "cheap," and that it is for "certain people." By contrast, "education" is for certain other people, and it is "expensive" (IG4–13). Another program analyst pointed out that middle-class parents were quick to extrapolate the results of early childhood research on the cognitive gains made by disadvantaged children in preschool programs to educational experiences for their own preschoolers. She sees flaws in that perception, however. In her view, middle-class children do not stand to benefit in the same way, but preschool programs for more advantaged children are "good in terms of social development. . . If by age six [children] do not develop significant social relationships, they are in trouble the rest of their lives. . . [I]n a small family, you don't have play groups, you don't have neighborhoods where the kids can run around and be together and learn from each other. . .then the school serves this purpose. . . [C]hildren by the time they get into kindergarten. . .will have been in school and comfortable with the surroundings. . . [I]t isn't that they are more developmentally ahead, . . .they've just had more [school] experiences." For disadvantaged children, the assumption is that they "don't have certain other experiences [beyond socialization] that middle-class kids have" (IG5 4–5).

AUSPICES AND FUNDING DIFFERENCES; OR, WHO WILL FIGHT FOR THE FUTURE: THE PROGRAM PERSPECTIVE

Although the policy and program professionals stated that early childhood programs, by whatever name, were alike in many respects, they also discussed what they perceived to be the differences. Paramount in descriptions of differences among programs were issues of funding and auspice.

The advocate for child care professionals pointed out that connecting child care to the State Education Department was important "to reinforce the perception that child care is education." Instead of increasing money for child day care through the Social Services Department, she was lobbying for creating a new early childhood education funding stream channeled through the education department. Because the education department sent money directly to service providers, rather than through parent subsidies as is the policy with social services, it could create stability within early childhood centers—wherever located—to impose teacher certification standards and upgrade salaries and programs. According to this advocate, it was difficult for policy participants to understand why she did not want the legislature to simply increase child-care subsidies and, at the same time, increase allotments for the pre-K program, leaving current funding streams and auspice in place. When pressed by policy analysts on the issue of whether "pre-K was 'better' than day care," particularly since day care standards are "more stringent," she said that she could not "tell them it is necessarily better, except they [pre-K programs] are better funded" (IG 4–8). While child day care has historically been associated with the "welfare system," pre-K is in the schools. As long as money for child day care is channelled through social services, this advocate felt that there would never be public support for what are viewed as welfare or private concerns. If money for child care is channelled through the education department, such programs become *education* and stand to benefit from the resources of the public schools, not the least of which is public funding and the perception of promoting the common good (IG 4–7). A problem with the governor's initial proposal to provide an educational component with "wrap around child care," she believes, was in the source of the funding. In this case, neither the Social Services Department nor the Education Department would be the source of the funding, but rather the "miscellaneous" category. This advocate strongly believed that this type of funding stream was the worst possible, because "there is nobody to fight for the future. . . [Who in "miscellaneous"] will fight DOB [Division of Budget] for more money [or] defend our dollars?" (IG4–20,21).

As two statewide administrators of early childhood education explained, the State Education Department considered itself in the child care business several years ago when federal money was available for day care. Title 4 of the Social Security Act "offered three dollars in federal money for every one dollar in state and local money that would provide day care. In New York State law, any program that runs for three hours or more a day is considered day care. Therefore, all pre-K programs for a brief time in the early seventies were three hours or longer. . . enabling the state and local school districts. . . to attract an enormous amount of money." In anticipation of attracting close to fifteen million dollars, the State Education Department published a brochure, entitled *School Plus,* designed to encourage child day care within the public schools, and opened nine new programs. However, as one program expert put it, "President Nixon saw that the door to Ft. Knox was open. . . and he closed down that law. . . and that money was no longer made available" (IG5–5,6). When pre-K programs became half-day again, about 2½ hours long, it was not a program decision related to whether or not child day care was an appropriate role for the schools but rather a way to conserve resources that were once again made scarce (EX3–12).

Analysts and program experts used auspices and funding streams to distinguish among the various preschool programs. One program expert viewed preschool programs for handicapped children as different because they "have three times more money. . .and a much lower staff ratio (IG5–31). When asked whether the children were different, the answer was yes because they are funded through a different source, although both Head Start and the pre-K program have typically allotted 10 percent of their enrollment to handicapped children. Children who are "slightly retarded" would use the same materials but the teacher would have to "be alert to [the child's] limits" and be prepared to spend more time in "interaction" than with children who are "capable of. . . more independent behavior" (IG5–32,33).

Even children who are viewed as needing the same type of interaction—those served in state pre-K programs and those served in New York City's Giant Step programs—are treated differently in terms of the resources available to these respective programs under two different agencies, the State Education Department and New York City. In the view of one statewide administrator, these programs have become "two distinct programs with the same philosophy" enrolling New York City's "very own four-year-olds" and they "can't even share a Social Services worker from one side of the district," let alone staff training or other resources (IG5–28). Apparently, Giant Step is completely funded by New York City, whereas the state pre-K program is only 89 percent reimbursed by the state, creating a situation in which one program has more funding than another. According to one interviewee, "They [Giant Step] had so much money they didn't know how to spend it!" (IG5–28).

Another program specialist pointed out that most of the "tremendous turf" and philosophical issues really "followed from the lack of funding rather than from a philosophical base." Because programs have different funding streams, it is assumed that the programs are different. For example, the purpose of the pre-K program is "to provide an educational experience for disadvantaged children;" the purpose of Head Start is to provide "an enriching experience for children." Both programs are viewed as "educational intervention" but Head Start comes through federal Social Services and "is framed as a service to the family rather than to the child," whereas the pre-K program is viewed as education because it comes from the State Education Department. Yet both of these programs target disadvantaged students from the same communities for basically the same school program (EX3–11).

A CASE OF SEPARATE BOOKS: THE POLICY PERSPECTIVE

Policy professionals, particularly those concerned with funding and authorizing early childhood programs, were quite attuned to perceived differences among child-care and various education providers. Their views, however, were not unanimous. On the one hand, one policy expert thought that "auspice is just that [because] what you do with kids is not so different. . .whether it's child care or education, regardless of whose auspice it's in" (EX1–8).

On the other hand, another policy professional said that not only are child care and education different but this difference is "institutionally acknowledged inasmuch as day care teachers or day care personnel are certified through a different system that works through Department of Social Services, and their certification is not one that builds in the kinds of qualifications that are needed to teach." Child care services are registered with the Department of Social Services and not the State Education Department, illustrating, in his view, that the system does not acknowledge that kind of similarity. Although "it is certainly to the advantage of the day care institutions to convey the idea that they have an educational mission," this policy analyst believes that it is "wishful thinking" on the part of the child care lobby. Rather than merge the two systems, something that would exacerbate the turf issues between pre-K and child care providers, he suggested regulations that would facilitate "collaboration" between the two systems, allowing "both purposes and functions combined within the same facility and the same schedule" (IG1–10,11).

A legislative analyst agreed with this perspective. She commented that even though child care and education have many similarities, . . . they are not the same. That is not to say that child day care is not a "very valuable service" that "could have a pre-K element in it" but, at the present time, there is a distinction between the professionals certified in these two areas, with child care providers having a much "lower level" of training (LEG2–11,12). Part of the problem with the governor's early initiative, in her view, was the potential for "traditional turf [clashes] between day care providers versus experimental pre-K providers" and "no real sense of what we were trying to accomplish and what direction or mission or objective we wanted to accomplish at the state level." The legislature funded the coordinating study by the Council on Children and Families to "define the scope of what they should be doing" (LEG2–18).

A lack of consensus on what constitutes "education" among four-year-olds has implications not only for auspice or oversight but also for who foots the bill. When budget analysts visited a number of pre-K programs "just to get a feel for what they were doing," one analyst said he posed the same question to all of them: "How do you determine what is socialization and what is education?" In his view, the service providers did not have a good answer. Consequently, he believes that everyone is still trying to define what that is. He himself could not judge although "there was a component to play at that age that is education" and at the same time is "socialization." Perhaps, he thought, "socialization [is] part of education at any age." But the fiscal issue becomes one of "whether playing with blocks has to be taught by someone [who earns] $20,000 a year [who is] an early childhood specialist and certified teacher. . .or anyone off the street who isn't going to molest the child" (EX4–52,53). With young children, this analyst continued, it is difficult to sort out "social activities" that would be covered by "social [services] people" and those that are education. He supplied a constrasting example of differentiating "between education [tuition] and room and board" for college students. Federal and state governments are "thrashing out" the issue of "what is education responsibility and who should finance it" (EX4–27).

Although the resolution of what is education versus socialization for young children is not at the present time being determined in the courts, the analyst suggested that a related issue is. When dealing with handicapped preschoolers, the "financing streams and [federal] government's responsibility" are different. Rather than an issue of education versus socialization, the issue becomes education versus "habilitation." If handicapped preschoolers' needs are viewed as educational in nature, the state and local governments must pay for services, since education is not a federal responsibility but "up to the states and local governments to finance as you see fit." However, if such services are defined as "habilitation" implying a need for medical intervention, then "we are speaking to a significant federal responsibility" through Medicaid funds. Of course, the federal government then is motivated to make the definition of "services that are being termed habilitation. . .as narrow as possible" to minimize its responsibility for funding. Likewise, the state will try to narrow the scope of what is an educational responsibility for handicapped children. Because definitions are so difficult to formulate, both the state government and federal government "go with the most conservative definition," letting the courts resolve the issue of fiscal responsibility (EX4–53,54).

Neither handicapped nor nonhandicapped children younger than five-years-old are entitled to a 'free and appropriate' education in New York State unless the courts order it.[3] When Family Court orders preschool placement, the placement "has been construed more to be habilitation than education... [and] school districts have no finance law in that." But the federal government gives only a "Medicaid component," so now the financial responsibility is "between the state and the county." The county claims it has no role in education and tries to give the bill to the state. The state says that "the way we pay bills for education is we finance them [through the] school districts. The school districts say, 'The counties just gave us the bill and now it's education [so] here, share it with us.'" (EX5–64,65). Parents are not concerned whether a service for their child is called "education or habilitation... as long as it's being provided and they don't have to pay for it," but school districts can "barely serve" the children from five through seventeen now, let alone entitling younger children to education in New York State (EX4–65).

Although the issue of education versus child care or socialization has not gone before the courts—nor has an entitlement for four-year-olds under New York State law—the same fiscal obligations are at stake. Another budget analyst described it thus: "You could say 'socialization' and we shouldn't pay for it [because] it's not education, and they'd say " 'Well, if this is education—not socialization, not child care—then we shouldn't pay for it' " (EX4,5—53,54). And a legislative analyst concurred that "you don't give money out of the education budget to run a Social Services program" (LEG2–24).

WHAT'S RIGHT FOR THE CHILDREN AND COMPLEMENTS THE EXISTING SYSTEM: A RATIONAL APPROACH TO EARLY CHILDHOOD POLICY

On the positive side, these budget analysts thought the question was how to get the "different systems... into sync." They wanted agreement on what type of background providers should have, how much compensation, what services and in what setting, and which standards—educational, therapeutic, or Social Services—should apply to those services. But they did concur that the "bottom line [was] what's right for the children" (EX4–56).

A policy analyst who has surveyed national programs for four-year-olds felt that there is in fact a "merging" of the two systems.

Pointing out the historic roots of the child-care system in day nurseries where the care was strictly custodial, she claimed that an observer "would be hard pressed to find organized programs now that say [they are] merely custodial." Whereas several years ago there was "some not so good education" in the child care system, there is now a "deeper understanding. . .that early education is beneficial for children." Because child care workers are trained in early childhood education now, they are "infusing that [education] beyond the nursery school into day care centers." The entry of public schools into child day care affirms the educational nature of child care, thus child care and education are "getting closer to being the same thing." However, in her view, an enduring problem rests with the bureaucracies that surround these programs. People who make policy "don't tend to think of those connections, so you've got one whole bureaucracy that's connected to subsidized child care, and another whole bureaucracy connected to education, and they're not the same. And they don't communicate very well." While one set of legislators may be "cooking up welfare reform and another set cooking up educational programs for four-year-olds," they don't "quite get it that they're aimed at the same kids." Preschool programs for handicapped children are theoretically open to handicapped children of all income levels, she explained, but early childhood education for disadvantaged children is "somehow only for certain kids, and it's not always clear where the line is between the kids who are eligible for special education and kids who are eligible for some non–special ed early childhood program. . . it's real fuzzy. [I]f you're at risk of school failure because you score low on. . .one of the favorite tests. . . in the lowest third or something, then how is that different from being developmentally delayed, which is a criterion for being eligible for special education programs?" (IG2–5,6).

Resources are wasted when "cumulative knowledge" such as curriculum and standards "doesn't get transferred and translated into these other programs," she continued. For example, children in a six-hour Chapter 1 class get breakfast and snacks, but in the same building the pre-K program gets no food. The same lack of coordination applies to the training. Each program has a "different system," so that Head Start offers training only for its staff, pre-K only for pre-K teachers, and child day care only for its staff (IG2–20). Yet "walking into" one program or another, this research analyst was not able to differentiate which programs belonged to which system. Programs could be differentiated according to curriculum philosophy or degree of child-centered interaction, but not according to auspice (IG2–38–45).

In New York State, one legislative analyst suggested that there has to be a better sense of the distinctions among programs that serve four-year-olds so that they can be better coordinated. On the one hand, the pre-K handicapped, child care, Pre-K, and Head Start are all separate programs that, in budget terminology, are "separate books" with different funding streams, eligibility requirements, and mechanisms for fiscal accountability. On the other hand, both legislative and budget analysts see their role as minimizing "overlap" and "duplication" but are loathe to isolate one program from another by decreasing the level of fiscal support. Of particular concern to budget analysts in any discussion of new initiatives for four-year-old children was that "a lot of support systems that are in place for the more affluent children" might be displaced (EX4–21). According to these analysts, "any time you increase an existing program, there are questions about how the funds should be allocated. . .we want to make sure that we weren't duplicating an existing effort such as the federal Head Start program or that we were in no way conflicting with it either. . .We want to complement the existing programs [yet] we would [want] a cost-effective approach to enriching services or expanding the opportunities to more children" (EX4–7,8).

Rather than view these programs as all serving children with very similar needs, the policy goal appeared to be one of establishing "rationality" or a continuum of services that basically keeps the present bureaucratic structure intact. In order to ensure that "we've got a rational process out there," the question becomes which agency should assume responsibility for which four-year-old children (LEG3–19). According to budget analysts, if the service is "day care, it's obviously DSS [Department of Social Services], with Experimental Pre-K, it's been the State Education Department, with pre-K handicap [it is either] the Health Department or the State Education Department" (EX4–33). One legislative analyst feels that "at this juncture we [haven't] got any real sense of the direction we should go in [except]. . .we've got to provide for a greater coordination" (LEG3–6,7). He believes that during the past several years there has been a movement toward a perception of these programs as a "continuum of services" with "links" to one other rather than as "separate entities" (LEG3–18). In contrast to the issue of day care versus pre-K, where "no one had any clear understanding as to what the difference was between one program and another"(LEG3–15), there are clearer distinctions between Experimental Pre-K and pre-K handicapped programs. In this legislative analyst's view, "disabilities are more tangible, more concrete than [being] disadvantaged. . . [and]

committees on special education will be able to...at a local level... define a handicapping condition versus a disadvantaged child who needs to be made school ready" (LEG3–16,17). In another analyst's view, the differences between pre-K handicapped children and the disadvantaged were "so obvious [as] to be self-evident" (EX2–3). Thus, the objective is not "to merge" but "to be able in a whole delivery system to provide a continuum of services that indeed each would be dealing with their separate populations, but we'll have a rationality and a logical sequence in the whole continuum of services" (LEG3–19,23).[4]

In response to this type of rational approach, an advocate for child care stated that her concern with public policy in general is that "we divide people up into categories and...only fund them according to categories" (IG4–31). In child day care, for example, she said that there are twelve funding streams, all with different income eligibility requirements for different funding formulas, and the same conflicting eligibility guidelines apply to Head Start and pre-K. For pre-K programs for the handicapped, of course, a child must be certified as handicapped in order to be placed in the program by family court. She felt that there is "too much labeling and too much categorizing...so that what happens is you find people twisting into contortions to become what the governments decided they should be in order to get money" (IG4–32).

Thus, when literacy is not the professed goal of schooling, and child care or socialization are not viewed as education, those who wish to broaden the scope of early childhood initiatives may be hard pressed to identify a legitimate role of government in this effort. However, ensuring equal opportunity for poor and minority groups, or at least equalizing access to resources—including education—has long been considered within the province of government. A major recommendation of the Governor's Task Force on Welfare, Poverty and Welfare Reform, for example, was to provide poor four-year-olds with an "earlier educational experience as a strategy to prevent dependence in the future" (EX1—1). The assumption behind these recommendations is that poor children do not have access to the preschool experiences that are available to middle-class children and that this disadvantage reduces the long-term ability of the poor to function independently within the state and the community.

9. EQUAL OPPORTUNITY FOR THE LEAST OF US AND POPULAR IN THE SUBURBS: PUBLIC SCHOOL FOR FOUR-YEAR-OLDS

I just know in my own case that my daughter is in the third day of first grade and she can read. I mean she can't read every word in every sentence but she can get through it, and she can read certain storybooks, and that is I think [because] of a combination of two years in nursery school, a year of kindergarten, and a mother and father who read with her and...[who] attach a great deal of importance to schooling and education. [But] youngsters who come from families where they don't have those three years—think of it—three years—[those] kids [are] already behind...[Free public school for four-year-olds] helps youngsters who might otherwise be behind—to be even.

—A policy analyst in New York State government

POLICY PROFESSIONALS AND program experts alike claimed that equalizing the opportunities of poor and disadvantaged children was the accepted rationale for publicly funded preschool for four-year-olds. One legislative analyst said that she did not want to sound "obnoxious" but she was "really very worried about the disadvantaged and the minority kids especially in New York [City]." A "terrible underclass" was being created with consequences that were already being reported in the newspapers: high school graduates who could not qualify for entry-level jobs, four hundred thousand school children in New York City schools alone who read more than two years below their grade placement, and finally, 40 percent of the young people who should have high school diplomas don't. She said, "It's very frightening to think of all those people who don't read well, who don't write well, who don't like [school] and can't pursue [their future]" (LEG2–46). This analyst believed that "these kids can be helped by being given programs that are useful, that will help them in school, and make sure that they are not handicapped" (LEG2–47). She echoed the beliefs of both policy and program specialists in her contention that to "do things right" resources must be targeted to young children to develop a "strong foundation" so that "the situation never occurs that you could be ten years old and you still can't read simple stuff" (LEG2–6,7).

HELPING THE LEAST OF US: A SHARED VALUE

What these policy and program experts viewed as important in the entry of public schools into preschool education was the access provided to those who otherwise would not attend early childhood programs. According to one research analyst, "middle-class kids are three times as likely to go to nursery school as low-income kids, so the public school system could be a way for those children who can't afford it, whose parents can't afford to pay for them to go, to get some kind of early childhood education and therefore be starting off with roughly the same preparations as other kids when they get to. . . kindergarten, first grade" (IG2–2–4). Similarly, a statewide early childhood administrator said she personally believes money for preschool should go to programs for poor children. Not speaking as a "company person" she exclaimed, "Forget universal [pre-K]!" With so many children living in poverty ("25 percent all over the state [and] 31 percent in New York City [including] ten thousand homeless children"), a situation akin to a "keg of dynamite" is being created among poor populations. She felt that her colleagues in the State Education Department shared her views that the need of poor children is so much greater now than it was when the Experimental Pre-K program was first established during the War on Poverty campaign of 1966 (IG5–40). According to this perspective, people have "lost sight of the fact" that early intervention in the form of preschool programs was initiated to help poor children in school—"not to be ahead of the middle-class kids, but to just stay above water" (IG5–41). Another program expert agreed. While poor children do have cultural, familial, and community connections that are not always acknowledged and respected, "they do not have many tangible resources that the middle class has, and those tangible resources buy experiences and comforts" that are lacking in the lives of poor children (EX3–23,24).

Budget analysts were also sensitive to "the needs of the least of us" in executing what they viewed as government's "traditional role... when you're dealing with an optional area" (EX4–25). Rather than "spread [state] resources more thinly across both [middle class and disadvantaged]...wouldn't it be best to focus on where the need is greatest, where [the children] are so far behind right now?" (EX5–29). If funding for preschool is extended to middle-class children, then "those who are disadvantaged in terms of coming from homes where they're not being read to because there are no reading materials or their parents are illiterate or speak another language...then their disadvantage just continues or will remain" (EX4–28,29). These analysts also emphasized that it was "not [their] intent to hold back the other group" but to extend opportunities to children with fewer resources (EX4–29). Citing language in Governor Cuomo's 1987 State of the State message, these analysts pointed out that it is a "state priority" to provide "early childhood education to every disadvantaged four-year-old child" (EX6–29). Further, these analysts believed that the Governor's statements "acknowledge that there should be a role by state government and perhaps local government to ensure...that we reach all [disadvantaged] four-year-olds...as soon as we can" (EX4–30). Nevertheless, how to provide these resources to disadvantaged children in a politically feasible way was—and is—a dilemma for policymakers.

On the one hand, early childhood education is often couched in cost-benefits terms: its present costs are less important than are its future benefits in the form of lower public outlays for welfare dependency. All policy and program experts pointed to the reductions in the number of high school dropouts, teen pregnancies and problems with juvenile delinquency that were attendant upon participation in early childhood education. As Representative Nicholas Paleologos from Massachusetts remarked in his address before the Legislative Symposium on Early Childhood Programs in New York State held on February 3, 1988: "Thank God for the Perry Preschool Project!" In his view—a perspective shared by the other symposium participants—the Perry Preschool Project provided justification for what policymakers believe is a valuable service for disadvantaged children. The advocate for local boards of education, for example, said that his group developed recommendations for public school for four-year-olds because "research findings have so strongly confirmed the advantage of early childhood intervention as...a dropout prevention mechanism" (IG1–3). Looking at the needs of children and the needs of "our society" in New York State, such as the "very severe" dropout problem and "changing demographics," budget analysts also see early intervention as a benefit that has been "proven" through research studies (EX6–45).

On the other hand, increasing the rates at which students graduate from high school and decreasing their future dependency on welfare may not be enough to garner the support of the middle-class for early childhood programs. Some program experts acknowledged that there was a tendency to "overstate" the benefits of early childhood education (EX3–50) and another claimed that it "frightened" her to think that the "whole future of society is lying on the backs of pre-K" (IG5–7). Lamenting what she perceived as the "quick-fix society," one program expert said that public preschool education is being "framed" as long-term intervention, yet "we want immediate solutions and we don't want them to cost very much" (EX3–5). Real support for either children or families, she believed, was lacking.

EDUCATION: THE RIGHT THING FOR POOR CHILDREN AND LOVED BY THE MIDDLE CLASS

One policy expert said she detected something of "an awakening" (EX1–12) about the increasing numbers of poor in this country and the seriousness of this situation for the future, yet she was skeptical "given the political perspectives around that we'll ever do the right thing for poor kids" (EX1–13). If she had her absolute preference this policymaker would opt for universal child care rather than education (EX1–4). Such child care would be available to all children and would be free for poor and disadvantaged children. Because the middle class would not perceive that service as a benefit to them, but rather as a welfare service for the poor, she did not think it would have enough political support. Sufficient funding would never be available to subsidize those who needed it, in her view. A compromise, she believed, would be to provide universal pre-K, a situation that could be potentially troubling because it would "expand the role and responsibility and universe of the public school system" (EX1–4). Even though the public schools have enough difficulty providing appropriate services to older children, this analyst concluded universal pre-K was the most politically feasible solution. Because the education establishment has a "constituency" and "clout" in New York State, the most workable solution to the child care needs of the poor, particularly the working poor ("we do precious little. . .for that group. . .up to 185 percent of the poverty level" (EX1–18)), would be to "broaden" the issue, making it "education." In her view, education is a "middle-class issue" and a "middle-class expenditure." People "love education" ('it's popular in the suburbs") but "hate it for the poor" (EX1–17). Given what she perceived as "political realities. . .,the reality of [today's] family" and also the recognition on the part of early childhood professionals that "socialization [is important] in educational experiences for children" and that "all children benefit from this. . .then I [say] why not do universal four-year-old education?" This type of maneuver would establish preschool services for families, a political constituency would develop to support it, "it's good for the kids [and] it will help families" (EX1–7).

Program professionals agreed with this perspective. One program specialist indicated that not only is there an "ever increasing population of women in the work force" but these women are returning to work when their children are at "younger ages." Additionally, this analyst predicted a "trend [at] the state and federal level to move young women from welfare to training to employment" (EX3–3). Poor women with young children would be "put from pillar to post" if the government were to say they "ought to be working [but] create [only] a 2½ hour preschool program" (IG3–3). Both these trends point to the need for more programs for young children, but as several program specialists cautioned, the programs must meet the needs of families "beyond the 2½ hours. . .usually sponsored by the schools" (EX3–3). An advocate for local boards of education concurred. The "overwhelming demand" is for child care for working mothers, and the "public demand" created by middle-class mothers who work is the "primary reason" public schools are seriously considering the issue of education for four-year-olds. Whereas a few years ago, scant attention was being paid to universal four-year-old schooling, this program advocate believed that a change in the public school role is being "driven by the demographics. . .change in the composition of the labor force, change in the composition of families, [change] in the character of family life" (IG1–34,35). A statewide administrator of early childhood programs also reported that the "huge need, the overall need, is for day care. . .[I]t has nothing to do with socioeconomic levels; it hits across all levels" (IG5). And an executive branch analyst said that the state has an interest in meeting the needs of families—"which means working families"—as well as poor children and "so we have to bring the school world up to the world of families today" (EX1–2,3).

It is not surprising then that the Council on Children and Families (1987) asserted that in the State of New York there is an "unprecedented demand for early childhood services...and the gap between the available supply and the demand continues to grow" (p. 3). A confluence of demographic trends has contributed to the need to both expand the number of programs and coordinate the activities of the multiple agencies that provide oversight and funding for early childhood (pp. 2, 11, 12). In 1970, according to the report, the majority of families in New York were headed by a father who provided sole financial support, but by 1987, only one-third of New York families fell into the "traditional" mode. Close to half of all mothers of preschool children were in the work force in 1987. Additionally, single-parent families have increased by 50 percent the last decade, and concurrently, the percentage of children living in poverty has increased to over 25 percent of the children in New York State (p. 2). Thus, given the "growing recognition of the short and long-term beneficial effects of high quality preschool experiences" the care of children in New York State cannot "simply be custodial but must incorporate elements that prepare children for the cognitive and educational requirements of school" (p. 3). Among the proposals submitted by the Council were expansion of the state pre-K program and school district sponsorship of day care.

Given that "much of [four-year-old] education doesn't now take place in the public schools" (IG2), it is interesting to note that the advocate for local boards of education felt that schools would respond to these initiatives or risk losing students to other institutions:

> The increased demand for early childhood education...can't be denied and there has to be a response from the public schools...[I]f the public schools don't do it, then private institutions are going to. Or day care institutions are going to get involved. So there needs to be an institutional response from the public schools on the issue. The opportunity is here, the demographics and the demand are such that something needs to be done. (IG1–4)

SUMMARY OF THE INTERVIEWS

One purpose of the study was to "unpack" contemporary New York State policymakers' definitions of school readiness and the role of literacy acquisition in current formulations of public school for four-year-olds. What these policymakers describe as important was compared with past influences on the establishment of school programs for children under the age of six. Although some differences emerged in the categories of expert knowledge, social values and demographic or economic conditions, these influences are recursive. Themes of equal opportunity, early intervention, and child care for working women are replayed in contemporary definitions of a public responsibility for four-year-old children.

In contemporary discussions of the role of the public school in the education of four-year-olds, however, the current influence of statewide bureaucracies appears more intrusive than was true in prior attempts to school young children, and expertise among policy participants is not confined to knowing what is good for children. Expert knowledge in terms of what children should be doing is vested in constituents, program specialists, and advocacy groups, not necessarily in the professionals who develop program legislation, oversight, and budgets. The question of readiness for school is not easily considered apart from the broader question of what should count as school or education, and what is socialization or habilitation—and thus someone else's responsibility to fund and administer.

Unlike some earlier periods in the history of preschool education, academic work in the form of reading and writing instruction is not currently viewed as developmentally appropriate for four-year-olds by either program or policy professionals in New York. Instead, the cognitive development and social learning associated with physiological maturation—a concept of readiness proposed in the 1920's and 1930's—were presented by contemporary program professionals as *the* content of education for four-year-olds. Whether such program content is considered education may depend upon the skill of early childhood advocates in legitimating socialization as a public expenditure under the aegis of education.

Actually, the curriculum of the early kindergartens emphasized the training of social skills and the formation of "good habits," according to historical accounts of the period. Although widely perceived by policy participants as academic in nature now ("doing the work of first grade," in the words of one interviewee), the kindergarten did not always teach reading. Rather, the work of the early kindergarten was very similar to the social learning and cognitive development espoused by contemporary program professionals. Just as the assimilation of the kindergarten into the public schools of the mid-nineteenth century was made easier by Dewey and the progressive education movement, the Perry Preschool researchers have effectively promulgated the benefits of an early childhood education that is broadly defined to include social learning. Every policy participant who was interviewed cited the research of the Perry Preschool Project as justification for an expansion of early childhood programs in New York State, whatever the aegis or funding stream. Beyond the Ypsilanti, Michigan, project, however, neither policy nor program professionals cited research to support their narrow view of developmentally appropriate practice that excludes literacy learning. A close reading of the curriculum sources cited by program professionals, in fact, appears to recommend activities that would support children's emergent literacy development—a concept that the program professionals did not address.

The following chapter presents a discussion of the models of agenda setting described in chapter 3. These models of agenda setting—interest group conflict, labeling the issue, and opening policy windows—are not intended to predict an outcome of the current discussion of public school for four-year-olds, but rather might help explain why this issue has attained such prominence and which parts are viewed as important.

Finally, I reexamine the role of literacy. I believe that the perceptions of the respondents regarding reading and writing among preschoolers are important not only for what they said but, by implication, what they did not know: the connections they did not make between social learning and literacy acquisition. In addition, I test the validity of the assertion by program professionals that kindergarten children are now required to do the reading curriculum of what used to be first grade. In order to examine evidence for the perceptions that kindergarten has become more academic, I analyze the beginning levels of a widely used reading series to detect change in difficulty over time. Chapter 11 presents the results of the analysis.

10. MAKING THE AGENDA: CONFLICTS, WINDOWS, AND LABELS

> *If there were no other reason than the interest of all civilized people, we should do all we can for our children. We need neither subtle philosophers nor sophisticated sociologists to tell us that government is duty bound to help protect, nurture, and encourage our children, especially those who lack the help they deserve from their own family situations.*
>
> *—Mario Cuomo, 1991*

THE ISSUE OF PUBLIC SCHOOL for four-year-olds has become an item on the political agenda in New York State. How it happened is the topic of this chapter. Borrowing from the literature on agenda setting as a political process, I present my interpretation of the seredipitious coming together of policy streams, open windows and the right labels to make public school for four-year-olds an idea whose time has come.

Through the perceptions and understandings of the participants in this study, I was able to describe the agenda-setting process at work—the process of defining and selecting those aspects of the issue to which New York State government is attending. Several theoretical stances on agenda setting helped to ground the present analysis: the group conflict and accommodation model (Cobb, Ross & Ross, 1976), the theory about labelling and defining issues to maximize public support (Nelson, 1978; 1984), and the idea of opportunities as open windows (Kingdon, 1984).

CONFLICTS, WINDOWS, AND LABELS: AGENDA SETTING THEORIES

One agenda-setting theory, proposed by Cobb et al. (1976), holds that issues can originate either with interest groups outside government or through mobilization by leaders within government (p. 127). Most issues must be supported by the public, even those issues that originate within government itself, if government is to act formally upon them. For issues to expand beyond narrow interest-group sponsorship to public sponsorship, they must evoke a positive emotional response, require little redistribution of material resources, and be associated with a high-status group (p. 128).

Nelson's (1978; 1984) agenda-setting hypotheses were developed around the history of child abuse legislation. She holds that issue adoption requires slack resources (1978, p. 35) and high-valance overtones (1978, pp. 36, 37), arguments that are similar to Cobb, Ross and Ross' (1976) ideas, and those of Kingdon (1984). In order for an issue to be recognized, adopted, and ultimately incorporated into the governmental agenda, she argues, it must be defined as a legitimate function of government and it must have few political and economic costs associated with it. Nelson notes that when equity is a concern, government expands its scope of responsibility. By contrast, a concern with efficiency influences the government to contract its purview.

Labelling an issue is of utmost importance, according to Nelson, because only those issues with a high degree of positive consensus will receive priority on the policy agenda (1978, p. 26). At times, policy leaders will align themselves with a high valance issue in order to facilitate their own professional careers (Nelson, 1978, p. 37), an idea similar to Cobb, Ross and Ross' within government "mobilization" (p. 132) and Kingdon's "visible participants" (p. 189). Often issues arise from research activities that are supported by the government, and these same research activities maintain the issue's visibility within the professional and mass media, thus increasing the likelihood that substantive decision making will ultimately take place on the issue (Nelson, 1978, p. 30).

Another theory, that of Kingdon (1984), proposes a pattern of agenda setting that is less orderly than the others but, as noted, incorporates many of the same elements. Kingdon believes that agenda setting is a different process than selecting a course of action from among alternative proposals once an agenda item has been acknowledged (p. 4). In order for government to acknowledge an issue, something must happen to call attention to it (p. 95). A condition or a crisis may focus concern in a particular area, and government may feel it can do something about it, thus turning a condition into a problem that needs a solution (p. 97). Sometimes conditions become redefined into more important categories that, in turn, are viewed as needing government action (p. 99). Whether or not issues—redefined as problems—receive action depends upon two other elements in the political stream: a climate of receptivity and the visible participants (p. 155). In Kingdon's view, and that of Nelson and Cobb et al., the issue must be well analyzed, it must not violate social values, and it must adhere to budgetary constraints (p. 19). Elected officials or high-level appointees are more effective than interest groups in achieving recognition on their issues, according to Kingdon, but policy entrepreneurs—advocates, bureaucrats, and researchers—greatly influence the form of the proposals that are ultimately selected as solutions to the problem. The latter group of policy participants may float their proposals long before the issue is defined as a problem, thus softening up the policy process to be receptive once a window is open for potential solutions (p. 190). Kingdon sees new policy developing when problems, politics, and participants converge at a particular point in history (p. 188).

Thus, the three models posit several common characteristics of issues that ultimately reach the "maintenance" (Nelson, 1984, p. 23), "decision" (Kingdon, p. 21), or "formal" agenda (Cobb, Ross & Ross, 1976, p. 126) stage where government officials take action on them. Through the efforts of interest groups, government-sponsored research, or high-ranking government officials, a condition must be perceived as a problem that government should address. The issue not only must be defined as a potential problem needing government intervention but also must be labelled in such a way that the public supports policy action on it. In other words, the issue must evoke positive public response. To insure public support, the issue should be consistent with widely held social values and should not require a redistribution of resources. Whether or not government actually makes substantive policy decisions on the issue, however, also depends on a serendipitous coming together of a feasible solution to a pressing problem and the right political conditions—a climate of receptivity for an issue whose "time has come" (Kingdon, 1984, p. 1).

NEW YORK STATE: CONDITIONS AND PARTICIPANTS

Two demographic "conditions" in New York State have focused the attention of policymakers on the issue of publicly funded education for four-year-olds. As discussed previously, the participation of women in the labor force, the concomitant need for child care services, and the high concentrations of poor and minority children who drop out of school and become burdensome to society are demographic facts that have become problems for New York State policymakers. Governor Cuomo tried to address both the problem of child care and the problem of educational disadvantage with a proposal for an "educational component" for disadvantaged four-year-olds with a wrap-around "child care component." Thus, an issue that was originally associated with Gordon Ambach (former education commissioner) and his 1983 proposal for early school entry and early school leaving was transformed in 1987 by Governor Cuomo into an education and child care proposal (1987) for all disadvantaged children that would combat dropout and welfare problems. When in 1988 Cuomo inaugurated the Decade of the Child, he again redefined the issue by proposing free and universally available school for all four-year-old children in the state of New York (see table 10-1 on the language of these visible participants as they redefine the issue). Since then, the governor has sought to expand the existing prekindergarten program for disadvantaged children. By virtue of the governor's personal association with the issue and proposed funding to initiate or expand programs, policy participants representing groups with a vested interest in the outcome of early childhood legislation have sprung into action.

A WINDOW OPENS TO THE PROBLEM, BUT WHAT IS THE SOLUTION? DEFINING THE ISSUE

As discussed in chapter 8, the 1987 proposal—an "open window"—precipitated a scramble on the part of child care providers to convey the idea that child care in any setting was education. Budget, legislative, and executive office policy analysts found themselves in a head-on confrontation over definitions, particularly the definition of education. Resolution of the problem of definition assumed importance for several reasons. As discussed previously, child care professionals and the

TABLE 10–1
Changes in the Views of Visible Participants on the Issue of Public School for Four-Year-Olds, from Child Development to Public Responsibility

From Child Development

The Regents have approved a legislative proposal that would provide state assistance for attendance of 4-year-olds in prekindergarten programs. This proposal reflects the commitment of the Board to offer an opportunity for school at public expenditure at an earlier age than now provided. . . A great change has occurred in early childhood education with the potential for excellent activities and providing more rigorous skill [*sic*] introduced at earlier times. Our experts in reading. . . indicate that. . . 40% of what was a part of the first grade reading program in the mid-1960s is now a part of the kindergarten program. . . This shift in the type of study and level of activity to earlier years should have an impact on the content of programs at later years. (NYSED, 1983)

To Equal Opportunity And Public Benefit

[The] Early Childhood Education Commission found average improvements of 38% fewer children retained in grade, 58% fewer placed in special education and 23% more graduating from high school. These gains not only help the children served but also mean real financial savings to all levels of government. . . [W]e set as our goal the provision of early childhood education to every disadvantaged 4-year-old in the State. (Cuomo, 1987).

To Public Responsibility

[T]o accept [the] challenge of building the future, we must start where the future always starts: with children. . . Now a staggering number of our children are undereducated. . . A large part of this entire generation cannot be impaired without severe consequences to the entire community. . . The problem of our children demands a bold and broad commitment of government at all levels, in partnership with the whole community. . . First, I propose that we adopt the goal of providing universal free kindergarten education for 4-year-olds within five years all across the state of New York. (Cuomo, 1988)

advocates representing this group believed an association with the State Education Department rather than with Social Services would help create stability, increased wages for providers, and public acceptance of the proposal as a legitimate government expense. Early childhood professionals already entrenched in the public school bureaucracy, the Experimental Prekindergarten providers, did not formally endorse this concept. According to the director of the lobbying effort, prekindergarten providers wanted to ensure that their program was not the object of a child day care takeover: educational arbitrage on the part of child care providers who wanted their full-day programs acknowledged as "school." At the same time, public school officials staked their claim to the proposed early childhood initiative lest the public schools lose ground to the private sector. In the absence of definitive answers from the statewide program experts, budget and legislative analysts asked their own questions about the differences between socialization, habilitation, and education so that a "rational coordination" of responsibilities among different bureaucratic players might be effected.

For the most part, policy professionals and program experts alike perceived the categories of "handicapped" and "disadvantaged" services to preschool children as serving distinctly different populations of children in programs with different content, thereby justifying separate funding streams, standards, and auspice. Within the broad category of "disadvantaged," however, there was little disagreement that the various educational programs for preschoolers targeted the same children, even though Head Start is administered through the Department of Social Services, Experimental Pre-K, through the State Education Department, and Giant Step, through the Mayor's Office in New York City. Regarding the conceptualization of all child care as education, thereby including child day care, all program experts agreed but few policy professionals were convinced. Although all policy professionals believed that child care was valuable and needed, they perceived child care services, regardless of the claim to socialization, as different from educational services and noted that this difference was acknowledged in the separation of the standards, funding, and oversight that are applied to their administration.

Legislation to fund a combination of the concept of education and child care was not passed, nor was the governor's subsequent proposal for universal education for four-year-olds. The proposal for education with "wrap-around" child care failed to pass in 1987, not because of "substantive issues," in the words of the director of the child care lobbying effort, but rather because of "political issues." In the director's view, the interests of preserving the aegis and funding of the Experimental prekindergarten program (which was immensely popular in downstate districts), prevailed over the notion that all child care was, in fact, education. Not wanting to alienate the day care constituency, however, the legislature has substantially increased funding for these centers through Social Services as well as the funding for Experimental Prekindergarten through the State Education Department. The legislature requested that the Council on Children and Families study the issue of "coordination" and make recommendations for a state initiative.

Subsequently, the Governor established a permanent interagency committee on early childhood education to help resolve some of the problems of "jurisdiction." Thus it may be said that, for the present, the legislature has "begged the question" of what is education and thereby fundable through state aid for education.

Whatever the ultimate resolution might be, it is abundantly clear that all policy participants paid a good deal of attention to how the issue is and has been labelled. Whether such programs were characterized as child care, socialization, habilitation, or education was crucial to all policy participants, not only because auspice and funding are different, but also because only education is viewed as having widespread public acceptance as an allowable—indeed, preferred—public expenditure.

But what counts as "school" in contemporary terms is made more complex by the isolation of content or program knowledge from policy planning. It may be a function of the contemporary bureaucracy that New York State policy professionals associate social learning or socialization with the Social Services bureaucracy, whereas they see education as a function of educational institutions and agencies. Similarly, they see child day care not as education but, at best, as socialization, because the Department of Social Services administers these programs. Programs administered through the Departments of Health and Mental Hygiene are likewise considered habilitation. Additionally, as policy and program professionals pointed out, the historical association of child day care with welfare and charity continues to undermine the attempts of early childhood advocates to characterize child care as socialization and socialization as education. Thus auspice and funding define what might be considered "education" in the minds of present-day policymakers, and concern with maintaining the separate bureaucratic structures of early childhood programs may override a concern with the similarities of either program content or the children served. A rational coordination of services that keeps existing aegis and monetary streams intact—and the interest groups at bay—appears to be the foremost consideration in developing a public responsibility for four-year-olds from the perspective of policy professionals.

ECONOMIC AND POLITICAL COSTS: A CLASS PERSPECTIVE

Agenda-setting models also suggest that issues must have broad public support as well as support from interest groups in order to be considered seriously by government. Issues with broad public appeal are those that have small economic and political costs and that do not require a redistribution of resources.

The agenda-setting theories about economic and political costs and resource distributions are interesting in light of the potentially high cost of preschool education to the public at large, should the age of public school entitlement be shifted downward one year. At first glance, such an issue may not appear to be publicly acceptable because it violates budgetary constraints. While the potential costs may indeed be too much for the legislature to support during tight fiscal years, there are several reasons why public school for four-year-olds may still be an idea whose time has come. Government support of the poor and equal access to educational resources were acknowledged values of all policymakers, but not necessarily ones they would support at the expense of the middle class. Public money spent on early childhood programs was billed not as good for the poor but as good for society, because such early intervention would save money in the long run. It would be a cost-effective way to combat welfare and crime among a school-aged population that is increasingly minority and poor. Further, the structure of the family in New York State has changed so that publicly funded programs for children under the age of school entry are a concern of mainstream families, not just an issue for the poor. Thus, in New York State a climate of receptivity may exist toward the expansion of the state's responsibility in early childhood.

According to 1985 data from Gordon Ambach, who was the State's education commissioner, the majority of middle-class four-year-olds in New York are already in educational programs, but the poor are not. Thus, middle-class families are already spending money on preschool programs. Publicly funded programs would relieve them as well as provide education for poor children who do not now have access to school. Although publicly funded school for four-year-olds would be expensive, it may come to be perceived as both a common good and one that does not require a redistribution of resources from the middle class to the poor. On the contrary, public school for four-year-olds may be viewed as financially beneficial to the middle class in terms of money saved in child care and private school tuition as well as in the reduced dependency of the poor on middle class tax dollars.

WHAT'S PAST IS PROLOGUE: BELIEFS WITH LONGEVITY

Another characteristic of issues that ultimately achieve agenda status and are acted upon is that they must not conflict with widely held social values. Contemporary policy participants affirmed several beliefs about early childhood education that have appeared at other points in history when a public responsibility toward the schooling of very young children has been invoked.

What were perceived as compelling reasons for sending children under the age of six to school in earlier periods of history were also reasons repeatedly cited by contemporary policy participants: commitment to equal opportunity for poor children and a belief in early intervention to dispel social and economic dependency. Public school for four-year-olds is being defined in terms similar to those articulated by the founders of the infant school and the kindergarten of the mid-nineteenth century, the Lanham nursery education centers of the 1940s, and the poverty programs of the 1960s. President Nixon, for example, said in 1969 that Head Start made the nation aware that "the children of the poor mostly arrive at school. . . already significantly behind their contemporaries."[1] Present-day discussions and the child-saving activities of the early preschools share the common goal of providing equal opportunity for children of the poor. As proposed by one New York State analyst, the "traditional role of government" in an "optional" area such as public preschool is providing for "the needs of the least of us." He believed, as did policymakers of the past, that it is best to "focus where the need is the greatest, where [the children] are so far behind right now" (EX 5–29). Both present-day policymakers and the advocates of the kindergarten, infant schools, and Head Start believed that equalized access to education as young children would lead the poor out of poverty and facilitate their economic independence as adults. In addition to supporting government sponsored education for children of the poor, these present-day policy participants, like those of the past, acknowledged a role for publicly funded early childhood programs when prevailing economic conditions changed the pattern of female participation in the labor force.[2] Nursery education in the Lanham centers and WPA school programs created during the depression and World War II were established to allow men and women, but mostly women, to work. In New York State, the majority of women with children under the age of five are now working. Additionally, workfare programs for dependent single-parent families are becoming increasingly common. Studies commissioned by the governor and legislature in New York demonstrated an overwhelming need for an increase in the number of publicly supported programs for children under the age of five. Clearly, contemporary policymakers, like those of the past, have acknowledged the influence of current demographics of women in the labor force and the changed structure of the traditional family as they consider the role of the public school in early childhood.

A final similarity between earlier attempts to define a public responsibility for schools for children under the age of school entitlement and current attempts is the displacement of literacy learning with social learning as the goal of early childhood education. When women's work was no longer needed for the war effort and the Lanham Act funding for preschool was about to expire, advocates of nursery education attempted, albeit unsuccessfully, to establish *socialization* as the goal of publicly funded early childhood education. However, not until the relatively recent research of the Perry Preschool Project has social learning been given equal billing with academic learning as a cost-effective benefit of early childhood education.

As Nelson (1978) suggested, research activities may provide support for particular issues and keep these issues before the public. In this case, the Perry Preschool Project was cited by all policy participants as justification for expansion of a public role in early childhood as well as proof that a developmentally appropriate curriculum—one that included social learning—was better than an academic approach. After testifying before the joint House Committee on Education and Labor and Senate Committee on Labor and Human Resources congressional hearing on early childhood education, Weikart (1988) himself commented that the committee "doesn't want more research . . . [T]hey have enough research information and are comfortable in acting upon it. The question they appear to be addressing now is how to act on the information" (p. 10).

In contemporary discussions of public school for four-year-olds in New York, knowledge of what children are ready to do, or can and should do, is left to the program professionals, who, in turn, inform the policy professionals. As these program professionals—the advocates, constituent group representatives, and early childhood specialists—indicated, the notion of teaching reading and writing among four-year-olds is not compatible with their idea of developmentally appropriate practice. Nonetheless, these program experts cited a relatively narrow range of research to build their interpretation of developmental appropriateness and appeared unaware that a larger community of researchers might not necessarily agree with either their perception of physiological maturation or their belief that literacy learning among preschoolers was inadvisable.

Of course, the construct of developmental readiness is not new to preschool education but, as noted previously, originated with the work of Pestalozzi and was "scientifically validated" in the early 1900s with the work of Gesell and his associates (see table 10–2). The concept of developmental readiness was applied to beginning reading instruction during the same era (Morphett and Washburne, 1931), and continues to influence the perceptions of many early childhood professionals. For example, the current president of the National Association for the Education of Young Children, David Elkind (1988b), cited Washburne's work as testimony to the futility of teaching reading and writing to preschool children. According to Elkind, children (in the Washburne study) who were taught to read at six and seven years old "were more interested, spontaneous readers than the early reading group" (p. 23). Elkind argued that only "about one or three per 100 [children]" have "a structural imperative [that is] a need to find stimuli to exercise their emerging mental abilities" in reading at the preschool age. These few children, Elkind continued, "teach themselves to read and ask adults for help when they need it" (p. 25).

PUBLIC SCHOOLS AND LITERACY LEARNING

What clearly emerged from the interviews with program specialists in New York State and what was also articulated by NAEYC president Elkind (1988) was the perception that public schools had pushed down the curriculum of first grade into the kindergarten, and that the kindergarten curriculum, the teaching of reading and writing, would be foisted on four-year-olds if they were in public schools. Related to this perception is the idea that early childhood is a distinct field with "its own curriculum, its own methods of evaluation and classroom management." Further, the early childhood curriculum is not a "downward extension" of elementary school, and "testing, workbooks, and group drill" (p. 27) are viewed as the curriculum of the elementary school. In the same article, Elkind cited "letters and numbers" as among the "core curriculum" that preschool children should know, along with a well-developed oral language vocabulary, colors and shapes, turn-taking, paying attention, completing tasks, and following directions (p. 26) Because early childhood education is not understood "by officials at higher levels of education" (p. 27). Elkind argued that an association with the public schools should be approached with caution, a view shared by an early childhood expert in New York:

TABLE 10–2

Slowly Changing Understandings about the Development of Children from Gesell to the National Association of Early Childhood Specialists/State Departments of Education

Beliefs from the Literature	*New York State Policy Participants' Beliefs*
The child must speak well before he can read well. (Pestalozzi, 1908)	
What does the 6-year-old care for print? His fingers are itching for contact with things, and his legs are set for chasing butterflies. . . Education cannot, by formulating courses of study, force intellectual functions. The laws which govern the growth of mind are as immediate and irresistible in their operation as those which govern the growth of the body. (Gesell, 1912)	There is a whole body of literature. . . that emphasizes the importance of developmental readiness. . . that kids not be put in school in formal learning situations until they are fully able to cope with it. (IG1)
The preschool teacher helps children consolidate their abilities in developmentally appropriate ways, through direct and representational experience, without trying to accelerate their development or push them along to the next level. (Hohmann, et al., 1979).	
All domains of development—physical, emotional, social and cognitive—can be described in terms of predictable, age-related sequences of growth and change. Developmentally appropriate program practice reflects the body of age-related knowledge about children's readiness and expected acquisition of skills and abilities (NAEYC, 1985).	Many 4-year-olds don't have the muscle development to hold a pencil and so one of the fears is that you're going to start to make demands on kids to do things before they are physiologically ready, that is, before they're developmentally ready . . . If you were to put a pencil in their hand. . . if you look at the scribbling of a 2-year-old, that's what you'd get. (EX3)
The notion that children unfold on an immutable timetable, however appealing, cannot be overgeneralized to intellectual, social, linguistic and emotional development. (NAECS/SDE, 1987)	

[W]hether or not a child is ready—that is, whether or not he will be successful in learning to read—depends not only on his own abilities but also on the kind and quality of instruction that is offered. (Durkin, 1970)

While research supports the idea that print-related learning results from informal experiences. . . the process is not one of children acquiring information about print via osmosis from a print-saturated environment. . . [C]hildren's attention needs to be directed to the print in these informal experiences. (Hiebert, 1986)

Lower-class and middle-class children face the same cognitive problems in attempting to compose their writing productions, but the two groups differ drastically in terms of information available to them. (Ferreiro, 1984)

Explicit teaching of words is a decontextualized form of tutoring. . . The literate parent is teaching the child an orientation to language [a metalanguage] which will not be relevant to learning to speak but which will be relevant to learning to read. The roots of literacy lie in how one learns to talk. . . The link. . . between the structures of society and the structure of the individual are to be found in their sharing of a common language which is the metalanguage for referring to language. It is in this common language that we may find an identity between what is taught and what is learned. (Olson, 1984)

[T]here is no value in 4-year-olds learning the letters of the alphabet, or 5-year-olds. (IG5)

I think [children] need to come to school with a certain experiential background that allows them to be ready to learn. . . but they shouldn't come to first grade knowing how to say their alphabet and why should they? (IG4)

The content of [preschool] experiences has to be rethought so we don't get into this craziness of teaching 3- and 4-year olds how to write and thinking we've done something because they write a year earlier or they can read words. (EX1)

> [O]n one hand it's good for public schools to get involved because it furthers the educational emphasis in programs for young children. On the other hand, public schools can be incredibly rigid and make things into overly structured and inappropriate kinds of programs. They tend to do that when they're taking on a program for children that they have not previously dealt with. In the same way that educators fear with kindergartners becoming too structured and rigid, in fact, that's what's happening to programs for four-year-olds. (IG2–16,17)

Teaching children to read and write is inextricably bound to the role of public schools. When in 1983 Gordon Ambach, the former education commissioner, proposed dropping the entry age to four, the rationale he presented was couched in terms of learning to read:

> The Regents have approved a legislative proposal that would provide State assistance for attendance of four-year-old children in prekindergarten programs. This proposal reflects the commitment of the Board to offer an opportunity for school at public expenditure at an earlier age than now provided. As the Head Start and experimental prekindergarten programs have demonstrated, a great change has occurred in early childhood education with the potential for excellent activities and providing more rigorous skill introduced at earlier times. Our experts in reading, for example, indicate that approximately 40 percent of what was part of the first-grade reading program in the mid-1960s is now a part of the kindergarten program. Much of what was formerly done in kindergarten is now part of prekindergarten. This shift in the type of study and level of activity to earlier years should have an impact on the content of programs at later years. (New York State Education Department 1983, BR8–33)

Although early childhood program professionals thought these statements were "outrageous. . .no one asked us" (IG5), contemporary policy participants still consider the idea that schools need more time to do their work a viable reason for lowering the entry age to four:

> [P]eople are continually complaining, "Well, we don't have enough time. There's not enough time in the school day to get students through the mandates and the curriculum dictates of the Regents Action Plan, let alone some of the options children want to pursue." If you're not going to expand the school day, and that's obviously something that's been discussed, but if we don't want to expand the school day, or the school year beyond 180 days, well, maybe the other option is that we look at the drop in the age requirement for education purposes to age 4. . .and that's what we're mulling over in and out of the legislature (LEG3–13).

Most program experts were in agreement that things have changed in kindergarten, that what "you used to know when you got out of kindergarten is now what you're supposed to know when you start kindergarten" (IG2–28). The curriculum is thought to have shifted downward, and it was stated over and over that the "objectives for first grade are now the ones for kindergarten." When children are not prepared for this shift ("kids have not changed a whole lot"), it is easy to say "Gosh, a lot of kids aren't ready. We should change the kindergarten entry age. So now we'll just say well it's not 5-year-olds who should go to kindergarten—it's 5½-year-olds" (IG2–29).

According to at least one program expert, policymakers respond to the easiest option. Changing the entry age to kindergarten can be viewed as "denying access to school to kids who previously were eligible, or you can look at it as the policymakers choosing the easiest thing. They change the entry age. . . It is much harder to rework the curriculum and say things have really gone too far" (IG2–29,30). Because as soon as the kindergarten curriculum changes—"more play, no they don't need to read"—the first-grade teachers object, and then [those at] the second grade. Instead of "dealing with the curricular shift and those kinds of changes," which are harder to remedy, "the entry age is going up [or down] all over the country. . . [T]hat's easier to legislate than it is to start attacking the entire curriculum in your school" (IG2–30).

On the one hand, then, many early childhood specialists have said that reading and writing do not belong in preschool, that workbooks and other reading and writing curricula are not developmentally appropriate, and that these same curricula materials, formerly used in first grade, are now being used in kindergarten. They believe that the reading and writing curricula is being pushed down to preschool. What is termed symbolic learning (NAEYC, 1986, p. 4) is not appropriate for preschoolers.

On the other hand, Elkind, the current president of the NAEYC, includes letters and numbers in the "core curricula" appropriate for preschool, and the widely promulgated curricula of the Perry Preschool Project also includes written language experiences for preschool children. A "Joint Statement" of concerns about present practices in pre-first grade reading instruction and recommendations for improvement (1986), published in *Childhood Education*, also set forth the belief that "literacy learning begins in infancy" and that "for optimal learning, teachers should involve children actively in many meaningful, functional language experiences including speaking, listening, writing and reading" (p. 110). This "Joint Statement" acknowledged the influence of children's diverse social and cultural backgrounds on language use and urged that these differences be respected and used as a "base for literacy activities." Since this "Joint Statement" was apparently endorsed by the Association for Childhood Education International, the Association for Supervision and Curriculum Development, the International Reading Association, the National Association for the Education of Young Children, the National Association of Elementary School Principals, and the National Council of Teachers of English, some consensus appears to exist that reading and writing are an appropriate part of preschool education. What the "Joint Statement" views as problems or "concerns" are primarily that children "are subjected to rigid, formal pre-reading programs with inappropriate expectations and experiences for their levels of development" (p. 110) and that such programs, apparently "commercial" reading programs, focus on "isolated skills," discourage "risk-taking," and do not accommodate children's "social, emotional and intellectual development" (p. 111).

Unfortunately, scant research has been done on current curriculum practices with respect to literacy activities in kindergarten or prekindergarten, child day care or nursery school centers. In kindergartens recently studied by Durkin (1987), there was little evidence of what might be termed the "emergent literacy" approach (such as that described by Schickedanz, 1982; Mason, 1986) recommended by the "Joint Statement" and discussed previously. Rather, traditional nursery school play activities and workbook activities from commercial reading programs both were incorporated into the kindergarten day. Initially, in the fall of the school year, Durkin saw instruction based on "colors, shapes and numbers." Reading readiness instruction, usually later in the school year, was based on the "beginning materials [usually in workbook form] in the basal series being used by the school." Such readiness work typically emphasized "letter names, auditory discrimination and eventually, letter-sound correspondences" (p. 767). Sometimes whole words were taught to kindergarten children, depending on the first grade reading book being used by the school.[3]

Few researchers have surveyed instructional practices at the preschool level. One recent survey of Midwestern preschool teachers found that they generally followed conventional methodology in their approaches to literacy (Robinson, 1990). Mostly, these preschool teachers read to children, teach them the alphabet, and how to recognize their own names. As in the kindergartens studied by Durkin, there was no evidence that preschool teachers provided instruction consistent with an emergent literacy approach: the majority did not create "print-rich" classrooms (p. 5), they did not provide opportunities for playful exploration of written language, nor did they believe in encouraging children to write. These preschool teachers were worried about creating "an unsuited academic environment for young children" (p. 6) and expressed concern that such practices were not developmentally appropriate. In an earlier survey of the literature on preschool reading activities, Collins (1986) also suggested that traditional methodology was widespread and that commercial materials[3] were a common form of instruction (p. 334).

Whether use of so-called commercial reading programs is as widespread as suggested has not been adequately addressed in the current literature, but this practice is apparently common enough to warrant the disapproval of virtually every policy statement on this issue—both those statements formally articulated by professional interest groups such as the NAEYC and the "Joint Statement" previously discussed and the informal commentary of the New York State program specialists. Thus the incursion of what are believed to be first-grade reading materials into the kindergarten and preschools was identified as a concern by all New York State program professionals. The program experts did not cite evidence for their belief that kindergarten, and some prekindergartens, were doing the work of first grade, except for their own observations. However, an examination of some of the reading materials themselves and the literature related to change in these materials, which is summarized in the next chapter, may provide evidence to refute or corroborate their perceptions.

11. BEGINNING READING MATERIALS: ARE THEY GETTING HARDER?

> *[T]wenty years ago...what you had to know, what you had to be able to do to go to kindergarten was different than what you have to be able to do [now]...[W]hat you used to know when you got out of kindergarten is now what you're supposed to know when you start kindergarten... [but]...the developmental level[s]... of the kids haven't changed a whole lot.*
>
> —*An early childhood policy expert and advocate for quality child care*

NILA BANTON SMITH traced the history of American reading instruction from the early nineteenth century to the beginning of the 1960s. One of the most significant trends discussed in that history is the "rapid and wide acceptance of a reading readiness concept [which] ushered in a new approach to reading" (Smith, 1965, p. 289). Smith located the first discussion of a 'readiness' concept as a "preparatory period" in the *Twenty-fourth Yearbook of the National Society for the Study of Education,* which was published in 1925. Beginning in the late 1930s and throughout the 1940s, the readiness concept not only was acknowledged but also was evident in the design and function of reading materials developed for the beginning levels of instruction:

> Wide acceptance of the reading readiness concept revolutionized beginning programs. Authors now considered the development of reading readiness so important that they provided material for and instructions to the teacher for use during a "readiness period." (p. 277)

Reading readiness books were introduced during this period. Usually two books were used, one for seatwork and the other for group practice with the teacher. Typical tasks, according to Smith, were picture-matching exercises involving shapes but sometimes letters and words, interpreting picture stories and other language experiences, and "getting acquainted" with the characters who were later introduced in the preprimer stories (p. 277). At this time, the number of preprimers published by the major textbook companies increased from one to as many as four (p. 278). The vocabulary of these preprimer books was "meticulously" controlled to match the high frequency word lists published by Thorndike, Gates, and the International Kindergarten Union, according to Smith. Further, there was "a drastic reduction in the number of new words presented to children before the first reader period" in preprimer and primer books published between 1935 and 1950 (p. 279). Smith extended the analysis of Selke and Selke (1922) and Beck (1928, in Smith, 1965) on the number of new words in preprimer and primer books to demonstrate this steady decline: In 1922, the average number of new words presented was 406, in 1928, it was 378, and by 1931 the vocabulary load had decreased by 25 percent, to 289 new words. This trend continued through the 1930s and 1940s, and new reading materials published during this period introduced even fewer words than in previous periods. According to Smith, the average number of new words in preprimers and primers declined to 174 by 1950 (p. 280).

This reduction in the number of words presented to children and the proliferation of prereading materials occurred at the same time as the child study movement, which emphasized a developmental or maturation readiness before cognitive learning could be expected to take place. In fact, although Smith does not directly attribute the change in the scope of reading materials to the concept of developmental readiness, she does acknowledge the influence of the child study movement in that "there was a trend toward recognizing general child development in the teaching of reading" (p. 289). David Russell, one of the authors of the 1948 *Ginn Basic Readers,* also indicated that the child study movement influenced the design of his particular program: "This series views the teaching of reading in the broad perspective of each child's mental, physical, emotional and social development" (Russell, cited in Smith, 1965, p. 289).

A close look at the beginning reading materials published by one textbook company, Scott, Foresman, between the early 20th century and 1950 also demonstrated the influence of the child study movement, particularly the concept of 'maturational readiness,' on the design and content of the material. In 1912, the beginning reading material consisted of the *Primary School Reader, Book One* (Elson, 1912–13), intended as a "first-year course in literature" with stories from children's literature selected "to arouse the strongest interest in 1st grade boys and girls." According to the manual, "attention [was given] to gradation" not only in vocabulary (578 new words were introduced) but in "story elements—plot" as well (p. 5). In 1914, the *Elson-Runkel Primer* was published for the first time, minimally revised as the *Elson Readers, Primer* in 1920 and 1927, and as the *Elson Basic Readers, Primer* in 1930. The 1914 primer presented 303 new words, and the 1920s revisions had 292 words, but the 1930 revision presented only 221 new words. However, in 1921, Scott, Foresman introduced the *Elson Pupil's Hand Chart,* the precursor of the preprimer book, which was minimally revised in 1927 but not called a preprimer until its revision as the *Elson Basic Readers, Preprimer* in 1930. The *Hand Chart* was intended for the child's use "from the first day of school" and presented 81 new words. By 1930, the *Elson Basic Readers, Preprimer* presented only 68 words. Thus the vocabulary load for these beginning materials was reduced from a high of 373 words in the 1921 and 1927 versions to 289 words in the 1930 revision.

A decrease in vocabulary was not the only change in the reading material; the methodology also was revised. For the preprimer and primer materials published prior to 1930, the method, called the "Elson-Runkel Method," established the "told story" as the starting point for instruction, "beginning where the home left off." An emphasis on building a "background of familiarity" before making "the transition from oral to visual interpretation" was presented in the manual:

> The child's delight in the oral story should be made use of in the very first steps of reading. Thus the school, beginning its work where the home leaves off and utilizing the capacities which the child brings with him, builds upon his previous experience. The use of the told story is the natural point of departure in teaching the child to read, for he has acquired in the home the power to translate spoken words into meaning and to visualize situations described by them. (Elson & Runkel, 1921, p. 160)

The Elson-Runkel Method as described in the manual suggests four steps in teaching beginning reading. The first step is the teacher's telling of the complete narrative, a story or poem found in the children's literature of the period including the Mother Goose nursery rhymes. The teacher was required to tell the story as many times as necessary to build children's familiarity with the plot and children were asked to follow and then retell the story using the illustrations in their preprimer and primer books. Although the student's text version of the story was simplified—the full story was only in the teacher's manual—each illustration in the student's book dealt with a major incident in the narrative ("an intimate connection between text and illustration" (p.161)). The second step in the manual was "dramatization" of the story which the children themselves planned and arranged to promote "teamwork" and "better seeing and keener appreciation" of the literature (p. 161). Actual teaching of sentences, words, and "phonetic elements" was the third step, and the reading of the simplified story was the fourth and last step (p. 163). Twenty seatwork lessons accompanied the primer and preprimer readers, and these were designed to "bring into action the pupil's play instinct" (p. 155). Three types of activities were presented: sheets of letters which the child was to cut apart and use to create words; reproductions of the illustrations and words from several of the preprimer and primer stories, which the child was to cut apart and rearrange in order to reconstruct the stories; and sheets with new illustrations followed by questions and answers using familiar words, which the child again cut apart and matched with appropriate illustrations. (The child was to keep his words from these tasks in separate envelopes to reuse).

With the 1930 revision (Elson & Gray, 1930) many of the preprimer and primer stories were dropped, reducing the vocabulary load as already noted, and although the primer manual emphasized that the reading selections were "real stories" from "literary sources" with a definite "plot structure [instead of] routine incidents," teachers were no longer asked to tell (or read) the fuller version of the story to children to build a background for reading. Rather, the manual suggested that the "stories are complete units in themselves" and incorporated a "sequential organization" including "simplicity in content, sentence structure and vocabulary to insure rapid progress, confidence and keen interest" (p. 5). (The 1930 revision of the preprimer introduced the characters Dick and Jane, who ultimately became the main elements in the reading materials published by Scott, Foresman for the next thirty years. The seatwork of the Elson-Runkel Method was replaced with the *Silent Reading Workbook* by 1930, a material that would later become *Think and Do Books,* very similar in format to contemporary workbooks).

In 1937, Scott, Foresman published its first prereading book, *Before We Read* (Gray & Monroe, 1937), because based on "experience and scientific investigations [it has been found that some children] entering 1st grade have not acquired the social adjustment necessary to work effectively with other children or have not developed habits and techniques of work [to] enable them to apply themselves attentively to. . .the mental processes of reading [or they are] speech. . .disabled [and others are] too mentally immature to begin reading." Other children, in their view, do not need prereading work because they have had "good kindergarten and home training and are ready and able to begin reading in early 1st grade." (in "Teacher's Notes and Directions", Gray & Monroe, 1937).

By 1951 when [*The New*] *Before We Read* (Gray, et al., 1951) was revised, the authors were recommending that this readiness book "should be used by *all* children immediately preceding the first pre-primer. . . [as] the final step before children begin 'real reading' " (p. 11). An "innovation" of The New Basic Readers Curriculum Foundation Series, as the 1951 revision of the Scott, Foresman reading program was called, was the introduction of two more prereading or readiness books, *We Read Pictures* and *We Read More Pictures.* According to the guidebook accompanying *We Read Pictures,* these materials were designed to do the following:

> [These materials are] designed to be the initial step in the prereading program for children who are chronologically young or physically, mentally or socially immature for their age. It is of value for children who are obviously in need of oral language development perhaps because of bilingual backgrounds. This book may be used in the kindergarten or preprimary grades in those localities where prereading materials are used before the child enters 1st grade. It may be used in the 1st grade with children who are not yet six years of age or with small groups of 6-year-olds who need a book that especially stresses language skills (Guidebook for *We Read Pictures* by Gray, Artley, Monroe, Arbuthnot, & Gray, 1951, p. 7).

The tasks presented in this book were characterized as "book handling," using "sentence patterns," and "interpreting simple pictures." Use of *We Read Pictures* would "foster success with *Before We Read,* the next step in the prereading program" (p. 7).

In the second readiness book introduced in this revision, *We Read More Pictures* (part of The New Basic Readers Curriculum Foundation Series, Gray et al., 1951), the influence of the maturational perspective espoused by child development theorists is even more apparent:

> Developmental differences are apparent in the ages at which children cut their first teeth or learn to walk and talk. As soon as the teacher begins to work with a group of youngsters at the prereading level, she is aware

> of wide variations in their stages of growth and in their abilities...[This book is designed for] children who are definitely immature and who need a prolonged readiness period. (Guidebook for *We Read More Pictures* by Gray, Artley, Monroe, Arbuthnot, & Gray, 1951, p. 2)

According to the authors, the emphasis was on "visual discrimination, eye-hand coordination, simple language patterns and those thinking and interpretative abilities that are difficult for many children whose mental maturation is slow" (p. 2). Not only were two additional readiness books introduced with this revision, but a "junior primer," *Guess Who,* was published for the first time as well, with the expressed purpose of giving "the slow learning, immature or frequently absent child" more time to master reading (Guidebook for *Guess Who* by Gray, Artley & Gray, 1951, p. 4).

During the revisions of the 1940s, the authors (Gray 1940–47) maintained the Dick and Jane characters but rewrote preprimer stories and, in the process, added another preprimer. (In the 1930s, the *Elson-Gray Basic Preprimer* became *Dick and Jane,* and another preprimer was added, *More Dick and Jane Stories*). In the 1940s, these revised preprimers were called *We Look and See, We Come and Go,* and *We Work and Play,* and the primer, *Fun With Dick and Jane.* These titles remained in the 1951 edition (except for "The New" preceding each title), and the number of new words presented stayed fairly constant: Preprimer vocabulary was 68 in the original *Dick and Jane* preprimer (1930) and remained at about that level through the revisions and additions of the 1930s, 1940s, 1950s and 1960s. Whenever a new level of readiness was introduced, the vocabulary of the preceding level was repeated. Whenever new words were borrowed from a subsequent level as, for example, the ten new words introduced in the junior primer, the vocabulary load was reduced in the next level. In other words, even though new books were added to the series, new vocabulary was not. Instead, the roughly 289 words that were found in the preprimer and primer books of 1930 were just spread out over more books with fewer words.

During the years between 1950 and 1965 a decline in the number of new words was noted by Smith (1965) in the revisions and new reading materials published during this period. For example, an average of only 89 new words was introduced at the primer level, and an average of 59 words was presented at the preprimer level. A study conducted by Klein in 1964 and cited in Chall (1967) on the 1956 revision of the Scott, Foresman reading materials suggests little difference between the 1951 and 1956 revisions with 64 words introduced at the preprimer level and 165 (presumably including the 10 junior primer words) at the primer level. In general, Chall demonstrated that the number of words introduced at the first reader level in Scott, Foresman materials declined by 100 words from 1920 (333 words) to 1962 (230 words), the year that the "Dick and Jane" stories were illustrated by "multiethnic" pictures in a multi-ethnic revision. The point that Chall was making (in addition to her discussion of the place of phonics instruction) was that reading materials had become less challenging for children. It may be argued that the introduction of materials for prereading instruction and the subsequent spreading out of a limited number of new words across many beginning reading books were both direct responses to the notion of developmental readiness and the belief that individual children mature at different developmental rates, some needing more readiness time than others. As early as 1937, the *Before We Read* readiness book was recommended for kindergarten classes, as were the readiness books published subsequently. It appears that these materials were designed for children who were not the requisite 6 years or 6½ years old, the age for "real reading," and thus were for children who participated in kindergartens. A relatively small proportion of children attended kindergarten then, as opposed to contemporary children, so that the use of readiness materials was also recommended for first grade.

An examination of the 1987 edition (Allington et al., 1987) of the Scott, Foresman reading materials designed for kindergarten and the beginning of first grade suggests that these materials are not substantially different from those of the thirties, forties, and fifties in the number of words or the type of tasks presented. For example, the 1987 kindergarten book introduces only four words, all of them color words, along with tasks involving visual discrimination and recognition of the letters of the alphabet, sound–symbol relationships for four phonemes, picture interpretation, color matching and recognition, and the language concepts representing directionality. The 1930 prereading book introduced 6 words and had the same types of tasks, with the exception of letter recognition and sound–symbol relationships. In the 1987 first-grade readiness book, 10 words are introduced as well as sound–symbol relationships. Thus, 296 words are introduced by the end of the primer level in 1987, compared to 238 in 1978, 164 in 1951, and 238 in 1937, a cumulative increase of about 50 words in a period spanning more than fifty years and many revisions. The number of words introduced at the very beginning levels, in the kindergarten and readiness levels, is quite consistent also. (Although the 1978 edition by Aaron et al. introduced an uncharacteristically high number of readiness words, it also introduced an uncharacteristically low number of primer and first-reader words and introduced only one word at the kindergarten level: the child's own name.) The very first readiness book (1937) required children to recognize 6 words, and the 1987 readiness book (which is suggested for first grade or the latter half of kindergarten, as the 1937 edition was) lists 10 (see figure 11–1).

Although the difficulty of the materials suggested for beginning reading in the kindergarten and first grade has remained fairly consistent since 1930, published materials other than Scott, Foresman may be considerably more difficult. Therefore, I examined another widely used contemporary beginning reading program: the 1989 edition of the Silver, Burdett and Ginn *World of Reading*. This program introduces skills similar to those seen in Scott, Foresman and a comparable number of words in materials at the kindergarten and beginning first-grade levels (Pearson et al., 1989). In the Silver, Burdett and Ginn kindergarten program, called *Hickory, Dickory, Dock*, there are no words taught, other than the child's name and, like the Scott, Foresman program, the skills focus on listening to stories, recognizing the letters of the alphabet, and associating letters with sounds. The Silver, Burdett and Ginn (Pearson et al., 1989) readiness materials, which are used either in kindergarten or at the beginning of first grade, introduce 16 words and provide a review of letter and sound discrimination. By the time children finish the end of the Silver, Burdett and Ginn primer materials—usually around midspring of the first-grade school year—about 330 words have been introduced to them, a number that is comparable to other publishers' materials.

Even though many policy participants believed that kindergarten children today are doing the work of first grade, the published materials that I examined did not appear to be more difficult than earlier editions. The reading tasks required of children before first grade, and through the primer level in first grade, have not changed significantly.

Nonetheless, materials that are more difficult than those that are recommended for kindergarten children may be used in kindergarten classes. Some researchers have also suggested that the total numbers of words introduced to children by the end of first grade is increasing (see, e.g., Barr, 1985). However, these are questions for future research.

Thus the perceptions held by many New York State early childhood professionals that the kindergarten is more academic than in the past and more focused on teaching abstract reading skills does not seem to be supported by an examination of the difficulty of the materials. Furthermore, these program professionals and the literature cited by

FIGURE 11–1
Cumulative Number of Words Presented by Level and Edition of the Scott, Foresman & Company Reading Materials from Early 1900s to Present

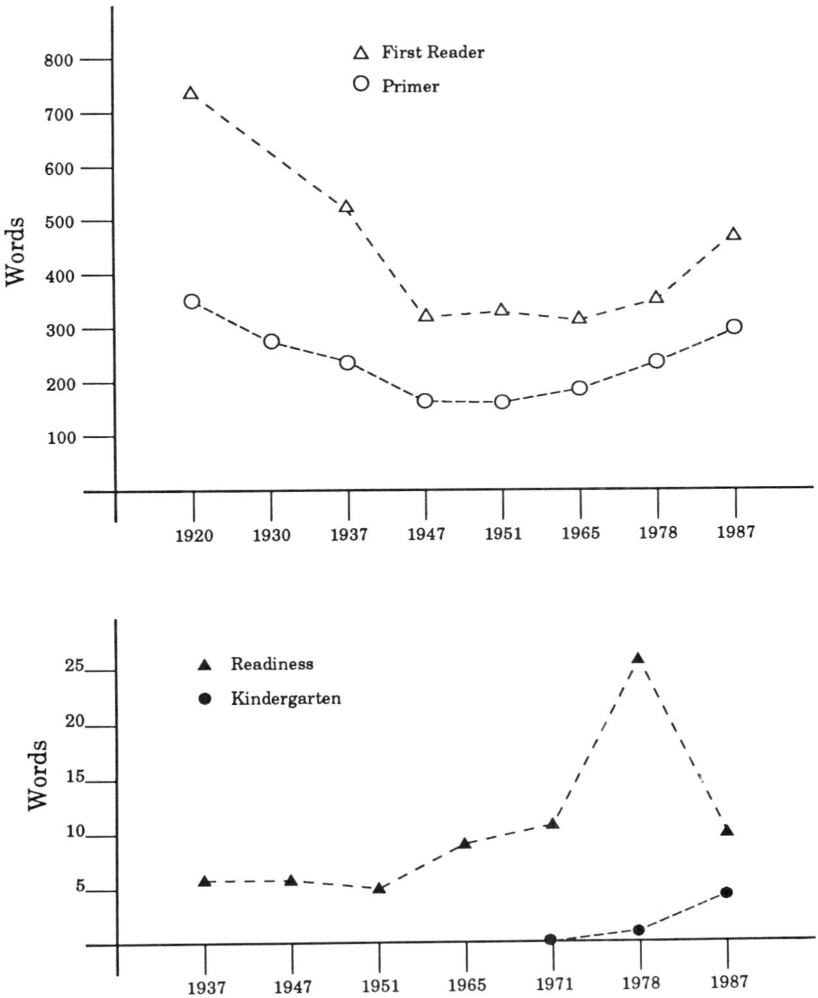

these professionals strongly suggest that traditional basal reading books, paper and pencil activities, and workbooks are inappropriate for children before first grade. It is ironic that these very materials, the prereading or readiness materials designed for kindergarten, are a response to the child development research of the 1930s in which physiological or maturational readiness became a preeminent concern of education. In the Scott, Foresman programs, these readiness materials replaced story reading, storytelling, and dramatization as prereading activities because it was believed that children younger than six years old were not ready for "real reading."

12. THE SHARED HISTORY: LITERACY, YOUNG CHILDREN, AND EARLY SCHOOLING

Preparing all children for school requires, above all, imagination and will—not vast amounts of money. It calls for a determination on the part of all citizens to build a better world for children, moving them to the top of the agenda. . . Nothing is more worth doing than easing the pain and improving the life chances of vulnerable, blameless children.

—Ernest L. Boyer, President of the Carnegie Foundation for the Advancement of Teaching

LITERACY, AMONG THE Puritans, was requisite for salvation. When they were without the benefit of schools, parents in colonial times were themselves held morally and legally responsible for teaching their very young children to read the Scriptures. Based on early records, particularly those in Massachusetts, historians also have established that young children between the ages of two and six frequently attended whatever schools were available, including the dame school and the common school (Kaestle & Vinovskis, 1980). Outside of New England and the mid-Atlantic region, however, any kind of schooling was less available for children of all ages. Literacy among Black children was rare prior to the Civil War and was forbidden for years in southern slave states (Cunningham & Osborn, 1979).

At the beginning of the nineteenth century, school bureaucracies were taking form in northeastern urban areas and the so-called grammar schools were gradually established. Children who could not already read and write were not allowed to attend these grammar schools but could and did attend private primary or "reading and writing" schools. Public school officials of this era believed that there were "few [parents] among us...unequal to the task of teaching the elements of the letters...[and] the office of instruction belongs to parents."[1] Further, school officials also believed there was sufficient "leisure" for parents, primarily women who were relegated to a domestic role, to discharge these educational responsibilities.

By the mid-nineteenth century, the responsibility for teaching children to read was gradually shifted from the home to the school. Additionally, public officials began to perceive that the resources available to poor parents for the education of their young children were unequal, and therefore such responsibility for early reading and writing instruction on the part of less advantaged parents was unduly burdensome.

With the advent of publicly funded primary schools—brought about because school officials ultimately realized that poor parents could not afford the tuition for private reading and writing schools—the entry of children under the age of four was prohibited. At issue was the cost and the increasing standardization of schools by age and grade, not whether schooling was beneficial for these young children. Nevertheless, children younger than four continued to attend private schools and common schools in areas where such schools were not highly bureaucratized.[2]

Expert knowledge, in the form of professional knowledge about the content of early childhood education, made its debut with the infant schools of the early nineteenth century.[3] Based loosely upon the ideas of Pestalozzi, schools were established for poor children as young as two years old in the belief that early childhood education would uplift impoverished children both intellectually and morally. Such early education would not repeat the "tedious pedagogy" of the common school but instead would relate to the developmental level of the child. Nonetheless, in an attempt to prove their efficacy these schools taught children as young as two years old to read. Widely heralded as a means to "banish" poverty "with all its attendant evils" (*5th Annual Report*, Infant School Society of the City of Boston, 1834, in May and Vinovskis, 1977, p. 62), and popular among middle-class parents who wished to enrich the experiences of their own children, the tenure of the infant school was nevertheless brief. A more balanced view of child development began to be articulated among educational professionals, and concurrently, medical literature on the deleterious effects of early reading ("precocity") on the later development of children gained currency among the middle class.

Unlike the infant school, the kindergarten—an educational experience for young children also based on Pestalozzian principles—survived, flourished, and continues to the present day as an established part of the public school system. Brought to this county in the latter part of the nineteenth century, the kindergarten[4] provided a group experience for children from three to six or seven years old in which they discovered nature through active manipulation of objects, rather than alphabet learning or book reading. Children "in the company of equals" were taught by mother figures who did the kinds of things mothers would do with children if they had the leisure and "strength": games, songs, and finger plays (Kraus-Boelte, 1907, p. 36). Like the infant school, the kindergarten was seen as social reform, a way to rescue the "vicious and improvident" immigrant children of that era from "drifting into our penal institutions" and enabling them to do "constructive work in our civilization" (W. T. Harris, Superintendent of the St. Louis Public Schools, 1880, in Bremner, 1971, p. 1458). The ideals of the kindergarten—to make it a "happy place" for children—contrasted with the traditional pedagogy of the nineteenth-century public school but merged nicely with the twentieth-century progressive view of education articulated by Dewey and the child study movement initiated by Hall. Professionals in education and psychology espoused notions of play being the work of the child and of the need for developmental readiness for cognitive tasks. Such beliefs insulated the kindergarten from reading instruction well into contemporary times. Most influential was the work of physician Arnold Gesell and his associates, who proposed the notion of a physiological readiness or maturation for learning. This construct of maturation was applied to written language learning with the classic study by Morphett and Washburne (1931), who believed that the mental age of 6½ years was the optimal age for beginning reading instruction.

Thus, by the late nineteenth century, publicly funded early childhood education had been proposed in terms that made it desirable to public officials: the equalization of educational resources for children of poor and immigrant parents who would otherwise be unable to obtain private early childhood education; the belief that early intervention would somehow eradicate poverty and make children of the poor contributing members of society; and congruence between the content of early childhood education and the prevailing expertise about what was beneficial for all children.

In the 1960s, a pressing societal concern about the children of the poor and an infusion of new knowledge gave rise to another preschool program: Head Start. As a result of the research of psychologists such as Benjamin Bloom and J. McVicker Hunt, policymakers of this era came to believe that cognitive deficits attributable to poverty could be ameliorated by education before kindergarten age. The federal government established publicly funded preschool programs to demonstrate this effect. An emphasis on basic skills such as reading was prevalent at this time, and schools were targeted for reform to undo what many viewed as the excesses of the progressive education movement. Hence the preschool programs of this period were evaluated on the extent to which the achievement of poor children was bolstered. Concern with the content or curriculum of early childhood programs was much in evidence during the period of the late sixies and early seventies, and different curricular approaches to preschool education were studied according to longitudinal or follow through models of evaluation. Although achievement in basic skills was the primary criterion for measuring the success of early intervention in the first Head Start studies, subsequent evaluations focused on the extent to which preschool participants were socialized into the culture of school. Socialization as a goal of early childhood education was not a concept that originated with Head Start, however; it had been cited often by advocates of the federally sponsored "nursery education" of the 1930s and 1940s as a reason to continue funding of these preschools after the depression and war effort ended.

Day nurseries—the precursor to the child day care center—were first established in the mid-nineteenth century to help poor working mothers. These centers did not represent mainstream middle-class values and were not perceived as an educational service. Rather, day nurseries were associated with social services and the welfare system; they were support for poor and "unfortunate" families.[5] By contrast, the nursery school, established in the early twentieth century, was clearly associated with education. Begun as a "laboratory" for universities engaged in child study, the nursery school became part of the middle-class child's educational experiences. A rapid increase in the number of nursery schools was attributable to government support during the depression of the 1930s, when funding was made available for WPA nursery schools and later, during World War II, for Lanham nursery schools.[6] These nursery schools were housed mainly in the public schools, but public schools were responsible for neither their administration nor their funding. Supporters of these nursery schools, seeking to have their tenure extended, emphasized that these early childhood programs were nursery *education* and not to be confused with child day care. The advocates of the Lanham centers wanted the nursery schools to become "institutionalized" within the public school system "like the kindergarten" had. In citing the reasons why public schooling should be "extended downward," these advocates were targeting middle-class children and clearly establishing the notion of socialization into "American habits or attitudes" as the goal of public preschool programs. Such habits could be learned only in group interactions under the "guidance of professionals" (as opposed to parents) and included "a spirit of cooperation and fair play, independence. . .self-confidence (Engleman & Nash, 1948, p. 363). . .being a good sport. . . taking it on the chin" (Levinger & Murphy, 1948, p. 18).

Despite their popularity, at the end of the war in 1945, all federal funding for the preschool programs was terminated, and these public preschools closed. Mothers "with their lean years behind them"—meaning the depression and their work on behalf of the war effort—were expected to return to the home in anticipation of their "dual role" of homemaker and mother (Gans, 1948, p. 11). Private nursery school education, however, expanded and flourished from the time of the Second World War to the present day.

Thus, twentieth century early childhood programs were reluctantly funded by the public and only in extraordinary historical times. They helped to put unemployed teachers to work during the depression and allowed mothers to participate in the labor force during the Second World War. Once these social conditions changed, all government support was terminated and no state except California continued the Lanham centers after federal subsidies ended. Clearly, a government role in early childhood programs even when it was touted as "education" and housed in the public schools was not viewed as legitimate at that time. In many respects, there was no consensus that early childhood programs belonged under the aegis of "education," an attitude that persists to the present day. Professional administrators were about evenly divided on whether "welfare" or the schools should supervise such programs, and the majority of these professionals in mid-twentieth century believed that the schools should not fund early childhood. As advocates of the Lanham centers were quick to point out, the fact that these centers were funded separately from the public schools hastened their termination. Issues of aegis and funding, which may be characterized as questions of bureaucratic responsibility, continue to define how early childhood is perceived, and these issues appear to have at least as much impact on policy in present day discussions of public school for four-year-olds as do issues of curricula or program content.

In the 1980s, the issue of publicly funded early childhood programs for four-year-olds came into prominence once again. The form that these programs would take—the actual program proposals and, particularly, the rationale for such programs—have changed significantly in New York State since the concept was first introduced in 1983 by Gordon Ambach, who was then the state's education commissioner. He proposed a program to accelerate children through the school system starting at age four, because kindergartens and nursery schools were purportedly teaching the reading curriculum of the first grade. The early childhood issue was next defined in terms of equal educational opportunity for poor children and intervention to reduce high school dropout rates and welfare dependency. In order to emphasize that poor women needed not only educational experiences for their children but also child care beyond the 2½ hour school day to enable them to work, Governor Cuomo in 1987 asked for a full-day program for disadvantaged four-year-old children, a day that included an educational component and a child care component. Because legislators could not agree on how to differentiate the education component from the child care component and, relatedly, on how to determine which bureaucracy should provide auspice and funding and set standards and oversight, the state legislature did not authorize the governor's 1987 proposal.

The legislature did acknowledge that early childhood programs were on the policy agenda, however, by authorizing the Council on Children and Families to prepare recommendations for a New York State initiative in this area and to report these recommendations.[7] In order to placate both interested groups, child care providers and education providers, the legislature increased funding for child day care through the Department of Social Services and for prekindergarten through the State Education Department.[8] During this period, prior to the governor's 1988 State of the State message to the legislature, I conducted my interviews with policy participants in New York to ascertain their perceptions of the issue of public school for four-year-olds and the role that literacy learning might play in the formulation of a public school responsibility in early childhood education.

As I noted previously, the scenario in New York State closely resembled the process of agenda setting described by Kingdon (1984); Cobb, Ross & Ross, (1976); and Nelson (1978). Kingdon's model, particularly the notion of a serendipitous coming together of policy, politics, and problems, appears to characterize the climate of receptivity in New York toward an early childhood initiative for four-year-old children. The demographics of New York State are such that the governor and the state legislature are looking at early childhood education as a way to reduce the dropout rate and welfare dependency among the increasingly large proportion of youth who are poor and minority. Women who work, now the norm rather than the exception in New York as elsewhere, have precipitated a demand for child care that far surpasses its availability, a fact noted by the Council on Children and Families in its 1987 report to the governor and the legislature. These two conditions have set the stage for a search for potential solutions. The governor himself has identified early childhood education as a priority, becoming a visible participant in the formulation of policy proposals to address these conditions, which are now viewed as problems requiring policy initiatives. Which proposals will ultimately be selected as solutions to these problems remains to be seen. By proposing universal and publicly funded education for all four-year-olds in his 1988 State of the State message to the Legislature, Governor Cuomo transformed the issue from one of equal opportunity and early intervention benefiting primarily the disadvantaged and the working poor to an issue of universal preschool entitlement. Because the Governor has now included early childhood priorities in the executive branch program proposals for several years, it may be said that the "policy window" is open to statewide initiatives in this area. Public school for four-year-olds has reached the stage—variously called "proposal specification" (Kingdon, 1984), "issue maintenance" (Nelson, 1978), or "formal agenda" (Cobb, Ross & Ross, 1976)—where substantive decisions may be made on this issue.

Looking back on the interview data, it is possible to observe the complexity of the process through which New York State policy participants defined public responsibility toward children under the age of school entry. As Cobb et al.(1976) suggested, the more heterogeneous the community—in this case, New York State—the more complex the process through which agendas are built. Further, as all three models suggest, the support of the larger society is crucial in order for any particular issue to become enacted into policy. Improving the opportunities of poor children has been a value espoused by contemporary policy participants, as it was those of the past. However, narrowly defining the issue as one of equal opportunity might limit middle-class support. Without the support of an interested middle-class public, it was seen as unlikely that substantive decision making could take place. Defining the issue as one of early intervention, not academic intervention as in Head Start but intervention in self-initiated learning that would have broad-based social outcomes, was also seen as limited by a lack of perceived benefits to the middle class, despite well-promulgated research on the benefits of such intervention for poor children. Given the second set of demographic indicators, that of women in the labor force as well as the high proportion of middle-class children already enrolled in preschool programs, an early childhood initiative that was targeted toward a broader, more mainstream constituency might have more support. The 1988 proposal of Governor Cuomo is such an initiative. According to the three agenda-setting models reviewed for the present study, however, high economic costs may limit the feasibility of issues. Universal schooling for four-year-olds has significant budgetary implications. Whether wide public support by broad-based constituencies will outweigh the high economic costs associated with such a program is not yet known.

As this issue has been reworked, from Ambach's floating of the early entry proposal in 1983 to Cuomo's 1988 policy initiative, it is informative to note how the definitions of public responsibility toward four-year-olds appear to have changed. Each of the agenda models attributes much importance to the way the issue is labelled or defined. Only those labels that evoke positive responses should be retained, according to Nelson (1978), and the issue of universal education for four-year-olds is testimony to the way problems can be redefined in a search for the best fit between public perceptions and feasible solutions.

In summary, the issue originally was cast as one of curriculum acceleration: kindergarten children were doing the work of first grade, and thus, prekindergarten children should do the work of kindergarten. It was then recast by Ambach (1985) as an issue of equal educational opportunity for children of parents without the resources to purchase preschool education. Cuomo continued to identify the issue with the disadvantaged but expanded it to include a child care component in 1987. The governor's proposal generated a great deal of activity on the part of lobbyists for child care providers, who saw an opportunity to associate child care with the education establishment rather than social services. At this juncture, policy professionals, as opposed to the program professionals, viewed education and child care as separate functions, primarily because each is administered by different bureaucracies. Program professionals, on the other hand, emphasized that child care was in fact education. In their view, an emphasis on social learning rather than literacy learning differentiated early childhood education from the primary grades. In the 1988 Message to the Legislature, Cuomo refocused the issue on education, but he expanded the proposal to include children from all families, not just the working poor or disadvantaged.

Interviews with policy participants suggested that even though education is viewed as an allowable, even preferred, expenditure on the part of government, the specific type of early childhood program that might be considered an educational program rather than a social services program is not yet clear. Thus, policy participants rely on funding and aegis to define an education responsibility. The content of early childhood education—what such programs should accomplish and for whom—is left to the program professionals in New York State.

Program experts decide what it is children should be doing in early childhood education and, according to the interview data, these experts do not see literacy development as a goal of preschool education. The construct of maturational readiness articulated in the 1930s has prevailed among these contemporary program specialists. Thus, reading and writing, narrowly perceived as "workbook" activities or "commercial" programs, are not viewed as developmentally appropriate for preschool children. The reading curriculum of first grade is thought to have encroached on preschool education, particularly the kindergarten, which is widely perceived to be teaching reading skills formerly learned in first grade.

Neither the narrow view of maturational readiness nor the narrow view of reading espoused by New York State program specialists is necessarily shared by the larger early childhood profession. The curriculum developed by the Perry Preschool Project as well as the most recent statement on developmentally appropriate practices prepared by the NAEYC appear to incorporate literacy development within the domain of language learning. Regarding the incursion of first-grade reading into the kindergarten and prekindergarten programs, there is scant research to justify the perceptions of these program specialists. Although the beginning materials associated with basal reading programs do appear to be commonly used in kindergarten classrooms, materials published by at least two major textbook companies do not appear to have changed significantly in what is presented at the beginning levels. Ironically, these very beginning reading materials—which are now universally rejected as developmentally inappropriate by early childhood specialists, were developed in the 1930s and 1940s in response to the theory of maturational development still espoused by the program specialists, at least in New York. In other words, the construct of reading readiness and concomitant "developmental" instruction[9] were created for children who were judged, then as now, not ready to participate in reading and writing.

Thus, public school for four-year-olds can be said to be an issue whose time has come in New York State. However, even as New York policy participants prepare to invest in what they believe to be the future competence of four-year-old children, literacy development is not viewed as having a prominent role in the school lives of the children. In an attempt to underscore the attitude that literacy is not taught, but somehow learned, the New York State Education Department Bureau of Child Development (1982) published this account by a third-grade "former non-reader":

> How come my other teachers couldn't teach me to read even spending all morning in a reading group, and this year you let me just fool around with all sorts of things and all of a sudden I can read? (p. 9)

It may very well be that this child agonized over learning to read for several years before he finally figured it out. It may indeed seem to him that his present teacher lets him "just fool around with all sorts of things" rather than recycling instruction that was obviously unsuccessful the first time and probably humiliating as well. It is possible that the child is right—the teacher let the child just fool around—but I doubt it. As the successful national literacy program in New Zealand has demonstrated (Clay, 1985) and, here in this country, as the national evaluation of Reading Recovery in the state of Ohio has confirmed, "recovering" children who fall behind their peers, even during first grade, is hard work (Pinnell, Fried & Estice, 1991). It requires intensive assistance by teachers who are sensitive observers of children and enormously knowledgeable about the process of learning to read and write. I wonder if the program professionals in New York really believe that children will "just learn" to read without assistance, whether by parent, peer or school teacher? More to the point, is the message a responsible one, particularly since so many children in this state are deemed at risk of failure in school?

EPILOGUE

I began this inquiry several years ago. Like many of the policy participants interviewed for the study, I believed that if public schools were to serve four-year-olds, they should do a better job than they had with many five- and six-year-olds. Like the policy participants in the study,

I also believed that four-year-olds and, indeed, all children, should be protected from inappropriate practices that could diminish their potential as learners and alienate them from school. I agreed with the early childhood professionals who said that literacy learning does not begin with the letters of the alphabet. Literacy learning cannot be pulled apart from the lives children live. Knowledge about written language—like all other knowledge—is personally constructed out of the everyday stuff of our lives.

Unlike many of the early childhood professionals in the study, however, I believed that reading and writing *do* belong in the preschool—absolutely massive amounts of playful, joyful, even raucous literacy activities. Yes, even letters of the alphabet. I still believe this.

Literacy is for all children, not just for those who come to kindergarten and first grade already knowing just about all they need to be readers. I believe in the tyranny of experience over development. Early childhood programs can be powerful equalizers of children's early literacy experiences—experiences that invite all children to become "makers of stories."

I know that children differ in the personal histories they bring to school and families differ in the resources they have to promote the well-being of their children. But anthropologists, linguists, and psychologists tell us that even the poorest children participate fully in the language and culture of their community. Such diversity among "ways of knowing" should be a resource for schools—including preschools—that must prepare children to take their places in an increasingly multicultural world. These differences should not become the rationale for not teaching all children whatever it is they need to know to participate fully in our literate culture. If we want to engage children in literacy and to have them value it, these differences should become the text that teachers weave between the culture of the home and the culture of the school.

I believe there is a trap for many children in the concept of 'developmentally appropriate.' For some 'developmentalists,' including several interviewed for the study, children's cognitive growth is biologically fixed and the timetable is not influenced by instruction. In the area of early literacy, such "nativist" (Smith & Shepard, 1988) perspectives might preclude reading to children who prefer to spend all of their time at the sandbox. Children who claim that they cannot write a story or their names might not be invited to explore with paper and pens if we believe that children's thinking passes through invariant stages regardless of how we support their learning.

On the other hand, those who hold a Vygotskian perspective, who are also called 'developmentalists', believe that instruction should move ahead of development and pull it along. With assistance, children are able to construct meanings for tasks that they could not understand on their own. This instruction or scaffolding enables children to perform tasks that they could not otherwise do. But such instruction actually *transforms* the child's development so that tomorrow the child is able to independently do what he could do *only with assistance* today.

The interaction between *instruction* and *development* is complex, and an uncontested definition of the relationship does not exist. Nonetheless, personal beliefs about the relationship between instruction and development are extremely important to the way teachers approach children and to their expectations for learning. For example, teachers who hold a "nativist" view do not believe that they can accelerate the development of an unready child, whereas teachers with "interactionist" views believe in themselves as able to "bring children along" (Smith & Shepard, 1988).

Often, under the guise of development, four- and five-year olds are screened and sorted into those who are ready and those who are not. Those who are deemed "ready" are often the children who are already privy to the literate culture of school. Like the mainstream children described by Heath (1983) and the middle-class preschoolers identified by Adams (1990), children who are ready to learn in school are those who can take the language of books and create their own texts; they are children who have had literally thousands of hours of one-to-one guidance in learning about written language at home and thousands more hours in private preschools.

Often, under the guise of development, those who are deemed "not ready" risk being further isolated from the very literacy experiences they need to become literate. All too often, these children are poor children.

Low-income children described by Teale (1986), for example, rarely participated in storybook reading with their parents or received guidance from them on the uses and form of print. Nonetheless, low-income parents care about the education of their children and want them to learn to read and write (Lareau, 1989). Unlike many mainstream families, however, they often do not know what it is that schools expect of their children upon entry to kindergarten, nor do schools tell them.

One very articulate African-American mother, for example, recently spoke at a forum on improving the schools in the city where she lives because she was concerned about her own kindergarten child learning to read and write:

> Nobody says, "This is what she should be doing in kindergarten. This is what she should know for 1st grade." By third or fourth grade I know more about reading levels. I don't know if she's on target [now]. I am uneducated to the system about what to expect. . . [In] Head Start all she did was play. It could be a good program but a child shouldn't just be beginning [to learn about reading] in kindergarten. Our kids need basics. If you can read and comprehend [you can succeed] (Albany Citizens for Education, Albany, N.Y., January 30, 1989).

Although I did not question this mother about her child's particular preschool experience, she is likely right that many preschool programs provide precious little guidance in reading and writing. This is so because, as I suggest in the study, reading and writing have been narrowly defined and frequently misconstrued as developmentally inappropriate and as passive learning. At the time of my study, program professionals viewed reading and writing as academics taught through a "skills workbook" approach, rather than as language processes deeply embedded in the cultural life of the child.

Unfortunately for low-income children, who are the majority of those eligible for publicly funded preschool, the idea that reading and writing are developmentally inappropriate could prevail upon the providers of such services. A teacher in one publicly-funded preschool program told me, for example, that unlike the middle-class preschool where she had taught previously, the program for disadvantaged children was not "academic." She said that she "can't teach" the letters of the alphabet:

> But I do with their names. Whenever I write their names on their pictures or whatever art work they are doing, I reinforce the letters and my afternoon class, you know, sings "A, B, C, D". If I was ever observed. . .

When I asked incredulously whether she was really not allowed to teach the alphabet, she said:

> Well, they say if they're ready for it. I can't have an alphabet up in my room, but I can teach letters [in their names]. . .They want to see lots of art work, they want you to have all of your centers, but they don't want to see too many educational things.

I asked who was the "they" who forbid the alphabet and "educational things." She replied, "the state."

In an interesting juxtaposition of philosophy, a typical school day in the life of a four-year-old child named Ben who attends the most exclusive private preschool in the same metropolitan area was recently described in a local newspaper article (Preller, 1991). Ben, the child of professional parents, participated in storybook reading at least three different times during the day and had not one, but two "lessons" on the letter K! Such discrepant practices exist because private preschools, such as the one Ben attends, do not have to conform to the state curriculum guidelines promulgated for publicly funded programs for low-income children.

My argument here is not about teaching the letters of the alphabet. I suspect that the ban on displaying the alphabet is symbolic. Letters of the alphabet represent academic learning—the purview, if you will, of the elementary school. Merely lifting the ban on alphabet teaching will not suddenly transform publicly funded prekindergarten programs into communities of children and teachers who value literacy. As skilled observers of children have told us, children value literacy and learn to read and write in *responsive* literacy environments.

My argument is instead about *responsibility*—responsibility in the sense of "promise in return." What is the *promise* of education for four-year-olds, particularly four-year-olds from families who are poor or themselves illiterate? I submit that the preschool must celebrate and affirm what each child knows but also extend and elaborate this knowledge so that each child can become literate. To do less would simply maintain the "home advantage"[10] of children who are "ready to learn" and abort the promise of education for those who are not.

APPENDIX

DATA COLLECTION AND ANALYSIS PROCEDURES

The study is "naturalistic inquiry," based in large part on the data collection and analytic procedures described by Lincoln and Guba (1985). In naturalistic inquiry, exploratory questions are posed but the design of the study is not completely specified at the outset. However, naturalistic inquiry develops in characteristic ways and these patterns are described by Lincoln and Guba as "successive iterations" of purposive sampling, inductive analysis, theory-building, and the "projection of next steps." The researcher is the human instrument "doing what comes naturally"—using tacit or intuitive knowledge in addition to "propositional" or theory-based knowledge and using methods that are suited to "humanly implemented inquiry," such as interviewing and examining documents and archives (p. 187). The research steps are repeated until the information becomes redundant and an explanatory theory or description can be constructed from the analysis (p. 188). The final step is the writing of the case report—an interpretation of what was found in the study (p. 189).

The purpose of the study was twofold: (a) to describe and explain the part that literacy learning plays in discussions of public school for four-year-olds, an issue that is said to be on the contemporary policy agenda, and (b) to relate contemporary perceptions to the past. It was assumed that an historical analysis of the role of literacy learning in early schooling would inform the contemporary analysis and that themes of literacy learning and early schooling may be recursive. Thus, the historical analysis of relevant educational literature produced over approximately the last century became one part of the data collection; contemporary documents and interviews became another part.

Unlike "experimentation," which isolates the phenomenon under investigation from its context in order to manipulate and observe (or "control") variables, the present research strategy is an attempt to "deal with the entangled situation between phenomenon and context" (Yin, 1989, p. 23). In particular, the language of the participants—both participants in the history of early schooling who left a legacy of their writings and present day policymakers whose perceptions were recorded and transcribed—constitutes the data base (explained more fully below) from which my categories emerged.

Apriori models of agenda setting (Cobb & Ross, 1976; Kingdon, 1984; and Nelson, 1978, 1984) were reviewed at the outset of the study, not to predict how the issue of public school for four-year-olds came to be prominent at this point in history, but rather to help formulate patterns in the interaction of issues with contexts that might lend explanatory or descriptive power to the analysis. Thus, instead of theoretical propositions to guide the analysis, a *descriptive framework* guides the analysis. The historical analysis is a description of what was important to those who wrote of earlier attempts to teach young children and how the perceptions of these activists reflected the events and knowledge of their times. (See Babbie, 1986, for similar examples of analytical techniques used to develop "historical/comparative perspective.") A chronology of early preprimary schooling was developed, along with a chronology of the prevailing notions of literacy learning for young children as explained in the educational literature of the period. The introduction of different preprimary-type institutions for children—including the present public school for four-year-olds— were compared across time periods to determine what "classes" or categories marked participants' understandings of how and why children should go to school, what reading had to do with early schooling, which children or whose children they were talking about, and the convergence of these perceptions with the social conditions or values of the era. With the perceptions of contemporary participants in particular, categories are expressed in their own professional and personal terms, not translated into the analytic language of the researcher, a distinction that Spradley (1979, pp. 17–18) feels is important to make.

Although naturalistic inquiry depends on the trustworthiness of the human instrument for much of its credibility (Lincoln and Guba, 1985), there are steps in the collection and analysis of the data that can also establish the validity of the case report. Yin (1989, p. 95) cites the use of multiple sources of evidence to provide multiple measures of the same phenomenon, commonly referred to as "triangulation" (p.

97) by qualitative methodologists. In the present study, three sources of information were used and compared to construct links or "chains of evidence" (p. 102) across time periods and ideas:

1. Documentation. These sources included documentary histories of American children (Bremner, 1970–74) and American education (Cohen, 1974)—original documents produced at different points over the last two hundred years and compiled in two multivolume collections—as well as secondary analyses that related the issues of early childhood education and literacy learning. Research on this topic reported in the contemporary educational literature, and education news stories in the mass media and specialized education newspapers were also reviewed. Memoranda, speeches, legislation and other documentation submitted by informants or referred to in interviews were also analyzed for thematic content. In addition, curriculum materials, in particular, those published by High/Scope and Scott, Foresman and Company which were designed for children and teachers to use at preprimary and primary levels were analyzed for their treatment of literacy learning.
2. Archival records. The Yearbooks of the National Society for the Study of Education published from the beginning of the twentieth century to the present day were analyzed for historical trends in the education of young children and the emergence of ideas on literacy acquisition at the preprimary levels. Current Population Reports and the earlier Decennial Publications of the Bureau of the Census as well as other statistical reports published by the federal Department of Labor and the Department of Education were used to ascertain preprimary enrollment trends. Resolutions, position papers, and research reports on public school for four-year-olds published by advocacy and interest groups and professional associations were analyzed for thematic content.
3. Interviews. Open-ended interviews were conducted with three policy participants and focused interviews, with fourteen. Thirteen focused interviews were tape recorded and transcribed. Interview time ranged from thirty minutes (the last interview) to 3½ hours. Purposive sampling to ensure representative perspectives was employed. An interview format with questions designed to elicit structural, contrasting, and explanatory information (such as the ethnographic interview described by Spradley, 1979, p. 60) was submitted to participants beforehand.

TABLE A-1
New York State Policy Participants Interviewed for the Study

Policy Participants	*Representing*
Executive Office	
EX 1	
EX 2	
EX 3	
EX 4	
EX 5	
EX 6	Education
	Human Services
Legislative Office	Budget
LEG 1	
LEG 2	
LEG 3	
LEG 4	
LEG 5	
Interest Groups	Schools
IG 1	Early Childhood Professionals
IG 2	Public Advocacy Research
IG 3	Children
IG 4	State Education Agency
IG 5	

Besides establishing validity, concerns with the reliability of case reports can be mitigated by maintaining an "evidentiary base" separate from the report itself and retrievable by an auditor (Yin, 1989, p. 98). Notes, transcripts, tabular material, archives and documents should be organized and categorized in a way that is not elaborate but provides enough information so that the data base may be inspected. In the present study, all original transcripts, tapes and interview notes are dated and coded for the affiliation of participants and filed; documents either cited by the participants or submitted by them are indexed on each participant file. Other documents are indexed and filed alphabetically by type of information (research, interest group position paper, etc.) as are notes and abstracts of archival materials. Copies of the transcripts and historical writings are cut up and sorted into matrices that attempt to track the persistence of ideas (represented by the language of the participants) on early schooling and/or literacy over time and the convergence of these ideas with other historical events. These matrices or charts, graphs, and other visual collections and tabular material are appropriately indexed and filed as part of the data analysis procedure and retrievable from the author for review.

NOTES

CHAPTER 1

1. This commitment appeared again in the text of the goals statement adopted by the National Governors' Association several weeks later (NGA, 1990, in *Education Week,* Mar. 7, 1990).

2. Children are behind schedule when they are unable to successfully do the tasks required by the classroom teacher. The tasks vary according to teacher, school, and district, but they are likely to include being able to fluently read the books used in first grade and, ultimately, achieving a score on standardized tests that falls into the general range of scores earned by other first grade children in the same school.

3. Literacy activities include any activities involving reading and writing.

4. William Teale (1986) recently described the home literacy activities—including storybook routines—experienced by low-income children that he had been observing over the past several years. Few of the children from Teale's study participated in storybook routines. Extrapolating from Teale's data, Adams estimates that by the time such children reach first grade, they will have experienced only around twenty-five hours of storybook reading and only about two hundred hours of additional "guidance" about print.

5. Early cognitive and emotional gains demonstrated by Head Start participants were not maintained, at least in the numerical estimates of effects produced in this metanalysis of extant Head Start data reports.

6. The three curriculum models were DISTAR (Bereiter & Englemann, 1966), High/Scope Perry Preschool Project (Weikart et al., 1971), and traditional "nursery school."

CHAPTER 2

1. The selection of literature that actually was reviewed from the three centuries of writing potentially available is itself a sampling process, and as such I should make it explicit. Because access to historical records is limited, particularly school records and the very early literature, this review relies heavily on the analyses of educational practices in seventeenth- and eighteenth-century Puritan New England written by Moran and Vinovskis (1986), Kaestle (1983), Strickland (1982), and Soltow and Stevens (1981), and accounts of education in early nineteenth-century Massachusetts by May and Vinovskis (1977) and particularly Kaestle and Vinovskis (1980). For my history of early childhood education among Black children I am endebted to Cunningham and Osborn (1979). In these very focused descriptions of the evolution of early school arrangements, many if not all of the important issues of literacy and preschool education in contemporary America are discussed. Besides this body of work on early American education, two documentary histories also helped me define important problems, locate these problems in history, and choose literature with representative perspectives. The first is *Childhood and Youth in America* (Bremner, 1970–74), a four-volume compilation of original documents covering topics from the early seventeenth century through 1972, and the second is *Education in the United States* (Cohen, 1974), a five-volume documentary history covering roughly the same centuries. Other sources helped me to frame questions about the changing knowledge base in psychology and education and to determine which interpretations of literacy or child development were prominent at various points in history. The *Yearbooks of the National Society for the Study of Education* (or *Scientific Study,* as it was called early on) from 1907 through contemporary volumes on reading, learning, and early childhood education were valuable not only for the text and citations but also because the selection and distribution of topics over the course of this century is important in and of itself. For current conceptualizations of literacy and the preschool, I sampled the research journals and multiple edition collections including *Current Topics in Early Childhood Education* (Katz, 1977–86), *Handbook of Research in Early Childhood Education* (Spodek, 1982), *American Childhood: A Research Guide and Historical Handbook* (Hawes & Hiner, 1985), *Handbook of Child Psychology* (Mussen, 1983), *Reading Research* (Waller & Mackinnon, 1979, 1981), *Reading Research Revisited* (Gentile, Kamil & Blanchard, 1983), and *The Handbook of Reading Research* (Pearson et al., 1984; Barr et al., 1991).

CHAPTER 3

1. A reading readiness workbook would include activities such as being able to identify visual patterns that are the same or different. The idea behind readiness workbooks was that learning to read required prerequisite knowledge, which workbooks could provide.

2. Because child development experts of that era believed that children needed a mental age of 6 1/2 years in order to successfully learn to read, "readiness" referred to the period before this mental age was achieved. Reading readiness instruction was usually planned for the end of kindergarten or the begining of first grade. Children were not given books to read until they were deemed "ready."

3. The types of visual and auditory discrimination skills that appeared on readiness tests and in workbooks also appeared in teachers' checklists of skills that were important for children to learn in order to read successfully.

CHAPTER 4

1. This special message was delivered to the Congress on January 12, 1965. Johnson's entire speech may be found in the *Public Papers of the President*, 1965, Book I, pp. 25–33. An excerpt, which I cite here, appeared in Bremner, 1974, p. 1800.

2. Instructional models for the Head Start programs were loosely referred to as belonging to one of three curriculum categories: traditional nursery school instruction; direct instruction based on behaviorist theories of learning and an hierarchical conception of the organization of knowledge, especially as set forth in the work of Bereiter & Engelmann (1966) and the so-called DISTAR materials; and instruction based on the theories of Jean Piaget (see, e.g., 1974), particularly the characteristics of preoperational intellectual development in children between the ages of three and seven (Schweinhart, Weikart & Larner, 1986).

3. These data are from Table 1. School enrollment of persons 2 to 34 years old, by level and control of school, race and Spanish origin: October 1960 to 1985, U. S. Department of Commerce, Bureau of the Census, 1986.

CHAPTER 5

1. The 1985 draft statement makes a more explicit connection between physical maturation and cognitive development than the statement ultimately accepted by the NAEYC and published in 1986. In later chapters I discuss changes in the language of the NAEYC statements on developmentally appropriate practices in literacy (see also table 5-1).

2. See, for example, Schweinhart and Weikart, 1988; Schweinhart, Weikart, and Larner, 1986; Gersten, Darch, and Gleason, 1988; and the other literature discussed in chapter 1 on this controversial issue. For a fuller discussion of changes in the theoretical underpinnings of the NAEYC position, also see chapter 7.

CHAPTER 6

1. All the various people that I interviewed for the study are participants in the policy process. I refer to all of them as "policy analysts" and "policy participants" and "policymakers."

2. If the policy participant defined his or her knowledge in terms of policy formulation alone, I refer to that person as a "policy expert" or "policy professional." If the policy participant assumed program or curriculum knowledge, I refer to him or her as a "program expert" or "program professional."

CHAPTER 7

1. It seems that making sense of other people's experiences, as presumably is required in reading, is appropriate when they are older, according to the view espoused here.

2. According to a broader, more "developmental" view, children participate in literate behavior and note the form and uses of written language, not only in preschools, but everyday as members of families and communities.

3. Virginia Adams summarized several research reports in an article in the summer 1978 issue of *Carnegie Quarterly*. Her article, entitled "New optimism about preschool education: Three reports from Ypsilanti, Michigan," was reprinted in an abridged version in the High/Scope curriculum written by Mary Hohmann, Bernard Banet and David Weikart in 1979. All citations of Adams (1979) refer to the abridged version of her article which appeared in Hohmann, Banet, and Weikart (1979) in an addendum titled "Research support for the curriculum" (pp. 283–290).

4. Forty-one three-year-olds were assigned to one of three curriculum treatments: (1) the "language training" curricula (known as DISTAR) based on the work of Bereiter and Englemann (1966) and described by Adams (1979, in Hohmann et al., 1979, pp. 285–6) as a "structured, didactic, traditional approach in which education is imposed from above with the teacher drilling the children

in language, reading and arithmetic skills"; (2) the "cognitively oriented approach [known as High/Scope] in which the child chooses his activities with adult guidance. . .proceeds at his own pace. . .as [his mentally abilities] emerge naturally in the process of growing up"; and (3) the "unit-based" or child-centered, "permissive" model (known as the traditional nursery school) of self-selected activities drawn from themes and emphasizing individual expression.

5. There is another way to look at this analysis. Children are referred to special education and retained in grade mostly because their reading achievement is behind their peers. This is probably more true now than in the recent past. If participation in preschool helps children to avoid being labelled as handicapped or "flunking," it is probably because preschool somehow helped children learn to read on schedule. When children are not isolated as failures, they are more likely to feel that they "belong" in school and more likely to stay there.

CHAPTER 8

1. See chapter 3 for a discussion of what the federal government counts as "school" according to the changing definitions proposed by the U. S. Department of Commerce, Bureau of the Census in 1920, 1950, and 1980.

2. Pre-K through grade three certification was approved by the New York State Board of Regents at its May 1990 meeting.

3. New York State Education Department distributes an undated reprint of federal legislation from 1970 through 1988 ("Education of the Handicapped Act, 20 U.S.C. 1400–1485") dealing with handicapped children. In addition, the office of the New York State Assistant Commissioner for Education of Children with Handicapping Conditions issues periodic memoranda to pertinent agencies describing the state's procedures and regulations for implementing federal laws (for example, see New York State Education Department, 1991). Public Law 94–142, which was passed in 1975, entitled all handicapped children between 5 and 21 years old to a free and appropriate education. Public Law 99–457, which was passed in October, 1986 (after I had already conducted many of the interviews reported here), entitled handicapped children between 3 and 5 years old to special education services as such services became available in the states. By July, 1991, New York was required to have special education services in place for 3 to 5-year-olds who were identified as handicapped. However, there is still no educational entitlement for non-handicapped preschool children. Although local school districts in New York State (through the Committee on Preschool Education) identify preschool children as handicapped and place them in special education programs, the cost of such programs is still largely borne by the county

in which the handicapped child resides. Since 1986 the cost of the Handicapped Children's Program (HCP) has risen dramatically in New York. For example, in the November 25, 1991 issue of *U.S. News and World Report,* Rensselaer County Executive John Buono complained that the cost of HCP has more than doubled since 1986; the county spent $2.9 million on the HCP program in 1986 and expects to spend approximately $6.5 million for 1991 (Boroughs, Black & Collins, 1991).

4. In January 1990, Cuomo established the Permanent Interagency Committee on Early Childhood Programs in order to help coordinate early childhood programs under the purview of the state agencies and the federal Head Start program.

CHAPTER 10

1. In a similiar vein, some twenty years later, David Elkind (1988–b) of the NAEYC held that early education is crucial for all children. In his view, the issue becomes "not whether preschool is important, but rather to what extent home schooling can duplicate what preschool has to offer. . . If parents possess the competence. . . then home schooling might suffice to prepare children for kindergarten."

2. The first reading book is called the "preprimer," which is an easy-to-read book with predictable sentence patterns. The introduction of the preprimer or other predictable books usually marks the beginning of commercial first-grade programs in reading.

3. Unless teachers make their own materials, virtually all their instructional materials are produced by commercial publishing companies. I think that the reference here is to materials that may look like traditional reading materials, such as workbook-type activities.

CHAPTER 12

1. This quote is cited in Kaestle and Vinovskis (1980, p. 52). It is attributed to Joseph M. Wightman, *Annals of the Boston Primary School Committee From Its First Establishment in 1818 to Its Dissolution in 1855* (Boston, 1860, p. 25–26).

2. These are the conclusions drawn by Kaestle and Vinovskis (1980).

3. This history of the infant school and the reasons for its demise are described in May and Vinovskis (1977) and in Kaestle and Vinovskis (1980).

4. Ross (1976) described the early history of the kindergarten and the progressive kindergarten movement. May and Vinovskis (1977) and Kaestle and Vinovskis (1980) compared the early history of the kindergarten with that of the infant school.

5. The beginnings of the day nursery and its separation from the nursery school were described by Scarr (1983).

6. Takanishi (1977) hypothesized the federal government's role in early childhood education based on her analysis of the conditions leading to the WPA nursery schools, the Lanham centers, and Head Start.

7. In January 1990, Cuomo established the Permanent Interagency Committee on Early Childhood Programs in order to better coordinate the various programs under state and federal auspice. Better coordination was one of the recommendations of the council in their report to the state legislature.

8. Since that time, the governor has recommended increased funding and the state legislature has provided increased funding for both child day care and prekindergarten programs in New York. With the passing of the federal Child Care and Development Block Grant of 1990, a significant new source of money is anticipated for child day care services for low-income families.

9. "Developmental" instruction, as I use the term here, means using curriculum materials that were designed for children who were judged too immature for tasks typically taught to their peers.

10. This is the title of Lareau's (1989) book on how middle-class families use their resources to compensate for an inadequate school curriculum in first grade.

REFERENCES

Aaron, I., Jackson, D., Riggs, C., Smith, R., & Tierney, R. (1978). *Basics in reading.* Glanview, IL: Scott, Foresman.

Adams, M. J. (1990). *Beginning to read: Thinking and learning about print.* Cambridge, MA: MIT Press.

Allington, R., Blachowicz, C., Cramer, R., Cunningham, P., Perez, Y., Robinson, C., Sebesta, S., Smith, R., & Tierney, R. (1987). *Scott, Foresman reading: An American tradition.* Glenview, IL: Scott, Foresman.

Ambach, G. (1985, May). *The challenge of excellence and equity in education.* Speech delivered at the Freedom Forum, Albany, NY.

Anderson. G. L. & Gates, A. (1950). Basic factors underlying learning. In N. Henry (Ed.) *The forty-ninth yearbook of the National Society for the Study of Education: Part 1. Learning and instruction* (pp. 12–35). Chicago: University of Chicago Press.

Anderson, J. E. (1948). The theory of early childhood education. In N. Henry (Ed.), *The forty-sixth yearbook of the National Society for the Study of Education: Part 2. Early childhood education* (pp. 70–99). Chicago: University of Chicago Press.

Association for Supervision & Curriculum Development. (1987). *Resolutions: 1987.* Alexandria, VA: Author.

Association of American Publishers (1990, Winter). Book sales hit $14.7 billion in 1989. *AAP Reading Initiative News, 1,* 4.

Babbie, E. (1986). *The practice of social research.* Belmont, CA: Wadsworth.

Barr, R. (1985). Observing first-grade reading instruction: Instruction viewed with a model of school organization. In J. Niles & R. Lalik (Eds.), *Issues in literacy: A research perspective,* Thirty-fourth Yearbook of the National Reading Conference (pp. 30–37). Rochester, NY: National Reading Conference.

Barr, R., Kamil, M., Mosenthal, P. & Pearson, P. D. (Eds.), (1991). *Handbook of reading research*. (Vol. II). NY: Longman.

Bennett, W. J. (1986). *First lessons: A report on elementary education in America*. Washington, DC: U.S. Department of Education.

Bereiter, C., & Englemann, S. (1966). *Teaching the disadvantaged child in the preschool*. Englewood Cliffs, NJ: Prentice-Hall.

Berrueta-Clement, J. R., Schweinhart, L. J., Barnett, W. S., Epstein, A. S. & Weikart, D. P. (1984). *Changed lives: The effects of the Perry Preschool Program on youths through age 19*. Ypsilanti, MI: High/Scope Press.

Bissex, G. L. (1980). *Gnys at wrk: A child learns to write and read.* Cambridge, MA: Harvard University Press.

Blair, T. R., & Rupley, W. H. (1983). A critique of Wiliam S. Gray and Arthur I. Gates's studies of teacher effectiveness in reading instruction: Early efforts to present a focus. In L. Gentile, M. Kamil, & J. Blanchard (Eds.), *Reading research revisited* (pp. 425–32). Columbus, OH: Charles E. Merrill.

Boroughs, D., Black, R. & Collins, S. (1991, November 25). An educational lesson. *U.S. News and World Report, III*, 55.

Borstelmann, L. J. (1983). Children before psychology: Ideas about children from antiquity to the late 1800s. In P. Mussen (Ed.), *Handbook of child psychology* (Vol. 1 pp. 1–40). New York: John Wiley & Sons.

Boyer, E. L. (1991, December 8). Perspective on children: America has orphaned its young. *Los Angeles Times*, p. M5.

Bremner, R. H. (Ed.), (1970–74). *Children and youth in America: A documentary history* (Vols. 1–3). Cambridge, MA: Harvard University Press.

Bruner, J. (1986). *Actual minds, possible worlds.* Cambridge, MA: Harvard University Press.

Caldwell, B. M. (1981). Day care and the schools. *Theory Into Practice, 20*, 121–29.

Caldwell, B. M. (1986). Day care and the public schools—Natural allies, natural enemies. *Educational Leadership, 43*, 34–39.

Caldwell, B. M. & Freyer, M. (1982). Day care and early education. In B. Spodek (Eds), *Handbook of research in early childhood education* (pp. 341–74). New York: Free Press.

California State Department of Education. (1988). *Here they come: ready or not! Report of the School Readiness Task Force.* Sacramento, CA: Author.

Carroll, J. (1964). The analysis of reading instruction. In E. Hilgard (Ed.), *The sixty-third yearbook of the National Society for the Study of Education* (pp. 336–53). Chicago: University of Chicago Press.

Chall, J. (1967). *Learning to read: The great debate.* New York: McGraw-Hill.

Chall, J., Jacobs, V., & Baldwin, L. (1990). *The reading crisis: Why poor children fall behind.* Cambridge, MA: Harvard University Press.

Clay, M. (1966). *Emergent reading behavior.* Unpublished doctoral dissertation, University of Auckland, New Zealand.

Clay, M. (1985). *The early detection of reading difficulties.* (3rd Edition). Portsmouth, NH: Heineman.

Clay, M. & Cazden, C. (1990). A Vygotskian interpretation of Reading Recovery. In L. Moll (Ed.), *Vygotsky and education: Instructional implications of sociohistorical psychology.* (pp. 206–222). Cambridge: University of Cambridge Press.

Cobb, R., & Elder, C. (1983). *Participation in American politics: The dynamics of agenda-building.* Baltimore, MD: Johns Hopkins University Press.

Cobb, R., Ross, J., & Ross, M. (1976). Agenda building as a comparative political process, *The American Political Science Review, 70,* 126–38.

Cochran-Smith, M. (1983). *The making of a reader.* Norwood, NJ: Ablex.

Cohen, R. (1985). Child-saving and progressivism, 1885–1915. In J. M. Hawes & N. R. Hiner (Eds.), *American Childhood* (pp. 273–309). Westport, CT: Greenwood Press.

Cohen, S. (Ed.). (1974). *Education in the United States: A documentary history* (Vols. 1–4). New York: Random House.

Collins, C. (1986). Is the cart before the horse? Effects of preschool reading instruction on 4-year-olds. *Reading Teacher, 40,* 332–39.

Committee for Economic Development. (1987). *Children in need: Investment strategies for the educationally disadvantaged.* New York: Author.

Corder, L. J. & Quisenberry, N. L. (1987). Early education and Afro-Americans. *Childhood Education,* 154–58.

Cravens, H. (1985). Child-saving in the age of professionalism, 1915–1930. In J. Hawes & N. R. Hiner (Eds.), *American childhood* (pp. 415–88). Westport, CT: Greenwood Press.

CSR. (1985, June). *The impact of Head Start on children, families and communities* (Contract No. 105–81–C–026). Washington, DC: Author.

Cunningham, C. E. & Osborn, D. K. (1979). A historical examination of blacks in early childhood education. *Young Children, 34,* 20–29.

Cuomo, M. (1987, January). *State of the state.* Annual message to the legislature, Albany, NY.

Cuomo, M. (1988, January). *State of the state.* Annual message to the legislature, Albany, NY.

Cuomo, M. (1989, January). *State of the state.* Annual message to the legislature, Albany, NY.

Cuomo, M. (1990, January). *State of the state.* Annual message to the legislature, Albany, NY.

Cuomo, M. (1991, January). *State of the state.* Annual message to the legislature, Albany, NY.

Decade of the Child. (1988, January 7). *The Times Union,* p. A15.

Delpit, L. (1988). The silenced dialogue: Power and pedagogy in educating other people's children. *Harvard Educational Review, 58,* 280–98.

Donaldson, M. (1978). *Children's minds.* New York: Norton.

Downs, A. (1972). Up and down with ecology: The "issue—attention cycle." *Public Interest, 32,* 38–50.

Duckworth, E. (1972). The having of wonderful ideas. *Harvard Educational Review, 42,* 217–31.

Durkin, D. (1966). *Children who read early.* New York: Teachers College Press.

Durkin, D. (1968). When should children begin to read? In H. Robinson (Ed.) *The sixty-seventh yearbook of the National Society for the Study of Education: Part II. Innovation and Change in Reading Instruction* (pp. 30–71). Chicago: University of Chicago Press.

Durkin, D (1970). What does research say about the time to begin reading instruction? *Journal of Educational Research, 10,* 52–56.

Durkin, D. (1974–75). A six-year study of children who learned to read in school at the age of four. *Reading Research Quarterly, 10,* 9–61.

Durkin, D. (1987). Testing in the kindergarten. *Reading Teacher, 40,* 766–70.

Durrell, D., & Nicholson, A. (1961). Preschool and kindergarten experience. In N. Henry (Ed.), *The sixtieth yearbook of the National Society for the Study of Education: Part I: Development in and through reading.* (pp. 257–69). Chicago: University of Chicago Press.

Early Childhood Commission (1986, March). *Take a giant step: An equal start in education for all of New York City four-year-olds.* Final report of the Early Childhood Commission submitted to Mayor Koch, New York City.

Edelman, M.W. (1990, June). *Memorandum: Update on CDF's current efforts and accomplishments for children.* (Available from Children's Defense Fund, 122 C Street, N.W., Washington, DC 20001).

Edmondson, B. (1986, February). Education. *American Demographics,* 26–54.

Education of the Handicapped Act (EHA), 20 U.S.C. 1400–1485. (n.d.) Distributed by the New York State Education Department, Albany, N.Y.

Elkind, D. (1988–a, February 3). The "miseducation" of young children. *Education Week,* pp. 24, 16.

Elkind, D. (1988–b). Educating the very young: A call for clear thinking. *National Education Association Today, 6,* 22–27.

Elson, W. H. (1912–13). *Elson primary school reader, Book one.* Chicago: Scott, Foresman.

Elson, W. H., & Gray, W. S. (1930–31). *Elson basic readers.* Chicago: Scott, Foresman.

Elson, W. H., & Gray, W. S. (1936–38). *Elson-Gray basic readers.* Chicago: Scott, Foresman.

Elson, W. H., & Keck, C. (1909–11). *Elson grammar school readers* (Books 1–4). Chicago: Scott, Foresman.

Elson, W. H., & Runkel, L. E. (1914). *Elson-Runkel primer.* Chicago: Scott, Foresman.

Elson, W. H., Runkel, L. E., & Keck, C. (1920–21). *Elson readers.* Chicago: Scott, Foresman.

Engelhardt, T. (1991, June). Reading may be harmful to your kids. *Harper's Magazine,* pp. 55–62.

Engleman, F. E., & Nash, H. (1948). Organization, administration, and finance. In N. Henry (Ed.), *The forty-sixth yearbook of the National Society for the Study of Education: Part II. Early Childhood Education* (pp. 362–84). Chicago: University of Chicago Press.

Farnworth, M., Schweinhart, L., & Berrueta-Clement, J. (1985). Preschool intervention, school success, and delinquency in a high-risk sample of youth. *American Educational Research Journal, 22,* 445–64.

Ferreiro, E. (1984). The underlying logic of literacy development. In H. Goelman, A. Oberg, & F. Smith (Eds.), *Awakening to literacy* (pp. 154–73). Exeter, NH: Heinemann Educational Books.

Fiske, E. (1986, April 13). Early schooling is now the rage. *New York Times* (Education Life, Section 12), pp. 25–30.

Fox, B. (1987). Literacy and state funded prekindergarten programs: Speaking out on the issues. *Reading Teacher, 41,* 58–64.

Fuller, E. M., Christianson, H., Headly, N., Landreth, C., Peterson, A. D., & Wood, S. L. (1948). Practices and resources in early childhood education. In N. Henry (Ed.), *The forty-sixth yearbook of the National Society for the Study of Education: Part II. Early childhood education* (pp 101–71). Chicago: University of Chicago Press.

Gans, R. (1948). Young children at the turn of this era. In N. Henry (Ed.), *The forty-sixth yearbook of the National Society for the Study of Education: Part 2. Early childhood education* (pp. 6–13). Chicago: University of Chicago Press.

Gates, A. (1983). The necessary mental age for beginning reading. In L. Gentile, M. Kamil, & J. Blanchard (Eds.), *Reading research revisited* (pp. 415–23). Columbus, OH: Charles E. Merrill. (Original work published 1937.)

Gentile, L., Kamil, M., & Blanchard, J. (Eds.). (1983). *Reading research revisited.* Columbus, OH: Charles E. Merrill.

Gersten, R., Darch, C. & Gleason, M. (1988). Effectiveness of a direct instruction academic kindergarten for low-income students. *Elementary School Journal, 89,* 227–40.

Glaser, B., & Strauss, A. (1967). *The discovery of grounded theory.* Chicago: Aldine.

Glass, R. S. (1986). Early childhood education: A sound investment. *American Teacher, 70,* 8–9.

Goelman, H. (1984). The discussion: What was said. In H. Goelman, A. Oberg, & F. Smith (Eds.), *Awakening to literacy* (pp. 201–13). Exeter, NH: Heinemann Educational Books.

Goelman, H., Oberg, A., & Smith, F. (Eds.). (1984). *Awakening to literacy.* Exeter, NH: Heinemann Educational Books.

Goetz, J., & LeCompte, M. (1984). *Ethnography and qualitative design in educational research.* Orlando, FL: Academic Press.

Goodman, Y., Altwerger, B., & Marek, A. (1989, October). *Print awareness in preschool children: Development of literacy in preschool children. Research and review.* Occasional paper No. 4, Arizona Center for Research and Development, University of Arizona, Tucson.

Goodykoontz, B., Davis, M. D., & Gabbard, H. F. (1948). Recent history and present status of education for young children. In N. Henry (Ed.), *The forty-sixth yearbook of the National Society for the Study of Education: Part II. Early childhood education* (pp. 44–69). Chicago: University of Chicago Press.

Gray, W. S. (1927). Training and experience that prepare for reading. *Childhood Education, 3,* 210–14.

Gray, W. S., Arbuthnot, M. H., Baruch, D., & Montgomery, E. R. (1940–47). *Basic readers*. Chicago: Scott, Foresman.

Gray, W. S., Artley, A. S., Arbuthnot, M. H., & Monroe, M. (1951–57). *The new basic readers*. Chicago: Scott, Foresman.

Gray, W. S. & Monroe, M. (1937). *Before we read*. Chicago: Scott, Foresman.

Gregory, B., Merrill, J., Payne, B., & Giddings, M. (1908). *The seventh yearbook of the National Society for the Scientific Study of Education: Part II. The coordination of the kindergarten and the elementary school*. Chicago: University of Chicago Press.

Harris, A. J. (1961). Reading and human development. In N. Henry (Ed.), *The sixtieth yearbook of the National Society for the Study of Education: Part I. Development in and through reading* (pp. 17–34). Chicago: University of Chicago Press.

Harris, A. V. S. (1907). Introduction. In M. Holmes (Ed.), *The sixth yearbook of the National Society for the Study of Education: Part 2. The kindergarten and its relation to elementary education* (pp. 9–18). Chicago: University of Chicago Press.

Harrison, B. & Magri, M. (1985). Policies for preschoolers. *State Legislatures,* pp. 12–15.

Harste, J. C., Woodward, V. A., & Burke, C. L. (1984). Examining our assumptions: A transactional view of literacy and learning. *Research in the Teaching of English, 18,* 84–108.

Hawes, J. M., & Hiner, N. R. (Eds.). (1985). *American childhood: A research guide and historical handbook*. Westport, CT: Greenwood Press.

Hawkins, A. (1989, July 27). *Early Childhood Education and Development Act* (H.R. 3), Report from the Committee on Education and Labor, U.S. House of Representatives.

Heath, S. B. (1983). *Ways with words: Ethnography of communication, communities, and classrooms*. Cambridge: Cambridge University Press.

Heath, S. B. & Thomas, C. (1984). The achievement of preschool literacy for mother and child. In H. Goelman, A. Oberg, & F. Smith (Eds.), *Awakening to literacy* (pp. 51–72). Exeter, NH: Heinemann Educational Books.

Henry, N. (Ed.). (1948). *The forty-sixth yearbook of the National Society for the Study of Education: Part II. Early childhood education*. Chicago: University of Chicago Press.

Henry, N. (Ed.). (1949). *The forty-eighth yearbook of the National Society for the Study of Education: Part II. Reading in the elementary school*. Chicago: University of Chicago Press.

Henry, N. (Ed.). (1961). *The sixtieth yearbook of the National Society for The Study of Education: Part I. Development in and through reading*. Chicago: University of Chicago Press.

Hiebert, E. (1986). Issues related to home influences on young children's print-related development. In D. Yaden & S. Templeton (Eds.), *Metalinguistic awareness and beginning literacy* (pp. 145–58). Portsmouth, NH: Heinemann Educational Books.

Hildreth, G. (1949). Reading programs in the early primary period. In N. Henry (Ed.), *The forty-eighth yearbook of the National Society for the Study of Education: Part II. Reading in the elementary school* (pp. 54–93). Chicago: University of Chicago Press.

Hilgard, E. (Ed.). (1964). *The sixty-third yearbook of the National Society for the Study of Education: Part I. Theories of learning and instruction*. Chicago: University of Chicago Press.

Hill, P. S. (1907). Some conservative and progressive phases of kindergarten education. In M. Holmes (Ed.), *The sixth yearbook of the National Society for the Study of Education: Part II. The kindergarten and its relation to elementary education* (pp. 61–85). Chicago: University of Chicago Press.

Hodgkinson, H. (1985). *All one system: Demographics of education, kindergarten through graduate school*. Washington, DC: Institute for Educational Leadership.

Hohmann, M., Banet, B., & Weikart, D. (1979). *Young children in action: A manual for preschool educators*. Ypsilanti, MI: High/Scope Press.

Holmes, M. (1927). Investigation of reading readiness of first grade entrants. *Childhood Education, 3*, 215–21.

Holsti, O. (1969). *Content analysis for the social sciences and humanities*. Reading, MA: Addison-Wesley.

Ilg, F., & Ames, L. B. (1950). Developmental trends in reading behavior. *The Journal of Genetic Psychology, 76,* 291–312.

Ilg, F, & Ames, L. B. (1964). *School readiness.* New York: Harper & Row.

Johnston, P., & Fleming, J. (1986, December). *Play and literateness.* Paper presented at the National Reading Conference, St. Petersburg, FL.

Kaestle, C. F. (1983). *Pillars of the republic: Common schools and American society 1780–1860.* New York: Hill & Wang.

Kaestle, C. F., & Vinovskis, M. (1980). *Education and social change in nineteenth-century Massachusetts.* Cambridge: Cambridge University Press.

Kamerman, S. (1984). Child care services: A national picture. In U.S. Department of Labor, Bureau of Labor Statistics, *Families at work: The jobs and the pay* (Bulletin 2209, pp. 20–24). Washington, DC: U.S. Government Printing Office.

Katz, L. (1986, April 29). Edited transcript of keynote speech delivered at the New York State Education Conference On Early Childhood Education, Kingsborough Community College, Brooklyn, NY.

Katz, L. (Ed.). (1977–86). *Current topics in early childhood education* (Vols. 1–4). Norwood, NJ: Ablex.

Katz, L. (1987). What should young children be doing? *The Wingspread Journal, 9,* special section.

Kawin, E. (1948). Records and reports: Observations, tests, and measurements. In N. Henry (Ed.), *The forty-sixth yearbook of the National Society for the Study of Education: Part 2. Early childhood education* (pp. 281–315). Chicago: University of Chicago Press.

Kennedy, E. (1989, January 25). *Smart Start: The Community collaborative for early childhood education* (S. 123). U.S. Senate, Committee on Labor and Human Services.

Kennedy, E. (1989, April 12). *Act for better child care services of 1989* (S. 5), Report from the Committee on Labor and Human Services, U.S. Senate.

Kingdon, J. W. (1984). *Agendas, alternatives, and public policies.* Boston, MA: Little, Brown.

Kraus-Boelte, M. (1907). An interpretation of some of the Froebelian kindergarten principles. In M. Holmes (Ed.), *The sixth yearbook of the National Society for the Study of Education: Part 2. The kindergarten and its relation to elementary education* (pp. 32–60). Chicago: University of Chicago Press.

Krause-Eheart, B., Learitt, R., & Steinkamp, M. (1985, November). *Three- and 4-year-olds in public school: Prescriptions for practice.* Paper prepared for the National Association of Elementary School Principals by the Developmental Child Care Program, the University of Illinois at Urbana-Champaign, Champaign, IL.

Lareau, A. (1989). *Home advantage: Social class and parental intervention in elementary education.* Philadelphia, PA: Falmer.

Lazerson, M. (1972). The historical antecedents of early childhood education. In I. Gordon (Ed.), *The seventy-first yearbook of the National Society for the Study of Education: Part 2. Early childhood education* (pp. 33–54). Chicago: University of Chicago Press.

Levinger, L., & Murphy, L. (1948). Implications of the social scene for the education of young children. In N. Henry (Ed.), *The forty-sixth yearbook of the National Society for the Study of Education: Part 2. Early childhood education* (pp. 15–45). Chicago: University of Chicago Press.

Lincoln, Y., & Guba, E. (1985). *Naturalistic inquiry.* Beverly Hills, CA: Sage.

Literacy Development and Pre-First Grade: A Joint Satement. (1986). *Childhood Education, 63,* 110–11.

Martin, A. (1988). Screening, early intervention and remediation: Obscuring children's potential. *Harvard Educational Review, 58,* 488–501.

Mason, J. M. (1986). Kindergarten reading: A proposal for a problem-solving approach. In B. Spodek (Ed.), *Today's kindergarten: Exploring the knowledge base, expanding the curriculum* (pp. 48–66). New York: Teachers College Press.

Mason, J. M., Kerr, B. M., Sinha, S., & McCormick, C. (1989, December). *Shared book reading in an early start program for at-risk children.* Paper presented at the National Reading Conference, Austin, TX.

May, D., & Vinovskis, M. (1977). A ray of millennial light: Early education and social reform in Massachusetts, 1826–1840. In T. Hareven (Ed.), *Family and kin in urban communities, 1700–1930* (pp. 62–99). New York: New Viewpoints.

McCathren, R. R. (1981). The demise of federal categorical child care legislation: Lessons for the 80's from the failures of the 70's. In H. Wallach (Ed.), *Approaches to child and family policy* (pp. 101–143). Boulder, CO: Westview Press.

McGill-Franzen, A. & Allington, R. (1991). The gridlock of low reading achievement: Perspectives on policy and practice. *Remedial and Special Education, 12,* 20–30.

McLane, J. B., & McNamee, G. D. (1990). *Early Literacy.* Cambridge, MA: Harvard University Press.

Merrill, J. (1908). Ways and means for securing organic continuity between the kindergarten and the primary school in the development of the child. In B. Gregory, J. Merrill, B. Payne, & M. Giddings (Eds.), *The seventh yearbook of the National Society for the Study of Education: Part II. The coordination of the kindergarten and the elementary school* (pp. 9–34). Chicago: University of Chicago Press.

Michan, E. J. (1977). *The economic growth debate.* London: George Allen & Unwin.

Mills, H. (1907). The evolution of the kindergarten program. In M. Holmes (Ed.), *The sixth yearbook of the National Society for the Study of Education: Part II. The kindergarten and its relation to elementary education* (pp. 86–114). Chicago: University of Chicago Press.

Mitchell, A. (1987, April). *Public schools and young children: A report of the first national survey of public school districts regarding their early childhood programs.* Paper presented at the American Educational Research Association Conference, Washington D.C.

Mitchell, A. (1989). Old baggage, new visions: Shaping policy for early childhood programs. *Phi Delta Kappan, 70,* 664–72.

Morado, C. (1985). *Prekindergarten programs for 4-year olds: State education agency initiatives.* Washington, DC: National Association for the Education of Young Children.

Moran, G., & Vinovskis, M. (1986). The great care of godly parents: Early childhood in Puritan New England. In A. Smuts & J. Hagen (Eds.), History and research in Child Development, *Monographs of the Society for Research in Child Development, 50,*(4–5, Serial No. 211) 24–40.

Morphett, M., & Washburne, C. (1931). When should children begin to read? *Elementary School Journal, 31,* 496–503.

Morrow, L. M. (1988). Young children's responses to one-to-one story readings in school settings. *Reading Research Quarterly, 23,* 89–107.

Mussen, P. (Ed.). (1983). *Handbook of child psychology* (Vol. 1). New York: John Wiley & Sons.

National Association for the Education of Young Children. (1985). *Draft position statement on developmentally appropriate practice in early childhood programs.* Washington, DC: Author.

National Association for the Education of Young Children. (1986 September). NAEYC position paper on developmentally appropriate practice in early childhood programs. *Young Children*, pp. 3–29.

National Association for the Education of Young Children. (1989, May). [Kindergarten entry age data 1989–1985; State policies on kindergarten—April 1989]. Data tables available from NAEYC Information Service.

National Association of Early Childhood Specialists in State Departments of Education. (1987, November). Unacceptable trends in kindergarten entry and placement: A position statement. Washington, DC: Author.

National Association of Elementary School Principals (n.d.). *Statement on early childhood education*. Alexandria, VA: Author.

National Black Child Development Institute. (1985). *Child care in the public schools: Incubator for inequality?* Washington, DC: Author.

National Center for Children in Poverty. (1990). *Five million children*. New York: School of Public Health, Columbia University.

National Governors' Association. (1986, August). *Time for results: The governors' 1991 report on education, task force on readiness*. Washington, DC: Author.

National Governors' Association. (1990, March 7). Text of statement on education goals adopted by governors. *Education Week*, p. 16.

Nelson, B. (1978). Setting the public agenda: The case of child abuse. In J. V. May & A. Wildavsky (Eds.), *The Policy Cycle* (pp. 17–41). Beverly Hills, CA: Sage.

Nelson, B. (1984). *Making an issue of child abuse: Political agenda setting for social problems*. Chicago: University of Chicago Press.

New York State Council on Children & Families. (1987). *Early childhood services in New York state: A report to the governor and legislature* (Vols. 1–2). Albany, NY: Author.

New York State Education Department. (1983, July). *Proposed statement of Regents elementary and secondary goals for students—1983*. Albany, NY: Author.

New York State Education Department. (1986. March). *Prekindergarten improves pupils' performance throughout the elementary grades*. Albany, NY: Author.

New York State Education Department, Assistant Commissioner for Education of Children with Handicapping Conditions. (1991, June). *Memorandum: Updated information of preschool issues*. Albany, NY: Author.

New York State Education Department, Bureau of Child Development and Parent Education. (1982, June). *Play: The early childhood program*. Albany, NY: Author.

New York State School Boards Association. (1986, April). *Right from the start: A draft position paper of the NYSSBA*. Albany, NY: Author.

New York State United Teachers. (1986, March). Resolution 20: Early childhood education. *New York Teacher, 28*(Supplement: Fourteenth Annual Representative Assembly, Toronto. Ontario).

Ninio, A., & Bruner, J. (1978). The achievement and antecedents of labelling. *Journal of Child Language*, 5, 1–14.

Nourot, P. M., Henry, J., & Scales, B. (1990, April). *A naturalistic study of ''storyplaying'' in preschool and kindergarten*. Paper presented at the American Educational Research Association Conference, Boston, MA.

Olson, D. (1984). "See! Jumping!" Some oral language antecedents of literacy. In H. Goelman, A. Oberg, & F. Smith (Eds.), *Awakening to literacy* (pp. 185–92). Exeter, NH: Heinemann Educational Books.

Paley, V. G. (1990). *The boy who would be a helicopter: The uses of storytelling in the classroom*. Cambridge, MA: Harvard University Press.

Pearson, P. D., Barr, R., Kamil, M., & Mosenthal, P. (Eds.). (1984). *Handbook of reading research* (Vol. 1). New York: Longman.

Pearson, P. D., Johnson, D., Clymer, T., Indrisano, R., Venezky, R., Baumann, J., Hiebert, E., & Toth, M. (1989). *World of reading*. Needham, MA: Silver, Burdett & Ginn.

Pellegrini, A. D., Galda, L., Dresden, J., & Cox, S. (1990, April). *A longitudinal study of the predictive relations among symbolic play, metalinguistic verbs, and early literacy.* Paper presented at the American Educational Research Association Conference, Boston, MA.

Pellegrini, A. D., Perlmutter, J. C., Galda, L., & Brody, G. H. (1990). Joint reading between black Head Start children and their mothers. *Child Development, 61*, 443–53.

Pendleton, A. (1986). Preschool enrollment: Trends and implications. In U.S. Department of Education, Office of Educational Research & Improvement, *The Condition of Education*, (1986 ed.) (pp. 124–39). Washington, DC: U.S. Government Printing Office.

Piaget, J. (1974). *The language and thought of the child*. New York: Meridian.

Pinnell, G. S., Fried, M. D., & Estice, R. M. (1991). Reading Recovery: Learning how to make a difference. In D. E. DeFord, C. A. Lyons, & G. S. Pinell (Eds.), *Bridges to Literacy: Learning From Reading Recovery* (pp. 11–29). Portsmouth, NH: Heinemann.

Preller, M. B. (1991, March 3). Ben's day. *The Sunday Times Union Personal Magazine*, pp. 8–10.

Ramey, C. (1985, October). *Does early interaction make a difference?* Paper presented at the National Early Childhood Conference on Children with Special Needs, sponsored by the Council for Exceptional Children, Denver, CO.

Robinson, S. L. (1987). Kindergarten in America: Five major trends. *Phi Delta Kappan, 68*, 529–30.

Robinson, S. S. (1990). *A survey of literacy programs among preschools*. Paper presented at the American Educational Research Association, Boston, MA.

Ross, E. D. (1976). *The kindergarten crusade: The establishment of preschool education in the United States.* Athens, OH: Ohio University Press.

Rowe, D. W. (1989). Author/audience interaction in the preschool: The role of social interaction in literacy learning. *Journal of Reading Behavior, 21*, 311–49.

Russell, D. (1949). Reading and child development. In N. Henry (Ed.), *The forty-eighth yearbook of the National Society for the Study of Education: Part II. Reading in the elementary school* (pp. 10–32). Chicago: University of Chicago Press.

Russell, D. (1961). Continuity in the reading program. In N. Henry (Ed.), *The sixtieth yearbook of the National Society for the Study of Education: Part I. Development in and through reading* (pp. 226–56). Chicago: University of Chicago Press.

Scarr, S. (1983, October). *Child care*. Paper presented as a Science and Public Policy Seminar, sponsored by the Federation of Behavioral, Psychological and Cognitive Sciences, University of Virginia.

Schickedanz, J. (1982). The acquisition of written language in young children. In B. Spodek (Ed.), *Handbook of research in early childhood education* (pp. 242–63). New York: Free Press.

Schieffelin, B., & Cochran-Smith, M. (1984). Learning to read culturally: Literacy before schooling. In H. Goelman, A. Oberg, & F. Smith (Eds.), *Awakening to literacy* (pp. 3–23). Exeter, NH: Heinemann Educational Books.

Schumacher, D. (1990, June 22). Special supplement: H.R. 3, the early childhood education and development act; S. 5, the act for better child care services. *Education Daily*, pp. 1–8.

Schweinhart, L. J., & Mazur, E. (1987). *Prekindergarten programs in urban schools.* Ypsilanti, MI: High/Scope Educational Research Foundation.

Schweinhart, L. J., & Weikart, D. P. (1988). Education for young children living in poverty: Child-initiated learning or teacher-directed instruction? *Elementary School Journal, 89,* 213–25.

Schweinhart, L. J., Weikart, D. P., & Larner, M. B. (1986). Consequences of three preschool curriculum models through age 15. *Early Childhood Research Quarterly, 1,* 15–45.

Scott, Foresman & Company. (n.d.) *The history of "Dick and Jane" publications.* [Mimeograph]. (Available from Scott, Foresman & Company, 1900 East Lake Avenue, Glenview IL 60025).

Scott, Foresman & Company. (1966, March). *The SCORE.* Glenview, IL: Author.

Selke, E. & Selke, G. A. (1922). A study of the vocabulary of beginning books in twelve reading methods. *Elementary School Journal, 22.*

Shepard, L. & Smith, M. L. (1988). Escalating academic demand in kindergarten: Counterproductive policies. *Elementary School Journal, 89,* 135–44.

Shields, P. M. & McLaughlin, M. W. (1986). *Parent involvement in compensatory education programs.* Stanford, CA: CERAS, School of Education, Stanford University.

Sigel, I. (1972). Developmental theory and preschool education: Issues, problems, and implications. In I. Gordon (Ed.), *The seventy-first yearbook of the National Society for the Study of Education: Part II. Early childhood education* (pp. 13–31). Chicago: University of Chicago Press.

Slavin, R. (1989). Students at risk of school failure: The problem and its dimensions. In R. Slavin, N. Karweit, & N. Madden (Eds.), *Effective Programs for Students at Risk* (pp. 3–22). Boston: Allyn-Bacon.

Smith, F. (1984). The creative achievement of literacy. In H. Goelman, A. Oberg, & F. Smith (Eds.), *Awakening to literacy* (pp. 143–53). Exeter, NH: Heinemann Educational Books.

Smith, M. L., & Shepard, L. (1987). What doesn't work: Explaining policies of retention in the early grades. *Phi Delta Kappan,* 129–34.

Smith, M. L., & Shepard, L. (1988). Kindergarten readiness and retention: A qualitative study of teachers' beliefs and practices. *American Educational Research Journal, 25,* 307–33.

Smith, N. B. (1950). Readiness for reading. *Elementary English, 27,* 91–106.

Smith, N. B. (1965). *American reading instruction.* Newark, DE: International Reading Association.

Snow, C. (1983). Literacy and language: Relationships during the preschool years. *Harvard Educational Review, 53,* 165–189.

Soltow, L., & Stevens, E. (1981). *The rise of literacy in the common school in the United States: A socioeconomic analysis to 1870.* Chicago: University of Chicago Press.

Sommerville, J. (1982). *The rise and fall of childhood.* Beverly Hills, CA: Sage.

Southern Growth Policies Board. (1990, January). *Preschool education for economic development: Practical steps for southern states* (SGPB Alert, No. 30). Research Triangle Park, NC: Author.

Spodek, B. (1982b). The Kindergarten: A retrospective and contemporary view. In L. Katz (Ed.), *Current topics in early childhood education* (Vol. 4, pp. 173–92). Norwood N. Ablex.

Spodek, B. (Ed.). (1982a). *Handbook of research in early childhood education.* New York: Free Press.

Spodek, B. (Ed.). 1986. *Today's kindergarten: Exploring the knowledge base, expanding the curriculum.* New York: Teachers College Press.

Spradley, J. (1979). *The ethnographic interview.* New York: Holt, Rinehart & Winston.

Steinfels, M. (1973). *Who's minding the children?* New York: Simon & Schuster.

Stone, C. A. (1985). Vygotsky's developmental model and the concept of proleptic instruction: Some implications for theory and research in the field of learning disabilities. *Research Communications in Psychology, Psychiatry and Behavior, 10,* 129–52.

Strickland, C. (1982). Paths not taken: Seminal models of early childhood education in Jacksonian America. In B. Spodek (Ed.), *Handbook of research in early childhood education* (pp. 321–40). New York: Free Press.

Suransky, V. P. (1977). *The erosion of childhood : A social-phenomenological study of early institutionalization.* Unpublished doctoral dissertation, University of Michigan, Ann Arbor.

Swenson, E. (1950). Applications of learning principles to the improvement of teaching in the early elementary grades. In N. Henry (Ed.), *The forty-ninth yearbook of the National Society for the Study of Education: Part I. Learning and instruction* (pp. 256–79). Chicago: University of Chicago Press.

Takanishi, R. (1977). Federal involvement in early education (1933–1973): The need for historical perspectives. In L. Katz (Ed.), *Current topics in early childhood education* (Vol. 1, pp. 139–63). Norwood, NJ: Ablex.

Taylor, D. (1983). *Family literacy: Young children learning to read and write.* Portsmouth, NH: Heinemann Educational Books.

Teale, W. (1986). Home background and young children's literacy development. In W. Teale & E. Sulzby (Eds.), *Emergent literacy: Writing and reading* (pp. 173–206). Norwood, NJ: Ablex.

Teale, W., & Sulzby, E. (1986). Emergent literacy as a perspective for examining how young children become writers and readers. In W. Teale & E. Sulzby (Eds.), *Emergent literacy: Writing and reading* (pp. vii–xxv). Norwood, NJ: Ablex.

Tyler, F. (1964). Issues related to readiness to learn. In E. Hilgard (Ed.), *The sixty-third yearbook of the National Society for the Study of Education: Part I. Theories of Learning and Instruction* (pp. 210–39). Chicago: University of Chicago Press.

U. S. Department of Commerce, Bureau of the Census. (1924). *Fourteenth decennial census publication.* Washington, DC: U.S. Government Printing Office. (Machine-readable film [1920, No. 10] available from Research Publications, Inc., New Haven, CT).

U. S. Department of Commerce, Bureau of the Census. (1953). *Seventeenth decennial census publication.* Washington, DC: U.S Government Printing Office. (Machine-readable film [1950, No. 1] available from Research Publications, Inc., New Haven, CT).

U. S. Department of Commerce, Bureau of the Census. (1986). *School enrollment—social and economic characteristics of students: October 1986* (Series P–20, No. 409). Washington, DC: U.S. Government Printing Office.

U. S. Department of Commerce, Bureau of the Census. (1982, October). *Current Population Survey Interviewer's Memorandum* (No. 82–21, Section II).

U. S. Department of Commerce, Bureau of the Census. (1987) *Who's minding the kids?* (Series P–70, No. 9). Washington, DC: Government Printing Office.

U. S. Department of Education, Office of Educational Research & Improvement. (1987). *Digest of education statistics—1987.* Washington, DC: U.S. Government Printing Office.

U. S. Department of Labor, Bureau of Labor Statistics. (1986, April). *Employment projections for 1995: Data and methods* (Bulletin 2253). Washington, DC: U.S. Government Printing Office.

Venezky, R. (1986). Steps toward a modern history of American reading instruction. *Review of Research in Education, 13,* 129–67.

Viadero, D. (1990, June 13). Gains from early intervention shown in study of low-birth-weight babies. *Education Week*, p. 5.

Vygotsky, L. (1986). *Thought and language*. Cambridge, MA: MIT Press.

Waite, L. (1981, May). U.S. women at work. *Population Bulletin, 36* (No. 2).

Waldman, E. (1984). Labor force statistics from a family perspective. In U.S. Department of Labor, Bureau of Labor Statistics, *Families at Work: The Jobs and the Pay* (Bulletin 2209, pp. 1–5). Washington, DC: U.S. Government Printing Office.

Walker, R. (1990, March 7). Governors aim to make schools "second to none." *Education Week*, pp. 1, 17.

Waller, T. G., & Mackinnon, G. E. (Eds.). (1979–1981). *Reading research: Advances in theory and practice.* (Vols. 1–3). New York: Academic Press.

Walton, M. (n.d.). *Statement on early childhood education*. Alexandria, VA: National Association of Elementary School Principals.

Weber, E. (1984). *Ideas influencing early childhood education: A theoretical analysis.* New York: Teachers College Press.

Weikart, D. (1988). David Weikart on hearings in Washington. *High/Scope Resource, 7,* 9–11.

Weikart, D., Epstein, A. S., Schweinhart, L. J., & Bond, J. T. (1978). *The Ypsilanti Preschool Curriculum Demonstration Project: Preschool years and longitudinal results* (Monograph of the High/Scope Educational Research Foundation, No. 4). Ypsilanti, MI: High/Scope Press.

Weikart, D., Rogers, L., Adock, C., & McClelland, D. (1971). *The cognitively oriented curriculum.* Ypsilanti, MI: High/Scope Educational Research Foundation.

Weir, R. (1962). *Language in the crib.* The Hague: Mouton.

Wertsch, J. V. (1985). *Vygotsky and the social formation of mind*. Cambridge, MA: Harvard University Press.

Whipple, G. (1949). Characteristics of a sound reading program. In N. Henry (Ed.), *The forty-eighth yearbook of the National Society for the Study of Education: Part II. Reading in the Elementary School* (pp. 33–53). Chicago: University of Chicago Press.

Whipple, G. M. (Ed.). (1925). *The twenty-fourth yearbook of the National Society for the Study of Education: Part I. Report of the National Committee on Reading.* Bloomington, IL: Public School Publishing.

Wittick, M. L. (1968). Innovations in reading instruction for beginners. In H. Robinson (Ed.), *The sixty-seventh yearbook of the National Society for the Study of Education: Part II. Innovation and change in reading instruction* (pp. 72–125). Chicago: University of Chicago Press.

Yin, R. (1989). *Case study research*. Beverly Hills, CA: Sage.

Zigler, E. (1984). Foreword. In B. Biber, *Early education and psychological development* (pp. ix–xi). New Haven CT: Yale University Press.

Zigler, E. (1987). Project day care. *Psychology Today, 21,* 32–38.

INDEX

A

B

C

I

J

K

L

M

P

R

U

V

W

Y

Z